Gilbert & Sullivan

Gilbert & Sullivan

The Creative Conflict

David Eden

Fairleigh Dickinson University Press
Rutherford · Madison · Teaneck
Associated University Presses
London

Associated University Presses
440 Forsgate Drive
Cranbury, NJ 08512, USA

Associated University Presses
25 Sicilian Avenue,
London WC1A 2QH, England

Associated University Presses
2133 Royal Windsor Drive,
Unit 1,
Mississauga, Ontario,
Canada L5J 1K5

The paper used in this publication meets the minimum requirements of the American Standard for Permanence of Paper for Printed Library Materials Z39.48–1984.

Library of Congress Cataloging in Publication Data

Eden, David.
    Gilbert and Sullivan, the creative conflict.

    Bibliography: p.
    Includes index.
    1. Sullivan, Arthur, Sir, 1842–1900. 2. Gilbert,
    W.S. (William Schwenk), 1836–1911.
    3. Composers—England—Biography.
    4. Librettists—England—Biography. I. Title.
    ML410.S95E3 1986 782.81'092'2 [B] 85–25297
    ISBN 0 8386 3282 3

Printed in Great Britain

For
CAROL

Contents

Acknowledgements

Although it is found at the beginning, the page of acknowledgements is in practice the last to be prepared of almost any book. When the acknowledgements are called for then it is time for the author to say goodbye to the work and to reckon up the debts incurred in preparing it. And, invariably, they are not easy to repay in full. I am grateful to Macmillan & Co, New York, for permission to print extracts from *Sir Arthur Sullivan* by Herbert Sullivan and Newman Flower, and to Messrs A.P. Watt for the same permission with regard to *Gilbert, His Life and Strife*, by Hesketh Pearson. Robert Hale Ltd have permitted me to quote from *Music In England* by Henry Raynor, and Alfred A. Knopf Inc of New York have allowed a quotation from *The Tenth Muse* by Patrick J. Smith. Grateful thanks are extended to the Royal General Theatrical Fund Association, 11 Garrick St, London WC2, as owner of the subsisting copyright in Sir William Gilbert's unpublished writings, to include in this book the first verse of the Duke of Dunstable's song from *Patience*. Mr F.W. Wilson, Curator of the Gilbert & Sullivan Collection at the Pierpont Morgan Library, New York, has kindly allowed me to make use of copyright material. The Society of Authors have allowed me to print a passage from the music criticism of G.B. Shaw. The Theatre Museum of the Victoria and Albert Museum, London, were helpful in selecting and providing the photograph of Madame Parepa which appears on p 114. The British Library Newspaper Library, Colindale, London, supplied the pictures from *The Tatler* (1904) which appear on pp 56-7.

My debt to Dr Terence Rees extends over many years and many projects. Only those who are privileged to know him will understand what I mean when I say that I have benefitted from his generous help at every turn. In particular he has supplied most of the illustrations for the present book, and has read part of it in typescript, saving me from many errors. I am grateful to Mr Patrick Kearney for guiding me through the treacherous reaches of erotic literature, where matters of date and authorship are so uncertain. Stephen Turnbull helped me greatly with the task of proofreading, and has clarified my thoughts for me in the course of many discussions. The favourable account of Sullivan's neglected music which is offered here would have been impossible but for the members of the Sir Arthur Sullivan Society, who by their effort have brought most of the composer's works to performance in recent years. I have been emboldened in my judgement of this music by knowing that it has the support, in general if not in detail, of George Hilton, Martin Yates, David Leslie, and Jonathan Strong. My understanding of Sullivan's life has been enhanced by the researches of John Gardner, selflessly communicated over a long period.

It is next to impossible to write about Gilbert and Sullivan without making mistakes. Many of the basic books do not meet modern scholarly requirements, and many points are subject to dispute. I must therefore apologise for any errors which remain in spite of the best efforts of my friends, and hasten to claim responsibility for myself alone. The same proviso covers all matters of judgement and opinion contained in the book.

1: Mainly Biographical

The Gilbert and Sullivan operas are part of the fabric of English and American life. From the moment of their first appearance they penetrated the national consciousness of both countries, where they have remained as near possessions of the folk as makes no difference. Their popularity brought into being the amateur operatic movement in Britain, and in America contributed substantially to the founding of the musical theatre. [1] It is given to few men to add a dimension to civilised life, yet Gilbert and Sullivan achieved this feat in both the Old World and the New.

The story of the collaboration between the two men is retold every time one of their works is performed; popular books on the subject are published regularly, and the mass media, allied to the recent revolution in production methods, have brought the operas to wider audiences than ever before. Nevertheless in many ways Gilbert and Sullivan remain unknown quantities. Sullivan, who left a large personal archive in the wake of a well-documented public career, can be seen clearly by those who wish to look. Gilbert is in a different position. He has been made the subject of two biographies, the second of which is by Hesketh Pearson, one of the finest of British biographers; but his highly idiosyncratic personality has been glossed over, as if the entertainment value of his behaviour absolved his admirers from thought. Everyone knows he was bad-tempered, litigious and autocratic: no one pauses to ask what sort of man conducts himself as he did. In the present study I have tried to take a fresh look at both Gilbert and Sullivan, to see them in terms prescribed neither by their eulogisers nor by their detractors. They are more stimulating, and more interesting, than either party seems ready to admit.

But first the plain unvarnished tale. As the older man Gilbert (1836-1911) naturally takes biographical precedence over Sullivan (1842-1900). The main facts of his professional career are well established; no researcher has so far been able to discover more of his early life than he himself divulged.

William Schwenck Gilbert was descended from yeoman stock living in and around Shipton Bellinger, near Amesbury, Wiltshire. One of these ancestors, the great grandfather, became a London grocer, and the grandfather established himself as a tea merchant, living at 17 Southampton Street, just off The Strand. It was at this house that Gilbert was born on 18 November 1836. His father, William Gilbert, began life as a naval surgeon, but retired on inheriting his patrimony to commence a life of leisurely travel in France and Italy. Nothing is known of the mother, Anne Morris, except that she was the daughter of a Scottish doctor. The unusual Christian name Schwenck was bestowed on Gilbert in honour of his great aunt and godmother, Mary Schwenck, a trustee of the grandfather's will.

If one could rely on it, William Gilbert's autobiographical *Memoirs of a Cynic* (1880) might furnish useful information about the family's journeys abroad. Unfortunately the work contains a fictional element, though clearly based on extensive travel in Italy, and to a lesser extent in France. One truth emerges beyond question, however: Gilbert the father was deeply attached to Italian opera and its singers. If he did not manage an opera house in Italy, like the hero of *Memoirs of a Cynic,* [2] he would clearly have liked to do so. His son, the future librettist, must have been exposed to talk about opera from the very beginning of his conscious life.

Suitably operatic is the one recorded incident of Gilbert's childhood. In about 1840 the family had travelled to Naples, taking with them the baby Gilbert, his three sisters, and a nurse. The nurse was out with the baby in the street when she was accosted by a couple of charming gentlemen who told her they had been sent to take the infant to his father. The nurse innocently handed her charge over, whereupon the family received a ransom demand for £25 (prices have risen since). The money was paid, and little Gilbert returned. Late in life he claimed to retain a memory of the incident, though he must have heard the story told and retold many times.

Further than this we hear nothing of the young child except that he delighted to play with a toy theatre. At the age of seven he was sent to school in Boulogne, and at thirteen he went to Great Ealing School. Here he showed himself intelligent but lazy; he was unpopular because he displayed a tendency to bully and beat those who disagreed with him. He wrote plays and acted in them, besides painting the scenery; according to Hesketh Pearson he knocked to the ground any boy actor who failed to meet his wishes. [3] An attempt to run away from school and go on the stage was foiled by the actor Charles Kean—a friend of his father's—who sent Gilbert forthrightly back to his studies. By the age of sixteen he was Head Boy of the school, with a reputation for his ability to translate the Greek and Latin classics.

Understanding of the next stages of Gilbert's career has been confused by his own faulty recollection, both in written statements and in verbal accounts given to his biographers. The true sequence of events has been discovered by Andrew

W.S. Gilbert 1836-1911

Goodman in the following entry from Foster's *Men-At-The-Bar:* [4]

GILBERT, William Schwenck, B.A. London Univ. 1857 and a member of
Convocation, dramatic author, clerk in privy council 1857-1862, late Capt.
Royal Aberdeenshire Highlanders militia (1868), author of the Bab Ballads,
etc., a student of the Inner Temple 11 Oct 1855, called to the bar 17 Nov
1863; only son of William Gilbert, Esq., of London; born 18 Nov 1836;
married 6 Aug 1867, Lucy A, youngest dau. of late Capt. T.M. Turner,
Bombay Engineers. 24, The Boltons, S.W.

By reading this entry in conjunction with a brief autobiographical essay
which Gilbert contributed to *The Theatre* 2 April 1883, it is possible to arrive at
the following narrative. On leaving school Gilbert began to study law at King's
College London, intending to proceed to Oxford. However, he was distracted
from his purpose by the Crimean War (1854-6) in which he took a lifelong
interest. He began to study for a commission in the Royal Artillery, but the
effective military end of the war in September 1855 prevented further progress in
this direction. He therefore registered as a student of the Inner Temple 11
October 1855 and continued his law studies at London, obtaining his B.A. in
1857. In order to subsidise his law studies he became a clerk in the Education
Department of the Privy Council Office (1857-62), but a legacy of £400 enabled
him to be called to the bar on 17 November 1863. He took pupillage with Sir
Charles James Watkin-Wilkins, and made his first appearance in the London
courts. However lack of success drove him to join the Northern Circuit
(Liverpool) in 1866. In the event success never came, and he averaged only five
clients a year during a period of four years.

The standard recourse of impoverished lawyers in Gilbert's day was journalism. By 1860 he had already written fifteen farces and burlesques, all of which
were rejected by the theatres. He tried poems and articles and eventually, in
1861, found acceptance in the pages of *Fun*, a newly-founded rival to *Punch*.
During his association with *Fun*, which lasted about ten years. Gilbert served as a
factotum, writing dramatic criticism, art criticism, and short stories. His work
on the magazine is remembered for the series of *Bab Ballads*, the first of which
appeared in May 1866. [5] A well known story tells how Gilbert submitted 'The
Yarn of the Nancy Bell' to Mark Lemon, editor of *Punch*, only to have it rejected
as 'too cannibalistic' for the tastes of *Punch's* readers. Gilbert might nevertheless
have become a *Punch* author, but Lemon compounded his original error of
judgement by refusing to offer a regular salary.

Some slight doubt surrounds the production of Gilbert's first play. The
honour is generally given to *Uncle Baby*, a short curtain raiser produced at the
Lyceum Theatre on 31 October 1863. However, this play is described in the bills
as 'By W. Gilbert'. No one would attribute it to W.S. Gilbert on stylistic
grounds alone, and the manuscript is only partly in Gilbert's hand. [6] This being
so, the possibility remains open that the little work is actually by the father, who
was always known as W. Gilbert, with collaborative help from the son. At this
time the father had a greater reputation.

W.S. Gilbert himself stated that his first play to be produced was *Dulcamara, or The Little Duck and the Great Quack* (St. James's, 29 December 1866). He received £30 for it, and was sufficiently emboldened by its success to propose to Lucy Agnes Turner (1847-1936), the daughter of an Indian Army officer. They were married on 6 August 1867, whereupon Lucy Gilbert passes into oblivion, except for a cookery book published after her husband's death. She was the recipient of some affectionate but not intimate letters, and can be glimpsed occasionally as an appendage to his social life. For the rest, no evidence survives to enable the biographer to gauge her contribution to the marriage. She remained childless.

Dulcamara is a burlesque of Donizetti's *L'Elisir d'Amore* (1832). It opened the way to a number of other burlesques which are all–significantly–of operatic subjects; in order they are: *La Vivandiere (La Fille du Regiment* - Donizetti) 1867; *The Merry Zingara (The Bohemian Girl* - Balfe) 1868; *Robert The Devil (Robert Le Diable* - Meyerbeer) 1868; *The Pretty Druidess (Norma* - Bellini) 1869. Though these works are not intrinsically superior to the output of the other men in the same genre, it is possible to trace in them a number of ideas later to be employed at the Savoy.

Victorian middle class opinion held with some reason that the theatre was not a place to be visited by respectable people. It was the achievement of Thomas German Reed (1817-88) and his wife Priscilla Horton (1818-95) to establish a type of drama which middle class people might attend with propriety. Eschewing the very word *theatre* they established a series of Illustrative Gatherings and Entertainments, first at the St. Martin's Hall, then at the Gallery of Illustration, Regent Street.

The Entertainments were innocent musical plays employing harmonium or piano, and introducing elements of impersonation, mimicry and burlesque; they were performed by a small regular company of versatile actors, one of whom was Corney Grain. Perhaps surprisingly in view of their respectable intentions, the Reeds did not foster mediocrity. Instead they employed the leading authors of the day to make a distinctive contribution to the Victorian Theatre. They produced Sullivan's *Cox And Box* (1866) and commissioned his *Contrabandista* (1867). Gilbert first worked for them in March 1869, when he wrote *No Cards*. Thereafter he produced the highly successful *Ages Ago* (1869), *Our Island Home* (1870), *A Sensation Novel* (1871), *Happy Arcadia* (1872) and *Eyes And No Eyes* (1875).

To read Gilbert's German Reed Entertainments is to see the Savoy libretti in embryo. *Ages Ago*, with music by Frederic Clay, contains a scene of walking ancestral portraits later to be resurrected in *Ruddigore*. *Our Island Home* introduces us to a Captain Bang who has been apprenticed to a pirate by his nurserymaid when she should have apprenticed him to a pilot. *Eyes And No Eyes* opens on a scene of a girl alone at the spinning wheel, later to be employed in *The Yeomen of the Guard*.

Having established himself firmly in the comic theatre, Gilbert began to reveal higher aspirations by writing substantial plays in blank verse. The list of

Great Victorians who attempted to write a tolerable blank verse play and failed dismally in the process is both long and distressing. Some of the most famous names in English literature are to be found here, submerged in impotence with the rest. It was Gilbert's bad eminence in this fallen company to have written blank verse plays which actually held the stage; they are devoid of durable literary qualities, but they were at least fit to perform, and were not without their significance as we shall see. The first of them was *The Princess* (1870) founded on Tennyson's poem of the same name. Next came *The Palace of Truth* (1870), followed by *Pygmalion and Galatea* (1871). This latter play was the most successful of all Gilbert's non-operatic works. Constantly revived for the benefit of beautiful actresses who wanted to play Galatea, the statue who comes to life, it made him a total of £40,000.

Pygmalion and Galatea was followed in the blank verse line by *The Wicked World* (1873), *Broken Hearts* (1875), and *Gretchen* (1879) a version of the Faust story. *Gretchen* was a failure and Gilbert, already beginning to be taken up by his work with Sullivan, abandoned his serious ambitions thereafter. He remained devoted to his blank verse however, turning *The Princess* into *Princess Ida*, and *The Wicked World* into *Fallen Fairies* (1909) with music by Edward German. Had circumstances permitted he would have converted his entire blank verse *oeuvre* into operatic libretti.

Blank verse apart, Gilbert occupied the seventies with work of many different kinds. His adaptation of *Great Expectations* appeared in 1871, and *Charity*, an early 'problem' play, in 1874. *Dan'l Druce*, a melodrama, came out in 1876, and in the same year he collaborated with Frederic Clay in the operetta *Princess Toto*, the most charmingly zany of all his works. [7]

The single most momentous event of Gilbert's career, his meeting with Sullivan, appears to have taken place in 1870, though the date is not established with complete certainty. Before dealing with this matter we should perhaps take the opportunity to recount the career of Sullivan to the same point. Once their association had fairly begun, the professional lives of the two men ran closely together.

Arthur Seymour Sullivan was born at 8 Bolwell Street, Lambeth, on 13 May 1842. In contrast to the long standing middle class affluence of Gilbert's forebears, the Sullivan family was acquainted with hardship, if not downright poverty. The grandfather, Thomas Sullivan, was a landless Irish labourer from Caherweeshen, near Tralee, County Cork. Born about 1777, he enlisted in the British army (57th Foot) in 1806, serving throughout the Peninsular War. After the defeat of Napoleon at Waterloo in 1815, he enlisted in the 66th Regiment and travelled to St. Helena as one of the Emperor's guards; he was finally discharged as 'worn out and undersized' after Napoleon's death in 1821. [8] He ended his days as a Chelsea Pensioner in 1838.

The composer's father, another Thomas Sullivan, was born in 1805. Since his father was away at the wars he was educated at the Royal Military Asylum, Chelsea, a school founded by Frederick Duke of York for the sons of British soldiers. Thomas, who must have shown musical talent, laid the foundations of a

Arthur Sullivan 1842-1900

career as a military musician at the Duke of York's School. At the age of fifteen he transferred as a bandsman to the Royal Military College, Sandhurst, where he remained till 1834.

Rather in Gilbertian fashion, Thomas appears to have known his wife from babyhood. She was Mary Clementina Coghlan (1811-82), a Roman Catholic of Irish and Italian descent, who was an interesting enough person to become in later life a friend and confidante of George Grove.[9] The couple married in 1836, producing two sons, Frederick, born in 1839, and Arthur.

In order to support his wife Thomas Sullivan became a clarinettist at the Royal Surrey Theatre, moving at the same time to the house in Lambeth where Arthur was born. In 1845, having failed to achieve prosperity outside the army, he returned to Sandhurst as Sergeant Bandmaster. As a consequence young Arthur grew up amid the sights and sounds of military music. Finally, in 1857, Thomas became Professor of Brass instruments at the Military School of Music, Kneller Hall. In this post he died on 22 September 1866.

Arthur Sullivan seems to have given evidence of musical gifts from an early age. No doubt impelled to continue the family tradition of wearing a uniform, he sought—and obtained—admission to the Chapel Royal in 1852. In 1856 he became the first holder of the Mendelssohn Scholarship, which enabled him to study at the Royal Academy of Music, while remaining a Chapel Royal chorister until 1857.

Sullivan's progress as Mendelssohn Scholar was so outstanding that the organising committee decided to send him as a student to the Leipzig Conservatory. He arrived there in the September of 1858 and remained till April 1861, winning golden plaudits from his professors at least one of whom, Robert Paperitz, considered his natural gifts greater than those of Brahms. It is worth bearing in mind that this judgement was made by an experienced teacher at what was then the leading institution for musical education in Europe. Paperitz can have had no ulterior motive for favouring a young Englishman.

On his return to England Sullivan faced the central dilemma of his career, namely the difficulty of earning a livelihood by composition in Victorian England. He won fame overnight, when his incidental music to Shakespeare's *Tempest* was performed at the Crystal Palace on 5 April 1862, but fame, as the saying goes, butters no parsnips. In order to live he became a teacher of the boys at the Chapel Royal, an ordinary music teacher, organist of St. Michael's Chester Square, Professor of Pianoforte and Ballad Singing at the Crystal Palace School of Art, organist at Covent Garden, and a member of the staff of the short-lived National College of Music. These unglamorous beginnings, necessitated by the plain fact that there was no money in most forms of musical composition, go far to explain the nature of Sullivan's creative output. If he wished to be heard at all, he had to write the kind of works the public would pay for.

During the 1860s, and for many years after, the most saleable form of music was the royalty ballad—a song which paid the composer a percentage of the purchase price whenever a copy was bought. Sullivan wrote about a hundred such songs, one of which was *The Lost Chord* (1877). This song was and is his most popular single composition. Royalty ballads were intended for the domestic drawing room; two other Victorian institutions were also consumers of music: the church and the provincial municipal music festival. For the former Sullivan provided a bookfull of hymns, including *Onward Christian Soldiers* (1871) and a number of anthems; for the latter he wrote substantial choral works and some orchestral music. He was thirty five before the theatre finally captured the centre of his attention. Up to this time his most important works were: *Kenilworth* (Cantata) 1864; *Irish Symphony* 1866; *Cox And Box* (Operetta) 1866; *In Memoriam* (Overture) 1866; *The Contrabandista* (Operetta) 1867; *The Prodigal Son* (Oratorio) 1869; *Di Ballo* (Overture) 1870; *On Shore And Sea* (Cantata) 1871; *The Merchant of Venice* (Incidental Music) 1871; *Festival Te Deum* (1872); *Light Of The World* (Oratorio) 1873.

Unlike Gilbert Sullivan never married, preferring to conduct a discreet but active sexual life in Bohemian London and in continental watering places. However, he underwent a traumatic love affair (1865-70) with Rachel Scott Russell, the daughter of one of the designers of the *Great Eastern* steamship. Rachel's letters to Sullivan have been preserved and published.[10] They reveal a passionate prig who absolutely demanded three things of him: the production of immortal masterpieces, a reciprocating rhetoric of sentiment, and a rock-solid middle class income. Any possibility of marriage was prevented by the Scott Russell family's rejection of Sullivan as a suitor for their daughter. He was considered too poor, and too lowly as a musician, to be countenanced. Rachel, no Elizabeth Barrett, was far too prudent to elope, and the affair gradually foundered as Sullivan failed to make the necessary *bourgeois* headway. Rachel's last letter to him is dated a couple of months before the meeting with Gilbert that was destined to enable him to fulfil at least the first and third of her demands. She married in 1872, and died of cholera in India in 1882 aged thirty-seven.

When, finally, Sullivan met Gilbert both men were well known in their professions. They must have known each other by repute for some time before the actual meeting took place; indeed, Gilbert had already expressed himself dissatisfied with Sullivan's music for *Cox And Box*, written with F.C. Burnand in 1866, 'Mr Sullivan's music is, in many places, of too high a class for the grotesquely absurd plot to which it is wedded.'[11]

The actual introduction was made by Frederic Clay at a rehearsal of *Ages Ago*, the score of which is dedicated to Sullivan. According to a familiar anecdote narrated by Gilbert himself, the librettist baffled the composer by quoting a piece of learned lumber from a musical encyclopaedia which he had just written into *The Palace of Truth*:[12]

Believe me, the result would be the same,
Whether your lordship chose to play upon
The simple tetrachord of Mercury
That knew no diatonic intervals,
Or the elaborate dis-diapason
(Four tetrachords, and one redundant note),
Embracing in its perfect consonance
All simple, double and inverted chords.

It is generally assumed that this encounter took place before the first performance of *Ages Ago* on 22 November 1869. However *The Palace of Truth*, from which Gilbert quoted, was not performed until 19 November 1870– a full year after the production of *Ages Ago*. Gilbert laboured long and hard on his blank verse plays, but it was not his custom to write a work a year in advance of production. It is therefore intrinsically unlikely that in November 1869 he would have been writing a play which was not seen until November 1870. Furthermore *The Princess*, Gilbert's first blank verse play, was produced at the Olympic Theatre on 8 January 1870. If he was working on any play in November 1869 that play was *The Princess*, not *The Palace of Truth*. For this reason a meeting between Gilbert and Sullivan in November 1869 is hard to sustain.

Much more likely is a date in July 1870, when *Ages Ago* was revived as a consequence of the poor performance of *Our Island Home*. The last night of the initial run of *Ages Ago* fell on Saturday 18 June 1870. *Our Island Home* commenced its run on Monday 20th, but failed to attract the public. Accordingly an abridged version of *Ages Ago* was offered from Monday 11 July, with *Our Island Home*, also abridged, as the afterpiece. [13] In other words *Ages Ago* was off the bills for three weeks. When revived, particularly in revised form, it would have required rehearsal.

The passage about music quoted by Gilbert at the *Ages Ago* rehearsal is found near the beginning of *The Palace of Truth*. It is perfectly credible that he should have begun work on a play in July for production the following November. This consideration, together with the evident need to rehearse the revised *Ages Ago*, suggests that the meeting between Gilbert and Sullivan took place on or shortly before 11 July 1870, when the combined performances of *Ages Ago* and *Our Island Home* commenced. To be even more specific, one might suggest that the meeting took place at a rehearsal held on that Monday afternoon in readiness for the evening performance.

Whatever the truth of the matter, collaboration between Gilbert and Sullivan was not discussed at the first meeting. In July 1870 Sullivan must have been working on his concert overture *Di Ballo* for the forthcoming Birmingham Festival. Despite the brilliance of his two comic operas *Cox And Box* and *The Contrabandista* it was by no means apparent to him or anyone else that his future lay in comedy. Nevertheless, a naturally genial personality had already predestined Sullivan to humour, and it was only a matter of time before he wrote another comic opera.

This time came in the winter of 1871 when John Hollingshead, manager of the recently opened Gaiety Theatre, asked Sullivan to provide music for a Christmas play, *Thespis*, to be written by W.S. Gilbert. Sullivan agreed, and so it happened that the Chapel Royal choirboy, the Mendelssohn scholar with a greater natural gift than Brahms, the organist of Chester Square, set out on the road to immortality by writing music for a Christmas entertainment.

The managerial policy pursued by Hollingshead was the opposite of the one which had brought success to the German Reeds. Arguing that the Lord

Chamberlain's Office relieved him of all responsibility for the content of his productions, he dealt frankly in pretty girls with scant clothing, and in what he called the 'sacred lamp' of burlesque. While most managers produced a pantomime for the Christmas season it was Hollingshead's policy to mount a Christmas novelty, much as modern civic theatres will present a children's play. What motivated Hollingshead to approach Gilbert and Sullivan is not recorded; he can hardly have foreseen the consequences of his choice.[14]

Thespis was produced on 26 December 1871. It was a hasty piece of work, for Gilbert was simultaneously engaged with two other plays: *On Guard* (Court Theatre, 28 October) and *Pygmalion and Galatea* (Haymarket, 9 December). Many statements to the contrary notwithstanding, *Thespis* was successful. It was withdrawn only at the end of the pantomime season, outlasting a number of other special productions.[15] Formally speaking the work was a classical extravaganza (p. 122), written to serve the great stars of the Gaiety, who at this time included J.L. Toole, Nellie Farren, and the Payne Brothers—the most famous Harlequin and Clown of their day. Nellie Farren appeared in tights as Mercury (she had popular legs), while the Payne brothers were given an opportunity to indulge in horse-play with food. Improbable as it sounds, it really is possible that in the first Gilbert and Sullivan opera the chief comedians threw custard pies into each other's faces.

Thespis cannot be performed today because the music, like several other of Sullivan's works, has been lost or destroyed. All attempts to find it have proved vain, including the services of a clairvoyant. A manuscript vocal score is said to have existed for many years at Chappells the music publishers, but it was destroyed—along with a cupboardful of Sullivan manuscripts—in a disastrous fire during the 1960s. Two numbers only survive: the chorus 'Climbing over rocky mountain', which was redeployed in *The Pirates of Penzance*, and a song, 'Little Maid of Arcadee', which was published separately.

Even the libretto of *Thespis* survives only in an imperfect form, for Gilbert died before correcting the proofs of what would have been the definitive text. He was a methodical artist, who achieved results only by the patient working and reworking of his material. He once said he could write a libretto in a fortnight, 'but it would be a precious poor libretto'. *Thespis* is not exactly 'precious poor', but it is not as fully achieved as the later operas. Some of the lyric writing is perfunctory, and parts of the dialogue appear to have been left to the improvisation of the actors. It is at its best in a song sung by Thespis in the first act:[16]

> I once knew a chap who discharged a function,
> On the North South East West Diddlesex Junction.
> He was conspicuous exceeding,
> For his affable ways and his easy breeding.
> Although a Chairman of Directors,
> He was hand in glove with the ticket inspectors.
> He tipped the guards with brand-new fivers,
> And sang little songs to the engine-drivers.

'Twas told to me with great compunction,
By one who had discharged with unction
A Chairman of Directors' function
On the North South East West Diddlesex Junction.

Once *Thespis* had come and gone Gilbert and Sullivan do not seem to have felt impelled to work with each other again. Sullivan turned to write his exuberant *Festival Te Deum* for the recovery of the Prince of Wales from typhoid fever (May 1872). For his part Gilbert gradually began to rise to a position of theatrical dominance, especially in the matter of the stage production of his own works. He was, if not absolutely the first, certainly the first really effective producer in the British theatre.[17] He kept at home a model theatre with striped wooden blocks for the performers. Using this he would work out all the stage directions for his play in advance, and arrive at the theatre with a perfectly clear picture in his own mind of what they should be. He would then proceed to drill the actors by rote until they conformed in every way with his wishes in the matter of stage position, gesture, and inflexion of voice. Since he could also design the scenery and costumes the result was a kind of total theatre, in which every part faithfully reflected the dramatist's intentions and personality. Modern directors, who take their dominance for granted, have Gilbert to thank for the revolution which first imposed on actors the discipline that subjects the individual performance to a larger artistic design.

If he could have known what Gilbert's production methods held in store for him it is quite possible that Sullivan would never have renewed the collaboration at all. The credit for persuading him to do so belongs to Richard D'Oyly Carte (1844-1901). Since he played such an important part in the success of Gilbert and Sullivan, it may be useful to glance here at Carte's career before proceeding with the narrative.

Richard D'Oyly Carte was born into a home in which intellectual culture, particularly French culture, was the norm. His father owned a musical instrument and publishing business (Rudall, Carte & Co) in which the young man commenced his career. He composed, and published through the family firm, some suave songs on parlour subjects before beginning to compose for the theatres. In 1871 his operetta *Marie* was produced at the Opéra Comique. In 1870 he had set up a theatrical and lecture agency, and in 1875 commenced the management of the Royalty Theatre for a season of Offenbach. It was for this season that he sought a work from Gilbert, and perhaps more especially from Sullivan.

Carte had seen *Thespis*, and been impressed by it. He appears to have realised that the combination of Gilbert with Sullivan was potentially a successful one, and deliberately set out to foster it. As a composer of operetta himself, Carte was in a position to understand Sullivan's superiority to other operators in the *genre*, and to appreciate what it would mean if an Englishman were to beat the French at their own game. It was not by accident, therefore, that he asked Gilbert to write an afterpiece for Offenbach's *La Périchole*, and asked Sullivan to set it. He was deliberately attempting to found an English school of operetta.

If *Thespis* was hastily contrived the second Gilbert and Sullivan opera, *Trial By Jury*, was fortuitous inasmuch as the libretto was not originally written for Sullivan to set. Gilbert had reworked an old idea from the pages of *Fun* for Carl Rosa,[18] whose wife, Euphrosyne Parepa, would have played the heroine if the performance had gone ahead (see page 113). However, Mrs. Rosa died in January 1874, and the project necessarily fell through. By the time Rosa was ready to begin again in opera Sullivan had already set *Trial By Jury*. The little work was produced on 25 March 1875 and was immediately recognised as a masterpiece. From now on it was certain that further works by Gilbert and Sullivan would be forthcoming.

Pleased with the success of *Trial By Jury* Carte set about trying to finance a revival of *Thespis* in a revised version, while Gilbert and Sullivan began to state their terms to other managers interested in their joint work. At length Carte found capitalists to back him in the formation of a company whose specific purpose was to promote English light opera; this was the Comedy Opera Company. He took a lease of the Opéra Comique Theatre, and here *The Sorcerer* was produced on 17 November 1877–the first deliberately planned Gilbert and Sullivan opera. Just how deliberately planned may be judged from a speech delivered by Gilbert in December 1906:[19]

> When Sullivan and I began to collaborate, English comic opera had practically ceased to exist. Such musical entertainments as held the stage were adaptations of the plots of the operas of Offenbach, Audran, and Lecocq. The plots had generally been 'bowdlerised' out of intelligibility, and when they had not been subjected to this treatment they were frankly improper, whereas the ladies' dresses suggested that the management had gone on the principle of doing a little and doing it well. Sullivan and I set out with determination to prove that these elements were not essential to the success of humorous opera. We resolved that our plots, however ridiculous, should be coherent, that our dialogue should be void of offence; that, on artistic principles, no man should play a woman's part and no woman a man's. Finally, we agreed that no lady of the company should be required to wear a dress that she could not wear with absolute propriety at a private fancy ball. I believe I may say we proved our case.

While there is no reason to suppose that Sullivan objected to these reforms, there is every reason to think they originated in the mind of Gilbert, whose criticism of the contemporary comic stage was always directed at its vulgarity. We must imagine the composer nodding in silent agreement while the librettist expounded long-cherished notions on what should be done to improve burlesque. Left to himself Sullivan would have taken the theatre as he found it–except in the musical department, where he would have been conscious of shortcomings.

Deliberately planned also was the cast of performers assembled for the new opera. The star system of the Gaiety was abandoned and in its place Gilbert, abetted by Sullivan, engaged only people who would not spoil the *ensemble* by self-assertion. Some of the best known names of the later Savoy operas were first seen at this time, including George Grossmith and Rutland Barrington. Grossmith (1847-1912) is also remembered as the co-author, with his younger brother Weedon, of *The Diary of a Nobody* (1892). In view of the librettist's deliberate attempts to destroy the star system it is ironical that the history of Gilbert and Sullivan as an institution has come to be written largely in terms of personalities, in particular those of George Grossmith and his successors in the comic 'patter' parts.

The months between the productions of *Trial By Jury* and *The Sorcerer* were eventful in the lives of both Gilbert and Sullivan. In June 1876 Gilbert became involved in a quarrel between his parents the letters pertaining to which provide almost the only documentary evidence for his family circumstances. It seems that William Gilbert, Tolstoy-like, had finally left his wife at the age of seventy-two. Gilbert the younger, writing to his mother, reveals a marked symapthy for his father's cause, even while trying to effect a reconciliation between them. Hesketh Pearson says that Anne Gilbert was a 'peculiarly repressed' and cold person, but as we shall see, the Gilbert father and son were as yolk and white of the same egg; faced with two such personalities a woman might be forgiven for anything.[20] At least, her husband did not return to her, spending the rest of his life with a daughter in the cathedral close at Salisbury. He died in 1890.

Later in the same year Gilbert became involved in a quarrel with the actress Henrietta Hodson which resulted in a short pamphlet war in April 1877. Miss Hodson's pamphlet affords a useful glimpse of Gilbert in the years before he achieved world fame (see page 55).

Sullivan in the same period had advanced to the threshold of the kind of academic career which was later to be followed by Stanford and Parry. At Easter 1876 he was appointed Principal of the newly founded National Training School For Music, a post he retained till 1881. The National School is now the Royal Academy of Music. To accompany the appointment he was given the honorary degree of Doctor of Music at Cambridge University on 1 June.[21] Sullivan disliked teaching, and was not gifted with the academic temperament, but it is worth reflecting that teaching and administration might nevertheless have claimed him, as they claimed Sterndale Bennett, if unexpected success in comic opera had not come to his rescue.

On 18 January 1877 Sullivan suffered the loss of his brother Frederic, who had played the Judge in *Trial By Jury*, and would have played *John Wellington Wells* in *The Sorcerer* if he had lived. *The Lost Chord* was written as Sullivan sat by his dying brother's bedside, but the composer did not expect it to succeed, as it continues to do in spite of every criticism that has been made of it.

The Sorcerer ran until the May of 1878, achieving 178 performances in all. Serious preparations for a successor to it began in January 1878, when Gilbert and Sullivan agreed to write a new opera for Carte and his capitalists. This was *H.M.S. Pinafore*, produced at the Opéra Comique on 25 May 1878. After an uncertain start caused by a heatwave in the summer, *H.M.S. Pinafore* became a huge success on both sides of the Atlantic. In America it created a sensation comparable only to the Beatles craze of more recent memory. At one time it was played in nine theatres in New York simultaneously, and in forty-two throughout the country, besides uncounted touring companies. John Philip Sousa met his wife in one such company. The impetus thus given to operatic performance laid the foundation of the American musical theatre, though exactly how much praise is to be bestowed on Gilbert and Sullivan for this achievement may remain a matter of conjecture.

In England the financial backers of the Comedy Opera Company made life difficult for D'Oyly Carte by wishing to withdraw the opera every time houses thinned in the heatwave. By the middle of August, however, the work was playing to packed houses. The capitalists now wished to maximise their gains, but were outmanoeuvred by Carte in a complicated legal arrangement which effectively gave him sole control of *Pinafore* after the end of July 1879.[22] On 31 July 1879 the financiers attempted to seize the scenery of the opera during the 374th performance with a view to opening their own rival show at the Imperial Theatre. The resulting legal battle was not settled—wholly in favour of Gilbert/Sullivan/Carte—until March 1881, but by that time the rival *Pinafore* production had foundered, leaving the triumvirate in possession of the field but forced to pay their own costs. As soon as a successor to *H.M.S. Pinafore* was required they decided to dispense with outside capital altogether. Each man put up £1000, and a new trading venture was begun.[23]

Owing to the state of copyright law in America very little of the money made by *H.M.S. Pinafore* in America reached the authors of the work. They therefore determined to produce their next opera, *The Pirates of Penzance*, simultaneously in England and America so as to obtain U.S. copyright. In October 1879 they sailed for New York, where, as the authors of *H.M.S. Pinafore*, they were received with something like unmodified rapture. Gilbert, however, soon became aware that Sullivan was the real centre of attention. He reacted by making jokes at Sullivan's expense, to the extent that Sullivan eventually confided to Frederic Clay that he thought he could not put up with it much longer.[24]

Exactly how much of *The Pirates of Penzance* was written in America is hard to determine. Sullivan left his sketches for the first act behind in England, and had to rewrite them from memory. This would have been a simple task for him, but the physical strain of completing the opera in the space of a couple of months almost exhausted him. He had suffered from kidney stones—one of the most agonising of all diseases—since 1872. *H.M.S. Pinafore* had been written through the spasms of an attack of kidney pain, and before going to America he had to have an operation (August 1879). In fact Victorian medicine knew no cure for an illness which was to affect him for the rest of his life. Rheumatism, too, seems to have affected him early. All in all he came to the Broadway opening of *The Pirates of Penzance* on 31 December 1879 more dead than alive. The work was nevertheless a great success, and one more step towards the establishment of Gilbert and Sullivan as an American institution.

In order to secure the English copyright of *The Pirates of Penzance* a makeshift performance had been given by a *Pinafore* touring company at Paignton, Devon, on 30 December 1879. The London opening, at the Opéra Comique on 3 April 1880 had to await the return of Gilbert and Sullivan from America. The resulting success silenced all those who said the furore of *Pinafore* could not be repeated. Carte's improbable dream of a worthwhile English comic opera was beginning to come true.

While still in America Sullivan had received an invitation from the committee of the Leeds Festival to conduct the forthcoming Festival. He was already committed to writing a work for the Festival, and had originally selected the subject of David and Jonathan. However he changed his mind and decided to set H.H. Milman's dramatic poem *The Martyr of Antioch* (1822). And, such was the temporary accord between the two men, he asked Gilbert to help him with the libretto. The resulting work was produced to great acclaim on 15 October 1880, becoming immediately established among the standard choral works of the day. Most of the text of *The Martyr of Antioch* is taken straightforwardly from Milman; Gilbert's contribution can at most have been a little dramatic carpentry. However he did write the lyric of 'Come Margarita Come', taking only a hint from Milman. This charming tenor aria may therefore legitimately be added to the corpus of the joint works of Gilbert and Sullivan.

For the text of his next libretto, *Patience*, Gilbert turned to the drawing room cult of aestheticism which flourished for a few seasons towards the end of the 1870s. The origins of the aesthetic movement lie ultimately in France, with Gautier and Baudelaire; in England Ruskin and Pater influenced a generation of artists and writers, of whom Rossetti and Swinburne, Oscar Wilde and Burne Jones are best remembered today. The works and opinions of these men, who did not necessarily agree with each other, created a general concern for beautiful things, to which were added such special fads as Rossetti's love of Botticelli, the vogue for Japanese prints and blue and white china, and the wish to live in a Queen Anne house.[25]

For the student of *Patience*, however, the reality of aestheticism is of rather less importance than George Du Maurier's caricatures of it which appeared in the pages of *Punch* from 1873-82. Oscar Wilde was accused by Whistler of having derived his aesthetic *persona* entirely from du Maurier,[26] and we need look no further than Mrs Cimabue Brown and her compatriots Maudle and Postlethwaite for the general inspiration of Gilbert's work.

Patience is in any case an aesthetic opera only by afterthought. According to a letter of November 1880, Gilbert had abandoned an early intention to write about aesthetes because the chorus would not be able to dress and make up appropriately.[27] He then developed his libretto for six months as a version of the ballad *The Rival Curates* (1867). A manuscript draft now in the British Library reveals *Patience* much as we know it in terms of plot and lyrics, but featuring a clergyman, Rev Lawn Tennison, as the hero.[28] Only when he began to feel hampered by his clerical subject did Gilbert return to aestheticism.

Oscar Wilde said that *Patience* is the tribute which mediocrity pays to genius. The audience who saw the work for the first time at the Opéra Comique on 23 April 1881 did not regard it as mediocre at all. Their applause set the work on the way to a total run of 578 performances. About a third of the way through this run, in October 1881, the production was transferred to the newly built Savoy Theatre, off The Strand. Even as early as September 1878 D'Oyly Carte had begun to investigate building sites for a theatre to serve as a permanent home for Gilbert and Sullivan. He purchased the Savoy site in 1880, and determined from the first that it should be the most sophisticated theatre in London. It is well known that the Savoy was the first theatre to be lit entirely by electricity, but D'Oyly Carte also included improvements to the safety of the public such as the stone staircase recommended by Sir Eyre Massey Shaw. [29]

Patience concluded its run in November 1882. The next opera was *Iolanthe*, produced at the Savoy on 25 November. The title of this opera is borrowed from *Iolanthe*, a one-act play by W.G. Wills produced at the Lyceum Theatre on 20 May 1880, with Ellen Terry in the name part. Wills' play is itself based on *King René's Daughter* by Henrik Hertz, which is in turn the source of Tchaikovsky's *Iolanta* (1891). Other versions of the same story had been seen on the English stage, but there is no need to look beyond the recent work of Wills for Gilbert's source. From his own works he made use of a *Bab Ballad* 'The Fairy Curate' (1870).

Sullivan's work on the opera was seriously disturbed by the death of his mother on 27 May 1882. As several biographers have noted, his feelings for his family were abnormally intense, even in the context of the close-knit Victorian home. This death severed his last remaining link with his near relations and left him, as he put it, 'feeling dreadfully lonely'. In June he travelled to Cornwall to stay as a house guest with Lady Andalusia Molesworth at Pencarrow House, near Wadebridge. Composition of *Iolanthe* proceeded apace in the congenial surroundings of the stately home, and the March of the Peers was written at Pencarrow on 4 August. Later he became dissatisfied with the libretto of Act 1, making a flying visit to Exeter to discuss it with Gilbert, who was yachting off the south coast. Finally, the composer received the news that his broker had gone bankrupt, taking with him £7000 worth of securities. This misfortune at least was soon repaired as Chappells the music publishers sold 10,000 copies of the vocal score on a single day.

Iolanthe ran until the beginning of 1884, to be followed at the Savoy by *Princess Ida*, an operatic version of Gilbert's earlier blank verse play *The Princess* (Olympic Theatre, 8 January 1870). The primary source of both play and opera is Tennyson's long poem *The Princess*, published in 1847. Since *Princess Ida* is not at all the simple mockery of feminism it is generally taken for (see p. 85), it may be worth sketching in its literary background here.

Tennyson began the composition of *The Princess* in 1839, at a time when the subject of women's rights was only beginning to enter the mainstream of public consciousness. In particular, his idea of an exclusively womens' college had hardly entered the minds of even the most advanced feminists, and was not therefore a really existing shibboleth to be attacked. The idea of a feminine university was actually broached by Tennyson's friend John Mitchell Kemble during the course of a bitterly antifeminist article in the *British and Foreign Review* for July 1838. Tennyson began the composition of his poem under the influence of Kemble but changed his stance in the course of composition. As a result the poem begins as a satire on feminine aspirations and ends as a celebration of marriage as the vehicle of the divine evolution of man. [30]

For the narrative part of his story Tennyson turned to two Persian tales, printed together in Henry Weber's *Tales Of The East* (1812). The first of these, *Calaf and the Princess of China*, is through its French original the source of Puccini's *Turandot*. [31]

Tourandocte, Princess of China, is aged nineteen and surpassingly beautiful. Her picture has caused havoc in the hearts of young men all over the world. In addition to her beauty, she is a prodigy of learning and skill in every possible department of knowledge. However the princess is extremely cruel, and in order to avoid marriage has set her suitors a number of riddles, to fail in which is to be put to death. Eventually Calaf Prince of Tibet guesses the riddle after the princess has been betrayed by Adelmule–a confidante who has been rescued from a raging torrent. At length Tourandocte softens towards the prince and marries him of her own accord.

The second tale, printed as a résumé in Weber's preface, concerns Ferokh-Faul, Prince of Serendib, and the Queen of the Amazons. The prince falls in love with the portrait of the queen of the Amazon kingdom of Shunguldeep, who besides being extremely brave detests all men. The prince and a companion disguise themselves as singing girls and set out for the Amazon city. They perform at court, but soon realise they will not gain their ends in disguise. They therefore collect a band of warriors and attack the queen, who yields willingly when she learns that the prince hates women as much as she hates men.

These two tales account for most of the plot of Tennyson's *Princess*, and hence for the plots of Gilbert's two versions of the poem. There is no evidence to suggest that Gilbert was directly acquainted with the *Tales of the East*, or that he went to any source other than Tennyson for his ideas. In adapting his play as an opera he made only the changes necessary to accommodate a chorus and provide musical scenes for the composer to set. The fairy-tale quality of the Persian sources emerges strongly in the opera, and no doubt contributes towards its continuing stage vitality.

Princess Ida was performed at the Savoy on 5 January 1884, with rather less than the usual success. Sullivan composed much of the music, and conducted the first night, through an attack of kidney pain. He was in any case displeased with the very idea of comic opera, wishing to write works of a musically more substantial nature. Sullivan's ambition is a subject in itself, to which we must return. In April 1884 it took the form of a decision to write no more operettas for the Savoy Theatre. The decision would have stood but for a binding agreement of 8 February 1883 by which the composer agreed to supply D'Oyly Carte with a new opera on request for a period of five years; Carte insisted on his bond, and

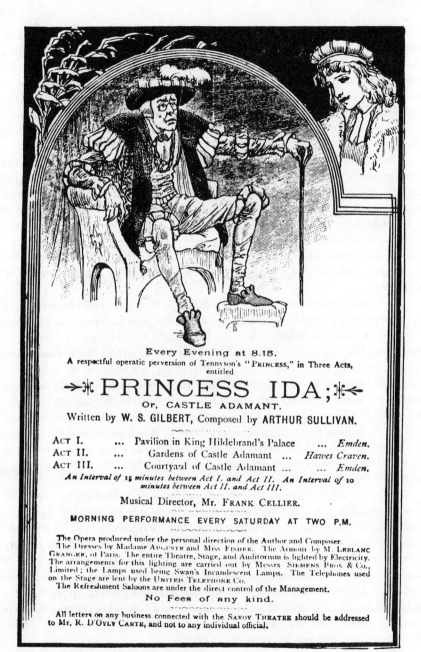

Every Evening at 8.15.
A respectful operatic perversion of Tennyson's "PRINCESS," in Three Acts, entitled

→⊁ PRINCESS IDA; ⊁←
Or, CASTLE ADAMANT.
Written by **W. S. GILBERT**, Composed by **ARTHUR SULLIVAN**.

ACT I.	...	Pavilion in King Hildebrand's Palace	...	*Emden.*
ACT II.	...	Gardens of Castle Adamant	...	*Hawes Craven.*
ACT III.	...	Courtyard of Castle Adamant	...	*Emden.*

An Interval of 15 minutes between Act I. and Act II. An Interval of 10 minutes between Act II. and Act III.

Musical Director, Mr. FRANK CELLIER.

MORNING PERFORMANCE EVERY SATURDAY AT TWO P.M.

The Opera produced under the personal direction of the Author and Composer.
The Dresses by Madame AUGUSTE and Miss FISHER. The Armour by M. LEBLANC GRANGER, of Paris. The entire Theatre, Stage, and Auditorium is lighted by Electricity. The arrangements for this lighting are carried out by Messrs SIEMENS BROS. & Co., Limited; the Lamps used being Swan's Incandescent Lamps. The Telephones used on the Stage are lent by the UNITED TELEPHONE CO.
The Refreshment Saloons are under the direct control of the Management.

No Fees of any kind.

All letters on any business connected with the SAVOY THEATRE should be addressed to Mr. R. D'OYLY CARTE, and not to any individual official.

Savoy Programme for *Princess Ida*

Sullivan was forced to yield. However he objected to the libretto proposed by Gilbert (see p 184), positively refusing to set it. Gilbert, who could see nothing wrong with his proposed subject, would not find another. For a time the partnership was actually in dissolution until Gilbert, in May, was inspired to *The Mikado* by the sight of a Japanese sword hanging on his study wall. It is the first of the Savoy libretti not to be constructed out of refurbished material, and it owes its existence to Sullivan's insistence that Gilbert should do something different.

The Mikado was, is, and presumably always will be the most popular of the Savoy series. It ran for two years in London, and conquered Europe into the bargain. No doubt the chief reason for this success is the splendid surge of inspiration which seems to have come jointly to author and composer after their earlier differences. In Pooh-Bah Gilbert created one of the memorable figures in comic literature—not a human being, certainly, but a magnificent grotesque. Sullivan was upset when Ethel Smyth told him she thought *The Mikado* his masterpiece, but the judgement has been endorsed by many generations of theatregoers.

The Mikado was produced on 14 March 1885. Its great success deprived us of the opera we might otherwise have had in 1886, and gave Sullivan time to devote himself once more to choral music. In June 1885 he travelled to America to supervise the New York production of *The Mikado* and visit his brother's wife and children in California, where, incidentally, their descendants are still to be found. He returned home in October, and at the beginning of 1886 began to consider the work he would write for the Leeds Festival in the coming October. This was *The Golden Legend*, written partly at Yorktown near Sandhurst, and partly at Stagenhoe Park, near Whitwell, Herts. When performed for the first time on 15 October 1886 it was immediately regarded as a masterpiece, except in Berlin, where it was greeted with a xenophobic 'What business has this foreigner here?'[32]

Gilbert's affairs during 1885/6 are not recorded. In October 1885 he proposed that the plot of the next opera should be the one Sullivan had already so firmly rejected. Once again Sullivan refused, but on this occasion Gilbert saved the situation by changing his mind voluntarily. On a snowy morning in January 1886 he travelled in haste to Sullivan's flat with the outline of the plot of *Ruddigore*, or as it was first spelt, *Ruddygore*. Gilbert wished to start serious work on the new subject immediately, but Sullivan, who was girding up his loins for *The Golden Legend*, did nothing until the Leeds event was out of the way. Gilbert finally delivered the completed *Ruddygore* libretto on 5 November 1886, whereupon the composer set to work in earnest.

Much has been made of Sullivan's habit of writing his scores under great pressure in the weeks immediately before production. In part this haste was a reflection of a taxing professional life punctuated by bouts of illness, but it was also a matter of deliberate policy. As anyone who has ever done it will know, the task of preparing a full orchestral score is exceedingly onerous, even when all the available short cuts are employed. Sullivan delayed the preparation of his scores simply because he knew that at any moment music might be lost through changes made at rehearsal; his delay was intended to ensure that he prepared the full score only of music which was actually to be performed. In the case of *Ruddygore* this policy was well advised, for the work was hastily revised after the first night.

The new opera was produced on 22 January 1887 to a reception of mixed cheering and boos. Sullivan's diary reports a friendly reception until the last twenty minutes of the second act, when parts of the audience took exception to Gilbert's revival of all the ghosts at the conclusion of the opera.[33] Given the premise that one ghost may return from the tomb to his childhood sweetheart, as does Sir Roderic Murgatroyd, there seems no reason in logic why a chorus of ghosts should not do likewise. Nevertheless Gilbert responded to the audience reaction of the first night by putting the ghostly aspect of the finale into its present form.

Considering the length of time available for its gestation *Ruddigore* is a surprisingly inept play, which has been subject to many cuts and alterations in the course of its performance history. Gilbert blamed the failure on the music for the ghosts, regarding it as insufficiently comic. Sullivan thought the music was ill provided for by the libretto, so much so that he left the score to Gilbert in his will—the only recorded malicious act of his career. On a happier note we may record the survival, in a hospital theatre in South London, of a number of the ancestral portraits from the first production of *Ruddigore*. One of the designs, a Jacobean falconer wearing a pale blue and brown costume, appears to have been used throughout the history of the D'Oyly Carte Opera Company.[34]

Ruddigore survived on the Savoy stage for less than a year—a poor run by the standards of Gilbert and Sullivan. Faced with the obvious need to provide a successor, Gilbert again proposed the plot Sullivan had so often rejected (May 1887). Sullivan agreed to look at it carefully if the librettist would provide a scenario, but reserved the right to reject it if it proved distasteful. In the meantime previous operas were to be revived to keep the theatre open.

In September Sullivan again rejected Gilbert's scenario, while Gilbert flatly refused to seek another theme. For a time it seemed there might be no new opera at all, but just as the chance sight of the Japanese sword made possible *The Mikado* so an advertising poster on Uxbridge railway station led Gilbert to another change of mind. On this occasion he saw a poster for the Tower Furnishing Company showing one of the yeomen warders of the Tower of London.[35] Gilbert at once recognised the possibilities of an opera set at the Tower, and by Christmas had completed a scenario which he read to Sullivan and Carte. After several changes of title this scenario was to be called *The Yeomen of the Guard*.

Sullivan expressed himself satisfied with the new idea, but early in 1888 he travelled to Algiers and Monte Carlo to meditate on his destiny, and on the rather more mundane subject of Alfred Cellier's *Dorothy* (Gaiety, 25 September 1886). *Dorothy*, an elegant and accomplished operetta, but hardly a great one, was destined to run for 931 performances—much longer than any work by Gilbert and Sullivan. Its success reminded the aggrieved composer of *Ruddigore* that talent as fine as his was not necessary to the making of a successful light opera, besides reinforcing the judgement—universally held by contemporary musicians— that his work with Gilbert was a prostitution of that talent. And, it must be said, no recent English composer, having written a work like *The Golden Legend*, would have thought it desirable to write another one like *Ruddigore*. In modern terms it is as though Benjamin Britten had written both the *War Requiem* and *Salad Days*. Who, in those circumstances, would have thought it right for him to spend his energies on even such a good show as *Camelot*?

In fact the desire to outstrip *Dorothy* preoccupied both Sullivan and Carte at this time. A letter written to Sullivan by Carte on 13 February 1888 reveals that both manager and composer had already sounded out Gilbert on the possibility of moving up-market into a more ambitious type of opera. [36] A new theatre was to be used, and a new company engaged. Late in February Sullivan wrote from Monte Carlo announcing to Gilbert his positive intention to abandon the present arrangements and begin again on more substantial lines. Gilbert's letter in reply is mostly an appeal to self-interest. It may have influenced Sullivan, but more likely the composer recognised in the historical romance of the *Yeomen* libretto the possibility of reconciling artistic ambition with financial reward. At least he decided to continue the collaboration.

Gilbert delivered the complete libretto 'in the rough' on 8 June, and in July Sullivan travelled to Fleet in Hampshire to begin composition. During August he insisted on some changes to the second act, and in September settled down to work in earnest. The opera was finally produced on 3 October 1888, not without apprehension from Gilbert, who carefully placed on record his view that the opening was too serious. In the event it ran for over a year, and was accounted their finest work by both partners.

With the exception of *The Yeomen of the Guard* all the Gilbert and Sullivan operas begin with a chorus. For the *Yeomen*, however, Gilbert chose to commence with the attractive picture of Phoebe Meryll sitting and singing at the spinning wheel. He had already employed this idea at the Gallery of Illustration in *Eyes And No Eyes*, wherein Clochette is discovered spinning outside her cottage. However, the decision to open with a solo may have had something to do with Gilbert's relationship with Jessie Bond, the actress playing Phoebe. In June 1887 Gilbert had been annoyed when Sullivan refused to allow the Savoy Theatre to be used for an afternoon performance of *Pygmalion And Galatea* in which Jessie Bond was to have enjoyed the solo spot as Galatea, the statue that comes to life. [37] When we find Jessie Bond entrusted with the solo opening of Gilbert's next libretto, is it too much to suppose that he was doing in one way something he could not do in another? For her part Miss Bond took her revenge on Sullivan in her memoirs, and in her conversations with Hesketh Pearson, who appears to have taken her at face value in his book on Gilbert and Sullivan.

During the course of 1888 D'Oyly Carte had bought a building plot for his proposed new opera house in Cambridge Circus, and on 15 December that year his wife laid the foundation stone of what was to become the Royal English

Opera. Sullivan's operatic ambitions were now supported in a positive way by the prospect of a building to house them, though it seems the opera house as such was Carte's personal plan. He, Sullivan, cemented his aspirations even further towards the end of 1888 by writing music for Henry Irving's production of *Macbeth* (Lyceum, 29 December). This production is remembered for Sullivan's fine overture, and for John Singer Sargent's portrait of Ellen Terry as Lady Macbeth, now in the National Portrait Gallery.

On 9 January 1889 Sullivan phoned Gilbert to explain to him his intentions for the future, expressing the hope that Gilbert would participate as librettist in the scheme. The discussions which ensued are part of a wider theme (see p 191). Essentially Gilbert refused to write words which could not be heard through the music, while Sullivan refused any longer to write music which gave primary consideration to the audibility of the words. Charge and countercharge went forth until the end of March, when Gilbert took refuge in the nobility of art and Sullivan was mollified by a promise from Carte that his work should open the new opera house. Until then, apparently, Carte had intended to open with an opera by another composer. By 24 April Carte was discussing terms for the renewal of the partnership, and all culminated in a handshake on 9 May. Sullivan asked Gilbert to develop a Venetian idea he had previously mentioned, whereat Gilbert produced the outline of *The Gondoliers* (8 June). The libretto was completed in October, and the music substantially written during November for production on 7 December 1889.

The Gondoliers ran at the Savoy for a total of 554 performances. Though the fact was hardly apparent at the time it was to be the last great success of the Gilbert and Sullivan collaboration. As far as the general public are concerned the collaboration enters limbo at this point; the better-informed enthusiast has heard the names of a few supposedly dull works perpetrated by both men during the 1890s; very few understand that the period is, if anything, the most interesting episode in their joint and separate artistic endeavour. In particular the efforts of Sullivan, struggling like a fly in marmalade to escape from the consequences of his Gilbertian past, are a source of fascination. Gilbert remained well content with himself, but the disastrous quarrel he perpetrated in 1890 was the source of all future ills. It should be remembered that *The Gondoliers* continued to be performed as a sunny background to the traumatic events which are about to be described.

During the preparation of *The Gondoliers* building work on Carte's new opera house was going ahead, placing on Sullivan the requirement to compose his opera forthwith. He therefore took his customary winter holiday abroad and returned home at the end of March 1890 to start the opera (*Ivanhoe*). Almost immediately a quarrel broke out between Gilbert and Carte over the question of preliminary expenses for *The Gondoliers*.

Like Sullivan, Gilbert had travelled abroad after the production of *The Gondoliers*. His trip took him to India, where he gathered a collection of seventy papier mâché heads for use as models if he should ever write an Indian opera. Returning home at the beginning of April 1890 he found that his first royalty cheque from *The Gondoliers* was smaller than expected. He called for a copy of the accounts and was appalled to find that Carte had spent £1400 on redecorating the front of the Savoy Theatre, including £500 on new carpets for the staircase and lobbies. Following an unpleasant scene with Carte, Gilbert wrote to Sullivan on 22 April setting out the grounds of the dispute and attempting to enlist the composer's aid against the manager.

The legal basis of Gilbert's position was an agreement of 8 February 1883 by which Carte, as the owner of the Savoy Theatre, let it to the business partnership of Gilbert-Sullivan-Carte for a rent of £4000 per annum. Any profit remaining after 'repairs incidental to the performances and rendered necessary from time to time by ordinary wear and tear' had been paid for was to be shared equally among the contracting parties.[38] Gilbert held that the carpets, not being 'incidental to the performance', should have been paid for by Carte alone as proprietor of the theatre, and not charged to the triumvirate of Gilbert-Sullivan-Carte. It should be said that this was not Gilbert's first brush with Carte in the matter of expenses; he had been suspicious of Carte's business methods since at least the days of *Patience*, and in 1885 had sought more control of the management side of the partnership. The £500 carpet was therefore not an isolated and unexpected grievance but the latest irritant of a series.

On 26 and 27 April Gilbert met Sullivan to discuss the situation, but when Gilbert suggested a new business agreement Sullivan proposed to let the matter rest for a week. By 3 May Sullivan thought it better to let the new contract wait until another opera was required (the contract of 1883 had been renewed on 8 February 1888). Exasperated, Gilbert wrote on 5 May terminating his collaboration with the composer, and forbidding Carte to produce any of his, Gilbert's, work after Christmas 1890. An attempted reconciliation in Carte's office ended in a display of hysterical fury on the part of Gilbert when Sullivan refused to sign a new contract, and openly sided with Carte over the carpet expenses.[39] By 9 May Gilbert had already entered into negotiations with Horace Sedger, manager of the Lyric Theatre, for the work that was to become *The Mountebanks*.[40]

On 4 July Carte was due to pay Gilbert's *Gondoliers* royalties for the April-July quarter. However, on the advice of his solicitors he decided to withold the sum until the carpet affair of the previous April was settled. On 16 July Sullivan refused to join in Gilbert's request for an examination of the Savoy bank account, and on 30 July Gilbert issued a writ for his unpaid royalties. Carte paid £2000 forthwith, but witheld the remaining part of the royalty, allegedly to cover the costs of an outstanding lawsuit brought by the American singer Lillian Russell at the time of *Princess Ida*.[41] Gilbert now applied for a receiver to be brought in at the Savoy, claiming that at least a further £1000 was owed to him.

Because of Gilbert's absence abroad—he was taking a cure for the gout at Carlsbad—the case was not finally heard until 3 September. After a day-long hearing, during which both Carte and Sullivan swore affidavits that the Lillian Russell lawsuit had not been settled, Gilbert was awarded £1000; Carte was ordered to present an account within three weeks, and to hand over all monies still unpaid within a further four days.[42]

Thus far the battle had been fought mostly between Gilbert and Carte, with both parties trying to enlist the support of Sullivan. According to his own statement,[43] Gilbert had in fact tried to keep Sullivan out of the court proceedings but had found it technically impossible to do so. However he now began to pursue two separate quarrels—a legal one with Carte over the theatre accounts, and a personal one with Sullivan over the composer's affidavit sworn in court on 3 September.

On 14 October Gilbert discovered that the affidavits sworn by Sullivan and Carte had been incorrect insamuch as the costs in the Lillian Russell lawsuit had actually been settled. As a substitute for accusing Sullivan of perjury, he claimed that Sullivan had accused *him* of perjury by swearing a contradictory affidavit. He demanded a retraction on the following humiliating terms:[44]

> I must ask whether you are willing to give me in writing a distinct retraction of the clause in your affidavit to which this letter refers, with permission to make such use thereof as may appear to me to be desirable.

Sullivan, who had followed Carte's advice not wisely but too well, declined to provide a written proclamation of his own mendacity. Would you? Gilbert subsequently modified his position, but pursued the matter relentlessly for months on end; he was still referring to it a year later. Sullivan, however, refused to submit. The two men drifted apart and were not formally reconciled until 12 October 1891, when they met at Sullivan's flat and shook hands.

Argument was not over yet, however. Late in 1892, when the question of a new collaboration was broached, Gilbert at once raised the old points about the division of profits. In a series of tart letters during November he reminded Sullivan of the dissensions of the past, and of the part he, Gilbert, had played in revealing the undeniable sharp practices of Carte over a number of years. The matter of profit sharing was not agreed until the end of November 1892, and not finally settled until January 1893, by which time work on a new opera, *Utopia Limited*, had already begun.

Before *Utopia Limited* could be written, however, both Gilbert and Sullivan had other work to do. Sullivan's *Ivanhoe* project was the culmination of much thought and long intention. As a young man he had written an opera called *The Sapphire Necklace* to a libretto by the critic H.F. Chorley; the work was never produced, and most of the music has disappeared. At another time he was reputed to be writing an opera to an Italian text on the subject of Mary Stuart. Sooner or later, with or without the association with Gilbert, he would have written an opera for one of the existing operatic outlets. What distinguished the *Ivanhoe* endeavour was not the fact that Sullivan was writing an opera but Carte's daring ambition (shared by Sullivan) to use *Ivanhoe* and the new opera house as the foundation of a glorious new chapter in the history of English opera. Ignoring all precedent and all experience it was hoped to make opera in English a commercially viable proposition by allowing each work a long consecutive run like a comic opera. Since there was no external financial guarantee it followed that if the opera house failed to make money it must close. Apparently this latter possibility did not occur to Carte, who was caught unawares when the cold light of reality began to break in on his dream.

The work on *Ivanhoe* begun in May and interrupted by the carpet quarrel was finally completed in December 1890. The first night, on 31 January 1891, was undoubtedly the climax of Sullivan's career: the military bandmaster's son conducted, in an opera house specially built for the purpose, the *magnum opus* which was to set English music on a new course of prosperity. For that night at least *Ivanhoe* was the still point of the turning world. Few artists can have experienced such a moment, and in Sullivan's case it was entirely self-generated.

The novelty of the event and generous praise in the press set *Ivanhoe* on a prosperous course. It became fashionable to go and see it several times, exactly as if it were an opera at the Savoy. The extended run lasted for six months, embracing a total of 155 performances—a number which only Rutland Boughton's *Immortal Hour* has ever surpassed. Nor, contrary to many statements, was the work forgotten thereafter. It was performed by the Carl Rosa Opera Company during the nineties, revived by Beecham in his 1910 season, and broadcast by the BBC in March 1929 (twice). The songs became standard items in the concert repertory, and two of them—'Ho Jolly Jenkin' and 'Woo Thou Thy Snowflake'—were constantly recorded in the years up to 1930. If a single work could possibly have established English opera, *Ivanhoe* was that work.

And yet the stigma of failure persistently attaches to *Ivanhoe*. In part this is because it has not become a repertory work, and never can; mainly it is because the unnatural success of Sullivan's part of the operatic project was immediately followed by the ignominious collapse of Carte's. When the initial run of *Ivanhoe* concluded, Carte followed it by running Sullivan's opera in tandem with Messager's *La Basoche*—a combination which failed to attract the public. Carte now found himself without resources. He negotiated in vain for operas by Cowen (*Signa*) and Bemberg (*Elaine*)[45]; rehearsals were begun for *The Flying Dutchman*, to be run with *Ivanhoe*, but the only piece actually to be produced was Sardou's *Cléopâtre* with Sarah Bernhardt in the title role. In short, the opera house made no money once the initial excitement of *Ivanhoe* had passed. To his great humiliation—but in entire consistency with his original philosophy—Carte was forced to sell his theatre for use as a music hall. The theatre, now called the *Palace*, is currently owned by Mr Andrew Lloyd Webber, who has musical ambitions of his own.

The collapse of the Royal English Opera had several consequences for Sullivan. It robbed him of his major platform for substantial operatic work and, more importantly, it placed him under a deep moral obligation to ensure that Carte's other theatre, the Savoy, remained viable. Ultimately this meant a renewal of the collaboration with Gilbert, whose activities must now claim our attention.

As we have seen, Gilbert commenced negotiations for a new opera almost as soon as his quarrel with Carte and Sullivan had begun. With Sullivan no longer obstructing it, he intended to produce the libretto which had been the cause of so much friction between them. The theme of this libretto, called 'the lozenge plot' by Sullivan, is one of transformation: by taking some kind of magic potion the characters become in reality the people they were formerly only pretending to be. A version of the libretto must have been in existence as early as 1882, for Sullivan had declined it then.[46] Now Gilbert offered it to Sullivan's pupil Arthur Goring Thomas (1850-92), the composer of an internationally successful opera, *Esmeralda* (1883).

Thomas commenced work on the libretto, subsequently called *The Mountebanks*, but in 1891 he began to show symptoms of mental disease, dying on 20 March 1892. Gilbert then turned as second choice to Alfred Cellier (1844-91), whose *Dorothy* had caused Sullivan so much heartsearching in 1888. Cellier had been musical director under Sullivan at the Opéra Comique before being replaced by his brother François in 1878; in addition he had contributed several curtain raisers for the Savoy operas.

Unfortunately for himself, Cellier was a dilatory worker, who had to be locked into his room to make him concentrate on his task. In 1878 he had been forced to pay £20 damages for the non-completion of a pantomime,[47] and now his slack attitude to rehearsals drew on him the full wrath of Gilbert, which wrath we must hope was withdrawn, for Cellier became fatally ill during the composition of *The Mountebanks*. He died on 28 December 1891 before he had completed the overture. A movement from his *Suite Symphonique* was used as a substitute, and the opera opened on 4 January 1892. It ran for eight months at the Lyric—a cheaper theatre than the Savoy—and has shown some power of survival, no doubt as a *quid pro quo* for the deaths of its two composers.

The Gondoliers finally left the Savoy stage in June 1891, at about the time *Ivanhoe* left the Royal English Opera. Sullivan refused a suggestion by Carte that he should set a libretto by J.M. Barrie, but in October agreed to write an opera called *Haddon Hall* with Sydney Grundy (1848-1914). Having completed some incidental music for Tennyson's *The Foresters*, he took the libretto of *Haddon Hall* with him to Monte Carlo in January 1892. Here he was joined by Grundy, with the intention that the opera should be ready by the spring.

Shortly after his arrival in Monte Carlo Sullivan was attacked by his kidney disease. He continued to write *Haddon Hall* through bouts of agony, as he had written many previous works, but at the end of February the illness took an acute, very nearly fatal, turn. Sullivan had already made the arrangements for his death when his nephew and servants placed him in a hot bath, an action which is supposed to have saved his life.[48] Returning home greatly weakened at the end of April, he took up *Haddon Hall* again in July, completing it for production at the Savoy on 24 September 1892. The opera ran until April 1893, a total of 204 performances. The music became extremely popular, and for half a century the work was a standard item in the repertory of amateur operatic companies.

By the gilt-edged standards of Gilbert and Sullivan neither *The Mountebanks*

Utopia Limited at the Savoy 1893
Photograph by W.S. Gilbert

nor *Haddon Hall* could be counted a profitable work. Already public taste had set in a mould which refused to accept the work of either man without the other. Gilbert first drew the logical conclusion by offering Sullivan a new libretto at the beginning of 1892, while the composer was still involved with *Haddon Hall*. Sullivan, who probably wished to be rid of Gilbert forever, prevaricated. He pleaded his involvement with the forthcoming Leeds Festival (October), and refused to involve himself in legal nit-picking over details of a new contract. Finally he took himself away to a winter villa at Cappé-Roquebrune near Monte Carlo, leaving Gilbert and Carte to sort matters out to their mutual satisfaction.

Over Christmas Sullivan's guest at Roquebrune was Sir George Grove, whose travelling expenses were paid by the composer. In January 1893 Gilbert settled his differences with Carte, and joined Sullivan and Grove. He brought with him a draft of a libretto called *The Happy Valley*, which he had first shown Sullivan earlier in the year. Both Sullivan and Grove declared this the best thing he had ever done, but Grove, who had several private walks with him, declared Gilbert, 'a hard cynical man of the world—a bitter, narrow, selfish creature'. [49]

In March 1893 Sullivan organised two concerts of English music at Roquebrune. The first, on 5 March, consisted of extracts from his own works, including the *Irish* symphony. The second, on 19 March, included works by Parry (*The Frogs*), Mackenzie (*Ravenswood*), Cowen (*The Language of Flowers*), and the newly famous scherzo from Stanford's *Irish* Symphony. [50] Returning home in April, Sullivan spent three days in May over the composition of an *Imperial March* for the opening of the Imperial Institute by Queen Victoria. At length, in June, he settled down to work on the new opera, now called *Utopia Limited*. The bulk of the music was written at Weybridge, where the score was completed on 29 September. Produced at the Savoy on 7 October 1893, it ran until June 1894—a total of 245 performances.

The principal soprano part in *Utopia Limited*, that of Princess Zara, was taken by a young American singer named Nancy McIntosh, whom Gilbert had heard singing at the home of Sir George Henschel during 1892. Gilbert's relationship with Miss McIntosh is a topic in itself; here it is sufficient to note that she could sing but not act, in spite of having been shown how to do so by Gilbert himself. Her unsuitability played its part in the relative failure of *Utopia Limited*, making Sullivan determined to have nothing more to do with her. Since Gilbert was devoted to her—his bound volume of her concert programme is in the British Library—the seeds of a further quarrel were soon sown.

Utopia Limited had begun life as promisingly as *The Mikado*, but by the third month of production word had got about as to the actual merits of the piece, and it became apparent that a successor would soon be needed. In January 1894 Gilbert visited Sullivan and begged him as a personal favour to write a part in the new opera for Nancy McIntosh, even though she could not claim it on merit. Sullivan did not refuse at first, though he wanted assurances that Gilbert would not attempt to settle any future differences in court.

With this proviso it was agreed to revive *The Mikado* until a new work by Gilbert and Sullivan should be ready. Gilbert, however, refused to allow a revival of *The Mikado* unless Nancy McIntosh sang Yum-Yum. Sullivan not agreeing to this, Gilbert withdrew permission for the performance of *The Mikado*. On 13 March 1894 Sullivan seems to have taken the initiative in breaking off future collaboration, whereupon Gilbert sought to work with Nancy McIntosh's teacher, George Henschel. Henschel, a famous singer himself, appears to have drawn the line at the hapless Miss McIntosh, and the proposal came to nothing. On the same day, 7 April 1894, Gilbert wrote to Sullivan expressing willingness to work with him again. Sullivan, however, was thinking of writing a ballet at this time; since Gilbert still withheld the performing rights of his works the Savoy did not see any operas by Gilbert and Sullivan for some while.

In the absence of the heavenly twins the Savoy was kept open by Messager's *Mirette*. Gilbert, with a libretto on his hands, arranged for it to be set by Osmond Carr (1858-1916), who had achieved success with the musical comedies *In Town* (1892) and *Morocco Bound* (1893). Produced as *His Excellency* on 27 October 1894, with the inescapable Nancy McIntosh in the cast, the work started well but soon faded owing to the inadequate nature of the music. Gilbert took the view that it might have been a second *Mikado* if set by Sullivan; we may agree with him to the extent of believing that Sullivan would have saved it from the oblivion which has fallen upon it. In fact *His Excellency* contains a higher proportion of intrinsically memorable verse than most of Gilbert's libretti. Anyone who thinks that the words of Gilbert are the cause of which Sullivan's music is merely the effect should obtain Osmond Carr's score and study it with care.

Under pressure from Carte to furnish the Savoy with a new opera, Sullivan attempted to oblige by reviving and revising his *Contrabandista*, written with F.C. Burnand in 1867. Having written the libretti of Sullivan's first two comic operas, Burnand always nursed the view that he himself might have filled Gilbert's place. Meeting for dinner in the late summer, Burnand and Sullivan discussed the situation at the Savoy; by the end of the meal they had agreed to resuscitate *The Contrabandista*. Sullivan must have seen the revival as an easy way to help Carte, Burnand as an opportunity to rival Gilbert. The new work was to be called *The Chieftain*.

The relationship between *The Chieftain* and *The Contrabandista* is not easy to summarise. Essentially the events of both acts of *The Contrabandista* are contained in the first act of *The Chieftain*; the second act of *The Chieftain* is written *de novo* as 'further adventures' of the characters from the first act. All of the re-used music from *The Contrabandista* is contained in the *Chieftain* first act; the second act is a fresh composition. The dialogue of both acts is written anew. Unfortunately Burnand proved incapable of improving on his earlier effort; by a clear margin the joint *Contrabandista/Chieftain* libretto is the poorest Sullivan ever set. British audiences, fixated on Gilbert, rejected it after 97 performances, though it did well in Germany.

The Chieftain ended its run at about the same time as *His Excellency*, neither work fulfilling the hopes of its creator. The inevitable effect was to draw Gilbert and Sullivan together again for a final attempt to win the favour of the public. It may be worth remarking in the context of the mediocre performance of *all* the works brought out at the Savoy during the nineties that public taste had undergone a distinct and permanent change with the invention of musical comedy. The first full-blown musical comedy is reckoned to be *The Shop Girl* (November 1894), closely followed by *An Artist's Model* (February 1895). These works immediately enjoyed the huge popularity which had belonged to Gilbert and Sullivan in the eighties, and made it harder for the Savoy style to stand up at the box office. *The Grand Duke*, for instance, which Gilbert and Sullivan were about to produce, had to contend with Sydney Jones' enormously popular *Geisha* (Daly's Theatre, 25 April 1896). Besides this, the Savoy was an expensive theatre to run; it could be kept open only by success—a *succès d'estime* like *Haddon Hall* was not enough to pay the gas bill, higher at this electricity-lit theatre than in the old Opéra Comique. In more ways than one the fat kine of the eighties devoured the lean kine of the nineties.

On 8 August 1895 Gilbert read to Sullivan an outline for *The Grand Duke* rather different to the final version,[51] and on 11th Sullivan agreed to set it. Gilbert now gave permission for his works to be performed once more. After a period of closure the Savoy opened on 6 November with *The Mikado*, followed on 7 March 1896 by *The Grand Duke*. When *The Grand Duke* collapsed in July, *The Mikado* returned to take its place. In this ignominious way the long collaboration of Gilbert and Sullivan came to an end. For Gilbert this was the effective end also of his creative life. He was sixty, and some way past his best. Sullivan, a man of much greater imaginative resource, still had music in him in spite of shattered health and the indifference of a public who could go to *The Geisha* for a kind of entertainment the Savoy did not pretend to provide.

Following the failure of *The Grand Duke* the official biography of Sullivan states that he spent the next couple of years in an alternation of royal visits, horse racing, and physical suffering. The Savoy Theatre was kept open by revivals of previous successes, by Offenbach's *Grand Duchess*, which actually did worse than *The Grand Duke*, and by *His Majesty*, in which F.C. Burnand, unabashed by *The Chieftain*, collaborated with Alexander Mackenzie.[52]

In fact the year 1896 seems to have been more complicated for Sullivan than the round of pleasure would suggest. The failure of *The Grand Duke* reinforced his desire to write music more substantial than operetta, but this time ambition was made urgent by the realisation that he had not long to live. If he was to do something further to fulfil his gifts time was short. Precise details of the course of events are lacking, but it is clear that Sullivan, in some agony of mind, attempted to resolve his problems by marrying a woman who would support him on the path of upward endeavour.

In the absence of his letters, it is hard to assess Sullivan's part in the affair with Rachel Scott Russell. Nevertheless it is probably true to say that while he had a full sexual appetite his affections were given to his family, and in particular to his mother. It is in this context that we should see his famous relationship with Mrs Mary Frances Ronalds, an American born on 23 August 1839. For reasons which it is not difficult to guess, Mrs Ronalds was pensioned by Napoleon III and described by the Prince of Wales as 'my very good friend'. Her social and musical gifts must have made her attractive to Sullivan, but her real value for him must have been that she could not ask him to marry her. As Victorian society was constituted she would have been ruined by the divorce proceedings necessary to separate her from a husband she had married in 1859, and from whom she had been separated in 1867. The benefit to Sullivan is clear: he could enjoy himself as a bachelor while allowing Mrs Ronalds to function as something very like a wife. In other words, she served as an emotional sheet-anchor, but was powerless to interfere in the composer's relationships with other women.

However, in terms of the events of 1896 Mrs Ronalds was definitely *persona non grata*, for she represented the past from which Sullivan desired to escape. While on holiday in Lucerne he had met Violet Zillah Beddington, the daughter of a wealthy and artistic family. Aged 21, Violet was obviously a gifted and distinguished woman, who in later life came to be called 'a miraculous flower' by Marcel Proust. Her sister Ada was a friend of Wilde and the artists of the nineties; her sister Sibyl became the confidante of Puccini. Sullivan must have seen in her a second Rachel Scott Russell—a beautiful and intellectual woman who would see to it that he wrote his missing masterpieces. He proposed to her, saying he had two years to live, which she had in her power to make fruitful. [53] She refused him apparently because she believed her parents would not consent to a marriage with a man in his fifties. [54] It is impossible to say how deeply Sullivan was touched by the affair, or whether marriage would indeed have altered his musical career. One thing may be said with some certainty, however: as Sullivan's widow Violet Beddington would have protected his interests more intelligently than his actual heirs; his manuscripts might not have been dispersed, and the ossifying post-humous influence of Gilbert on the D'Oyly Carte Opera Company might have been resisted.

The reaction of Mrs Ronalds to this important episode was understandably violent. She is said to have 'blown up' and 'made an awful scene'. [55] In August Sullivan forgot her birthday, and relations remained cool throughout the year. In January 1897 he was still sufficiently out of touch with her to enquire about her state of mind from a friend. [56] No doubt the failure of this attempt to break away ultimately bound him more securely to her.

In the meantime, he had contracted to supply the Alhambra Theatre with a ballet to celebrate Queen Victoria's forthcoming Diamond Jubilee. It had been his intention to complete the music by Christmas 1896, but the events of the year threw him off course. He therefore took his customary winter villa near Monte Carlo, and in January 1897 settled down to the composition of *Victoria And Merrie England*, as the ballet came to be called. It was a popular work, designed to make money, which it did.

The music of the ballet may be described as a Savoy opera without words; the story opens with a procession of druids and culminates in a *tableau vivant* of the coronation of Queen Victoria, incorporating on the way an 'Historical quadrille by Britons, Romans, Saxons and Normans', and 'Four Emblematic Pedestal Groups, representing Europe, Asia, Africa, and America', which are stated to have been 'exact reproductions of the Sculptures on the base of the Albert

Memorial, Hyde Park'.[57]

When the Jubilee was over Sullivan departed for Bayreuth and *The Ring*. He regarded *Die Meistersinger* as the greatest comic opera ever written, but could find little enthusiasm for *The Ring*. Returning home in September 1897, he began to talk about a new opera for the Savoy to be written with J.W. Comyns Carr (1849-1916). Carr was regarded as one of the wittiest men in England, but because he was little experienced as a dramatist it was decided to enlist the help of Arthur Wing Pinero (1855-1934). Pinero, whose work is not forgotten today, had a reputation for being able to construct a tight plot. A collaboration between Carr and Pinero should in theory have produced a brilliant libretto, for Sullivan could hardly have found two more distinguished men with whom to work. In fact they proved intractable collaborators, who refused to make alterations for the sake of the music.

Faced with these difficulties, Sullivan retired for the winter to the Riviera, where Comyns Carr joined him for a period of ten days. After many struggles with his health and with his text, which he described as 'a mass of involved sentences', Sullivan completed the opera, *The Beauty Stone*, for performance on 28 May 1898. His reward was a run of fifty nights—a hopeless failure by his own standards.

The Beauty Stone is unlike the other Savoy operas. In form it is a French opéra comique, made up of substantial musical scenes connected by dialogue. The formal Gilbertian placing of the chorus was abandoned, and the chorus functioned throughout as a crowd. As far as one can judge from their statements, the joint authors deliberately risked failure at the box office in order to produce a work of art. They may be said to have succeeded inasmuch as they supplied Sullivan with his first—and last—libretto of credible psychological motivation. Unfortunately the considerable merits of the libretto are disguised by a repellent mass of Wardour Street verbiage, which even Victorian contemporaries mocked. Sullivan for his part had to face the unpalatable fact that the Savoy Theatre was now associated exclusively in the public mind with comedy, and with his own earlier works with Gilbert.

Sullivan's main professional occupation during the remainder of 1898 was the conducting of the Leeds Festival in October. At this, his last festival, his physical state was such that Stanford and Cowen were retained throughout to take over his duties if he should collapse. The most important of the new works was Elgar's *Caractacus*, the production of which brought Sullivan and Elgar together, earning for Sullivan Elgar's lasting gratitude.

In the meantime plans for a new opera at the Savoy went ahead. This time the work was to be an undisguised comedy, as close to the familiar type as possible. On 11 November 1898 Sullivan had been introduced to Captain Basil Hood (1864-1917). Hood was a former military man, who had seen service in Ireland. Sullivan admired his ability, and the two men quickly decided on an oriental opera to be called *Hassan*. Sullivan was pleased with the new story, but before work could begin he became ill with influenza. As soon as he recovered he went to the Riviera, and thence to Switzerland. Here Hood joined him during the summer of 1899. Composition was begun in July, but a further deterioration in the composer's health again prevented progress. The opera, now entitled *The Rose of Persia*, was completed at Weybridge on 18 November, and produced at the Savoy on 29 November 1899.

Contrary to Sullivan's own expectation *The Rose of Persia* became the most profitable work to be seen at the Savoy since *The Gondoliers*. Good judges declared it his masterpiece in comic opera, and it has retained a permanent place in the repertory of amateur operatic societies. The libretto might reasonably be described as 'by W.S. Gilbert out of Sharazād.' Hood has taken the essence of his plot from the *Arabian Nights* tale *The Sleeper Wakened*, with hints from several other places, especially perhaps the tale of Alī Ibn Bakr and Shams al-Nahār. [58] The result is a pleasant evening's entertainment, which in a good production offers as much as *The Gondoliers*. The conclusion of the *Rose of Persia* libretto is the starting point of Weber's *Abu Hassan* (1811).

When *The Rose of Persia* ended its run in June 1900 the Savoy Theatre was kept open by revivals of *The Pirates of Penzance* and *Patience*, Sullivan having agreed in the meantime to write a new work with Basil Hood.

Contrary to his habit, Sullivan spent the winter of 1899/1900 in London. A recurrence of his kidney complaint drove him to Monte Carlo at the end of February, but he soon returned home via Paris, where he was forced by illness to break his journey. On 26 May he received a request from the Dean and Chapter of St Pauls for a *Te Deum* of Thanksgiving for the end of the Boer War, which was then regarded as imminent. This he agreed to attempt.

At the end of June Basil Hood brought the scenario and some lyrics of an Irish opera to be called *The Emerald Isle*. Sullivan was pleased, but the capture of Pretoria, also in June, seemed to promise a rapid end to the Boer War. He therefore took a house in Shepperton, where he completed the *Te Deum* in July. This *Te Deum* is his last completed work. Written in a straightforward massive style, it introduces the tune of *Onward Chrtistian Soldiers* in the final chorus.

Having completed the *Te Deum*, Sullivan went to Switzerland to begin work on the new opera. The first notes were written on 23 August. Between this date and the middle of September he composed the bulk of his contribution to *The Emerald Isle* as it now stands. Work on the opera was finally made impossible by 'violent neuralgia' and an inflamed throat. Sensing his approaching end, the composer set out for London, which he reached on 19 September.

October and the early part of November were passed in illness, during which it became apparent that Sullivan was dying. His inability to attend the opening night of the *Patience* revival on 7 November drew a friendly letter from Gilbert. Much has been made of his letter as evidence of final reconciliation between Gilbert and Sullivan, but it should not be forgotten that Gilbert had cut Sullivan dead on the last occasion they are recorded to have met, the previous June. [59] Gilbert had also refused to speak at the first night of the *Sorcerer* revival in September 1898.

Apart from the throat and kidney complaints, Sullivan was now suffering from bronchitis, exacerbated by a visit to his mother's grave on November 2nd.

The Rose of Persia, 1899
Walter Passmore as Hassan
Emmie Owen as Honey-of-Life
(*The Sketch*, 10 January 1900)

In the afternoon of 21 November his condition underwent a serious deterioration, and early in the morning of the 22nd he suffered a heart attack which killed him. It was the morning of Saint Cecilia's day, the patron saint of music.

Sullivan had expressed the desire to be buried beside his mother in Brompton cemetary. However, his will was set aside by the wish of the Dean and Chapter of St Pauls Cathedral, and he was buried in the Cathedral crypt. In the course of an extraordinary career Sullivan had created a position in English music which had not existed before him—that of a widely loved native composer. Since his day the succession has passed naturally to Elgar, Vaughan Williams and Britten, all of whom stood indebted to him for having brought about the change in attitudes which made their own recognition possible.

At his death Sullivan had written enough of *The Emerald Isle* to make reconstruction of the remainder a viable prospect. The work was entrusted to Edward German (1862-1936), who did it to such purpose that the posthumous opera became a great success when produced at the Savoy on 27 April 1901. Of all the works written by Sullivan apart from Gilbert it is the one which approaches most closely to the familiar style.

As for Gilbert himself, the 1890s may be seen in retrospect as a period in which the destructive consequences of the Carpet Quarrel began to work through. Gilbert won the quarrel in the legal sense, but it was a victory which cost him his artistic *rapport* with Sullivan. The traumatic court scene of 3 September 1890 remained as a permanent impediment to the marriage of true minds.

In that same September Gilbert had moved to his last home—Grim's Dyke, a large mock-Tudor mansion on Harrow Weald. Here, in large grounds surrounded by spring guns, Gilbert became a gentleman farmer, a Justice of the Peace (1893), and Deputy Lieutenant of the County of Middlesex. From 1893 he began to suffer from gout, so much so that the rehearsals of *Utopia Limited* had to be conducted from a wheelchair. However the gout left him in 1902, and he lived the rest of his life without major ailments.

Gilbert made his years at Grim's Dyke idyllic in his own particular way. The grounds of the house became something of an animal sanctuary as the librettist acquired a large collection of dogs and cats, a fawn, lemurs, monkeys and a donkey named after Adelina Patti. He tamed wild birds, and would allow no pheasants to be shot. At the amateur level he practiced photography, astronomy, and conjuring. He dressed up as a sheikh at fancy dress parties, and he danced the highland reel. During his earlier residence in London his house had been famous for children's parties, at which he spent more time with the children than with adults. At Grim's Dyke the children's parties apparently ceased, but he often welcomed children as guests at garden parties. He held regular dinner parties at which he surrounded himself with pretty women; in the privacy of his study he wrote fanciful letters to some of them. Fancifully also he selected a squirrel for his crest because his imagined ancestor Sir Humphrey Gilbert had been lost in the frigate *Squirrel* in 1583. At the end of the nineties he travelled to the Crimea to see for himself the scenes that had captured his imagination as a young man; at the death of Sullivan he was in Egypt with his wife and Nancy McIntosh.

Apart from the four libretti which have already been mentioned he wrote little. Even here it is apparent that *The Mountebanks* was substantially created in the 1880s, while *His Excellency* is said by Hesketh Pearson to have been a 'patched up' version of an old libretto.[60] In 1891 he produced a burlesque of *Hamlet* entitled *Rosencrantz and Guildenstern* (Vaudeville Theatre, 3 June). It is an amusing squib, the leading idea of which is that Claudius is annoyed by Hamlet's play because he is himself the author of it. Shortly before Sullivan's *Haddon Hall* he produced an operetta with music by George Grossmith called *Haste To The Wedding*. This work is based on *The Italian Straw Hat* (Criterion Theatre, 27 July, 1892). A play of 1897, *The Fortune Hunter*, is remembered because it became the occasion of a lawsuit in which Gilbert's powers of repartee were displayed to the full.

The Fortune Hunter opened in Birmingham on 27 September 1897. It was badly received, so much so that, when it moved to Edinburgh, Gilbert followed to oversee the production in person. To judge by his own account he was dissatisfied with his hotel, and this fact, together with the non-success of *The Fortune Hunter*, loosened his tongue. In an interview given to the Edinburgh *Evening Despatch* he took the opportunity to say that his favourites among his own works were *The Yeomen of the Guard, Gretchen*, and *Broken Hearts*, for into them he had put most of himself. Having attacked imported French plays because they kept respectable paying customers out of the theatres, he turned his attention to the great actors of his time: Irving, Tree, and George Alexander were unable to speak blank verse except in a dull and monotonous way. He slashed at musical comedy for its 'irresponsible comedians', and dismissed Sydney Grundy, the librettist of *Haddon Hall*, as a mere translator.[61] The interview soon reached London, drawing the following comment from *The Era*:

> Mr Gilbert's abnormal self-esteem has with advancing years developed into a malady. In his own estimation he is a kind of Grand Llama or Sacred Elephant of dramatic literature. The mildest criticism of his work, the most gentle disapproval of one of his plays, is a crime of lèse-majesté for which, if it were in his power, he would punish the culprit severely.... Mr Gilbert's career has been a succession of combats with the object, alas! unattained, of vindicating the Gilbert theory of the universe against sceptics and rebels.... his real kindliness and good-nature have simply been obscured by the abnormal protruberance of his bump of self-esteem.[62]

Gilbert immediately demanded £1000 damages in a lawsuit which brought him into contact with two of the leading advocates of the day—Marshall Hall and Edward Carson. His replies in evidence to these gentlemen are extensively quoted in books on Gilbert and Sullivan as examples of his wit, which indeed they are. A short single example must suffice here. Edward Carson questioned him about bad musical comedies:[63]

CARSON: Give me the name of one.
GILBERT: There are fifty of them.

CARSON: Give me one.
GILBERT: I would say such a piece as *The Circus Girl*.
CARSON: Would you call it a bad musical comedy?
GILBERT: I would call it bad. I believe the manager calls it a musical comedy.

Elsewhere Gilbert was less genial, revealing the unacceptable face of his power to destroy others with a word by a display of personal sensitivity. Sir Henry Irving had taken the opportunity to reply to Gilbert's criticisms at a dinner held by the Sheffield Press Club:[64]

CARSON: Did you observe that... Sir Henry Irving spoke good humoredly but warmly about the criticisms upon himself?
GILBERT: I do not admit that he spoke good-humoredly but warmly. I noticed that he spoke most angrily and spitefully concerning me. He described me as a librettist who soared to write original comedy.... I cannot conceive why he did so. I have never had an angry word with him, and I cannot conceive why he should be so spiteful.

Upset by the demise of *The Fortune Hunter*, Gilbert wrote nothing further until 1904, when he produced *The Fairy's Dilemma*, a clever burlesque which is to the conventions of pantomime what *A Sensation Novel* (1871) is to the conventions of the three-volume novel. The time for such things was long past, but Gilbert did, nevertheless, enter on a new period of theatrical prosperity with a series of revivals of his operas at the Savoy Theatre.

Following the death of Sullivan (22 November 1900) and Richard D'Oyly Carte (3 April 1901), the management of the Savoy devolved upon Carte's widow, Helen Susan Black (1852-1913).[65] Mrs D'Oyly Carte supervised the production of *The Emerald Isle*, and the first London revival of *Iolanthe*. The theatre was then let to William Greet, who was responsible, among other things, for the production of German's *Merrie England* (2 April 1902). On resuming the management of the Savoy in December 1906 Mrs D'Oyly Carte commenced a series of revivals of the Gilbert and Sullivan operas under the stage direction of Gilbert, who received £5000 for the five-year performance rights of his works, plus a £200 rehearsal fee for each opera.

These revivals marked the first dawning of public awareness that the Gilbert and Sullivan operas might be not simply successful entertainments but permanently durable works of art. They were rapturously received by audiences but excoriated by Gilbert, who found that Mrs D'Oyly Carte and her musical director François Cellier had engaged people who were primarily singers rather than actors for the principal parts. He raged at her, but had signed away the legal right to determine who should appear in his work. So disgusted was he that when the performing rights again became available for renewal in May 1910 he again sold them to Mrs D'Oyly Carte for £5000. Apparently he thought the quality of the productions had so far damaged the value of his libretti as to make them nearly worthless.

Sullivan had been knighted in May 1883 for the services he had rendered to the Art of Music in England. No one had any thought of knighting Gilbert until 1907 when, perhaps, someone thought it would be better to be safe than sorry. Gilbert treated the honour lightheartedly, saying it was a commuted old age pension. He accepted it mainly because it was the first knighthood to be conferred solely for dramatic authorship. His shoulder was tapped on 30 June 1907 by Sullivan's old Friend Edward VII. Characteristically, Gilbert called to mind the Royal Command performance of *The Gondoliers* at Windsor (6 March 1891) when his name had supposedly been omitted from the programme.

Though the dates speak for themselves, it is very hard to think of Gilbert as an old man. It comes as something of a shock therefore to realise that he embarked on his last operatic libretto at the age of 72. This was *Fallen Fairies*, an adaption of *The Wicked World* (1873). As was the case with *Princess Ida*, the blank verse text is taken largely from the earlier play, but on this occasion there was no comparable success. With music by Edward German the work was produced at the Savoy on 15 December 1909. Nancy McIntosh, given the leading role at Gilbert's behest, was dismissed from the cast by the manager (C.H. Workman) after only six days. Gilbert instantly took legal action on her behalf, but all was rendered null and void by the failure of the work, which ended six weeks later. Gilbert however was so annoyed with Workman that he refused permission for a revival of *Ruddigore*, which was to have been the next work performed. If this revival had gone ahead we would have had the benefit of Gilbert's own revision of the libretto. To judge from his stated intentions he would have cut out as much of the second act ghost music as possible, supinely assisted by the composer's nephew, Herbert Sullivan.

Little now remains to be told. Gilbert's life continued on its pleasant way, with trips to the Azores and Constantinople in 1910. Apart from loss of creative power there were few signs of diminished mental vigour. He mellowed to the extent of wishing some of the acerbic incidents of the past had never taken place, and he expressed himself in sentimental terms about his partnership with Sullivan. But these were momentary lapses; to the end he retained his faultlessly clear memory for ancient insults and his mastery of minatory prose. His decision (1897) to modify the illustrations of the *Bab Ballads* which is often treated as a sign of decay had in fact been taken in principle as early as 1875.[66]

Gilbert's last play was a short sketch entitled *The Hooligan* (Coliseum, 27 February 1911). Perhaps inspired by Dumas' *Derniers Jours D'Un Condamné*, this work depicts the last hours of a convict in the condemned cell.

On 29 May 1911, a fine day, Gilbert rose in good health and spirits. He visited some friends in Chelsea in the morning, paid a visit to the sick room of his friend May Fortescue, and lunched at the Junior Carlton Club with the Kendals, apparently as a gesture of reconciliation after a longstanding quarrel. In the afternoon he had an engagement to teach two young ladies to swim in the artifical lake at Grim's Dyke. The girls entered the water before he did, and one of them, an actress named Ruby Preece, got into difficulties. Gilbert swam out rapidly to rescue her, but his heart failed under the strain. He sank beneath her, and when finally pulled from the water was found to be dead. He had once expressed a wish to die on a summer day in his own garden; the wish had been fulfilled.

Unlike those of Sullivan, Gilbert's remains were not treated as a national relic. He was cremated at Golders Green, and buried in Great Stanmore church-yard. His wife survived until 1936—quite long enough to see him take his place among the fixed stars.

2: Gilbert's Personality

W.S. Gilbert once wrote of himself, 'I am an ill-tempered pig, and I glory in it.' This statement is wholly true; yet its implications have never been grasped by students of the librettist. There exists a mountain of evidence to suggest that he had a highly abnormal personality, was capable of hysterical anger, sustained vindictiveness, bullying, mental cruelty, and total selfishness. The story of his life is to a large degree the story of the way he expressed these characteristics in action: all the biographies and books on Gilbert and Sullivan record them, while contriving at the same time to deny them or treat them as a joke.

In the matter of denial the 'official' biography of Gilbert by Sydney Dark and Rowland Grey is as pious a piece of hagiographical whitewash as ever saw print. These authors deliberately censor the unpalatable aspects of Gilbert's nature in order to present the portrait of a benevolent despot, just but kindly, and devoted to animals and little children. 'The grim Gilbert of tradition,' they tell us, 'never existed'. [1] Much the same view is propagated by Hesketh Pearson, who did Gilbert the great honour of writing his life twice, once in his composite study *Gilbert And Sullivan* (1935), and separately, at full length, after Gilbert's papers had been made available to him (1957). Pearson made an honest record of what he found, but was determined to endorse the earlier opinion: [2]

> In fact, apart from his satirical genius and business acumen, he [Gilbert] was a typical, easy-going, unadaptable, independent, disrespectful, prejudiced, grumbling Englishman, who scorned everything he did not curse, accepted the conventions and made fun of them. He was cantankerous in manner and generous in deed. His sentimentality was screened with bluster. While looking at the face of a friend who had just died, he burst into tears, rushed from the room, pounded down the stairs to the accompaniment of loud oaths, seized the butler and bellowed wrathfully: "George, have you seen my bloody umbrella?"

Self-caricature by W.S. Gilbert:
'I am an ill-tempered pig & I glory in it'

This judgement, or a derivation of it, has become the standard account of Gilbert's behaviour. Writing at the height of Freud's fashionability, Hesketh Pearson made it a professional principle not to probe the subliminal depths of his subjects, preferring to let their own words and actions speak for them. He had, besides, an admiration for wits and men of action which made him disinclined to look sharply at Gilbert, who was both witty and active. In the case of Sullivan he had no such natural sympathy, and the result is a picture of the composer as unfriendly as that of the librettist is aimiable.

Gilbert himself had no interest in the workings of his own mind, or indeed of anybody's mind. His diary is mundane; the subjective is excluded from his correspondence. Nevertheless he stated on several occasions that his 'real' self was contained in his blank verse plays and in the character of Jack Point in *The Yeomen of the Guard*. Convinced as he was that Gilbert was actually a healthy Englishman, Pearson treated Gilbert's insight as a delusion, the sentimental self-deception of the clown who would be Hamlet. Once again he, Pearson, has been followed by the generality of writers, who cannot believe that Gilbert the amusing bully was 'really' the bloodless creator of the blank verse plays. The result is a double misconception: on the one hand Gilbert's genuine nastiness is denied, on the other the confessions of *Broken Hearts* are laughed off. The possibility that Gilbert might have been a truly ill-tempered pig with a truly broken heart is not even countenanced.

Hesketh Pearson's determination to have nothing to do with Freud was justified in many ways. Freud's theories are ultimately unscientific because they can be neither quantified nor falsified. On the other hand the middle class Viennese among whom Freud made his observations did not differ materially from the middle class Victorians from whom Gilbert sprang. Even if the ideas of Freud are restricted in time and place, therefore, their time and place are substantially those of Gilbert also. The Freudian analysis may or may not have value for modern child rearing practices—if it illuminates the nineteenth century that is sufficient. In the pages which follow I have embarked on a Freudian account of Gilbert's personality because I have come to find compelling the ease and simplicity with which Freudian theory accounts both for the pig in him and for the broken heart. Essentially I shall argue for an interpretation of him as a sadomasochist at the infantile level. It will of course be open to the reader to interpret the evidence in an entirely different sense.

But first the evidence itself. What was Gilbert like? What impression did he make when met face to face? The answer to this question is hard to find; many contemporaries recorded meeting him, few chose to dwell on the experience. The following extended account is given by that intelligent man Seymour Hicks, who was related to Gilbert by marriage:[3]

> ... wittily devastating to a degree was W.S. Gilbert, who had a strange personality if ever there was one. His small piercing eyes, which looked as if they had been long robbed of sleep, were generally fixed, maliciously it must truly be said, on big people and seldom directed towards the smaller fry. He

always gave me the impression that he got up in the morning to see with whom he could have a quarrel. I'm not sure this really was the case, for at heart he was a very kindly man, and above all things a very just one. Still, he seemed incapable of geniality, especially in the company of men, though being a great admirer of pretty women he took endless trouble to amuse them. But for the male species he seemed to trouble very little.

He was always extremely pleasant to me, but try as I would, I never got any further with him. He was full of harmless vanities and couldn't bear opposition of any kind, and I'm sure there were very few people, even his intimate friends, with whom he didn't, sooner or later, have misunderstandings. Most of the stories he told were of personal grievances, the battles they had caused, and the verbal victories he had won, but I'm bound to say that the constant repetition of his passages-at-arms and the stock jokes he indulged in, while being amusing at first, became very like one of his own flashes when someone said to him, 'Mrs So-and-so was very pretty once,' and he replied, 'Yes, but not twice.'

He was a local magistrate at Pinner, and nothing pleased him more than to be spoken to as 'Judge'. Those nearest to him always addressed him in this way, and it seemed amazing to me that so small a thing could tickle the vanity of one of the most critical men of his time. I should like to have heard the satyrical lyric he would have written about an acquaintance if it had been told him that the gentleman was really proud of being a member of a small country tribunal. It would have been such a literary surgical operation that the patient would have died of ridicule. Yet this observer of observers couldn't see himself.

He was invariably listened to by everyone with great deference, partly because of his position, and also because I never met anyone who wasn't rather afraid of him. I think that often he had no intention of being unkind and perhaps did not realise how much his cutting wit hurt. Jests came to his lips like lightning, and were fired off on the instant....

I well remember him some time before he received the honour of knighthood (which I rather gather he felt he ought to have received at the same time as Arthur Sullivan) being particularly bitter against the authorities, who, he said, handed out these things indiscriminately, by delivering himself of the following: 'It is not so much for my friends who ought to have an honour that I really mind—what's worrying me is that the Government may make my butler a knight. He's a damn good fellow and I'm afraid it may upset him.'

Six feet four, he delighted at the age of five-and-sixty to imitate Harlequin and, doing a *pas-bas*, he would often spin round and throw himself lightly into the third position. I always felt that, as he invariably did this for the edification of his lady friends, the performance was given to impress upon them the fact that his youth had not deserted him in the slightest degree. An easily-to-be-forgiven weakness, perhaps, but one, had he seen it in others, he would assuredly have held up to merciless ridicule.

One of his greatest regrets in life was his failure to achieve success in serious dramatic literature. His strong play *Daniel Druce*, with Herman Vezin in the leading part—an elocutionary type of histrion—pleased no one, but his own sense of humour helped him little in the disaster.

For its failure he was content to blame Vezin, the public and the Press, and indeed everyone connected with it but himself. He was extremely intolerant and, for a man of his enormous intellect, curiously childlike in being unable to see the other man's point of view....

I myself, unfortunately, met his displeasure just before his death in the most innocent way possible. He sent for me one morning and said, 'I hear that you and Charles Frohman are stuck for a play. You can have *Ruddigore* if you like, and I think, my dear Hicks, George Grossmith's part will suit you admirably.'

Knowing that the play was an extremely expensive one to launch—the uniforms alone in the second act having cost a small fortune on the opera's original production—I made many polite excuses in an endeavour, after thanking him for the honour he had done me, to convince him that the undertaking was one which neither Mr Frohman nor myself was in a position to embark upon. (As a matter of fact Mr Frohman at this time did not know which way to turn for money). Gilbert listened to my excuses and then, after a pause, said rather angrily, 'Oh, you don't want to do the piece because I suppose you think it was a failure at the Savoy. Well, so it was—it was the only failure I ever had with Sullivan. We made £7000.' Very confused, I tried to explain that such a thought had never entered my mind and that it was only a question of ways and means, but it was no good. The great man turned on his heel and walked away. I met him at the Garrick Club many times afterwards, but he either looked over my head or, if he found himself opposite me, as he did on one occasion at luncheon, very pointedly talked to the men on either side of me as if he was unaware of my existence. For Gilbert to do this to someone so immeasurably his junior struck me as extremely foolish. But I don't think he could help these things, for he was always manufacturing affronts against himself, and was really more of a spoiled child than anything else.

These memories of Seymour Hicks relate to Gilbert as he was in the early years of the twentieth century. For a picture of him as he was before he achieved wealth and fame in conjunction with Sullivan it is instructive to turn to a pamphlet published in 1877 by the actress Henrietta Hodson. The pamphlet was privately printed as part of a dispute with Gilbert over revivals of his blank verse plays at the Haymarket. As leading lady at the Haymarket, Miss Hodson (actually Mrs Henry Labouchère) naturally expected to play principal parts, but Gilbert did his best to prevent her appearing, as he had already done in connection with other plays of his. The actress decided to expose his behaviour publicly by printing an account of her relations with him since 1874. The full title of the pamphlet is 'A letter from Miss Henrietta Hodson, An Actress, to the Members of the Dramatic Profession, Being a Relation of the Persecutions which she has suffered From Mr William Schwenck Gilbert, A Dramatic Author. April 1877':

I had known Mr Gilbert for several years. In 1874 I saw a great deal of him, as I was then the lessee of the Royalty Theatre, and he wished to write a play for me. He told me that, somehow or other, he had invariably quarrelled with everyone with whom he had been professionally connected, and I took the greatest pains to prevent giving him any cause to quarrel with me. I agreed with him in all that he said, and I concurred with him in all his opinions. When he complained that Shakespeare had statues elevated to him, whereas he, who was in every way Shakespeare's superior, had none, I went so far as to console him with the assurance that, if only he would be patient, there could be no doubt that he too would live to see his own statue. When he abused all

"Come to interview me? It is what I have longed for"

"I have to be extremely strict at rehearsal"

Bab Found Out
(*The Tatler* No 162, 3 August 1904)

"No, you are quite wrong; this is not a family portrait"

"I always rehearse the ballet myself"

"I find this exceedingly useful in maintaining domestic discipline"

"These? Oh, they are only the heads of natives who annoyed me in India"

"Good-bye; thanks so much. Allow me—a trifling cheque"

"These pistols, I must explain, were used by my aunt at Malplaquet"

other dramatic authors, all critics who did not praise him, and the numerous actors and actresses with whom he had disputes, I did not defend them. Even when he told me stories, how he had "humiliated" actresses who had dared to resent his unprofessional behaviour, I kept my indignation to myself, and uttered no protest. When he said, that Miss Robertson had ventured, at a dinner party, to observe that she did not like one of his plays, in which she was acting, and that, before he forgave her, he had forced her to cry and humbly sue for pardon, I merely replied that anyone who questioned his great ability must be insane. Thus I kept on good terms with him, and it was settled that he should write a series of plays for me. The first was *Ought We To Visit Her*. It was adapted from a novel of Mrs Edwardes, and it was agreed that I should pay him £3 for each representation. The rehearsals commenced, and all went smoothly until the day before the appearance of the play. I was congratulating myself that I had managed not to have a single quarrel with my quarrelsome friend, by carrying out all his suggestions without even discussing them; for not only did I wish to avoid all disputes in the interest of my Theatre, but my *amour propre* was engaged in succeeding, where everyone else had failed.

The last rehearsal was going on when suddenly Mr Gilbert jumped up, and commenced pulling his hair and dancing like a maniac. 'Look,' he said, 'at that man reading a newspaper,' and he pointed to Mr Bannister, who was rehearsing the reading of a newspaper on stage. 'Do, pray,' I said, 'let the rehearsal go on quietly, and if anything goes wrong, make a note of it, and we will go all over it again.' On this he put on his hat, and, without a word, walked out of the theatre.

Gilbert's own privately printed reply to Miss Hodson tells us that he had had general disagreements with her at rehearsals, [4] but does not attempt to refute her other statements. In his fury he appears to have spoken a number of hard words about her, none of which were true. She had recourse to her solicitors, and he was forced to sign an apology which she made public. What is of psychological interest is her account of his behaviour in the solicitor's office, and of his sensitivity towards his own *amour propre* in seeking to prevent the publication of the apology:

Shortly after this I discovered that, whilst he had professed to be on the most friendly terms with me, he had been abusing me to my friends, and telling them, that I was in the habit of making use of bad language during rehearsals.... [At the solicitor's interview] Mr Gilbert vainly endeavoured, by subterfuges and quibbles, to avoid admitting what he had said. At last, when he had at length been brought to own that he had acted as I had been informed, and that his assertions had been entirely untrue, Mr Lewis insisted upon his signing a written apology. He appeared to be in a condition approaching madness, walked about the room, drank glass after glass of water, and, only when Mr Montagu Williams joined with Mr Lewis in urging him to comply, and told him there was no excuse for his misconduct, the ... document was drawn up and signed by him.... A few days afterwards I received a letter from Mr. Gilbert imploring me not to publish the apology, as, if I did, he said, that he could never show his face again.

The scene in the solicitor's office in 1876 may be compared with the following incident described by Hesketh Pearson as taking place in Richard D'Oyly Carte's office at the Savoy during the Carpet Quarrel: [5]

Carte continued to argue while Gilbert sat glowering. Suddenly Gilbert turned to Sullivan and demanded his opinion. Without hesitation Sullivan sided with Carte. Gilbert instantly saw red.

'You are no gentlemen,' he shouted, 'for you should answer to me. You are both blackguards!'

He then let loose a torrent of abuse that shocked Carte and hurt Sullivan, rushed at the door, wrenched it open, and bellowed a threat:

'I'll beat you yet—you bloody sheenies!'

The door banged, the atmosphere lifted, and the two remaining members of the firm breathed freely.

To return to Miss Hodson's narrative. The publication by her of Gilbert's unwilling apology was followed by a revival of *Pygmalion and Galatea* at the Haymarket. Gilbert tried to prevent her appearing in the play, but when this failed subjected her to the following treatment at rehearsals (December 1876):

> The rehearsals commenced. Mr Gilbert's whole behaviour to me was a studied insult. He neither spoke to me nor looked at me, but only recognised my presence by a distant bow. Mrs Arthur Lewis (Miss Kate Terry) used to sit on the stage, and, when I was rehearsing my part, he talked and laughed with her; when I was offstage all conversation ceased, and he paid attention to what was taking place. Others unconnected with the theatre were brought in, as well as Mrs A. Lewis. One day it was Mr Gilbert's father, another day Mr Arthur Lewis, another day Mr Hare, and Mr Gilbert never failed to show before them, the same marked inattention to rehearsals, whenever I was on the stage.

An actress is not necessarily on oath when she publishes a private pamphlet. One might ascribe her account to imagination if its entire truthfulness were not attested by Gilbert's behaviour to other actresses who annoyed him. The first actress to play the part of Galatea was Madge Robertson, later Dame Madge Kendal. She resisted Gilbert's wishes in connection with the play, leading him to take his own type of revenge. He would take a party to a box—presumably not during the public performance—pay great attention while the other members of the cast were speaking, but turn his back on the stage whenever Madge Robertson appeared. He would then 'talk audibly with his friends, punctuating the conversation with loud laughs'.[6] Another Galatea, Janette Steer, was threatened with a legal injunction to secure her conformity. Finally, in the eighties, he reduced Mary Anderson to tears because her conception of Galatea differed from his own. Eventually she secured a public triumph, only to be insulted by Gilbert, whose judgement had proved in error, and who now suspected that the success of the play was due to her rather than him.[7]

Just how far Gilbert was prepared to go in the matter of persecuting women is illustrated by the case of the Comtesse de Brémont. The Comtesse de Brémont appears to have been an early specimen of the liberated woman, who had published erotic verse (whatever *that* means in the Victorian context) and associated with actors and jockeys in South Africa. She was a journalist, who in October 1894 asked Gilbert for an interview. He told her that his interview fee was twenty guineas, whereupon she replied that she would be happy to write his obituary for nothing. This tart reply enraged Gilbert. He wrote to *The Times* and *The Daily Telegraph* about what was, after all, a private correspondence, calling it an example of 'feminine spite'. The Comtesse brought an action for damages, whereupon he sought information in New York—she was American by birth—Paris and Cape Town to prove that she was not a countess at all and that her previous life was not above reproach. This evidence he produced in court, winning his case after the lady had been in his words 'vivisected in the witness box'.[8] Having won he became conciliatory, waiving his costs and ending by calling the countess his sister. No doubt he would have described any further resistance on her part as an example of feminine ingratitude.

Persecution of a different but hardly less humiliating kind was characteristic of Gilbert's methods of rehearsing the actors and actresses who appeared in his plays. He preferred to work with novices, who would be in no position to hold inedependent ideas on how the parts should be performed. It was his habit to rehearse repetitiously until the lines were delivered with the exact inflexion he required, accompanied by precisely the gesture he had predetermined. As long as he encountered no resistance he was infinitely patient; when resistance came he was ruthless in supressing it. Many anecdotes exist describing his methods, which were sufficient in 1885 to reduce George Grossmith to the use of drugs to calm his nerves.[9] The following incident, narrated by Seymour Hicks, well shows the degree of public humiliation he was prepared to inflict in order to have his will:[10]

> At rehearsal once the story is told of him that, having gone back and back in a part with a well-known actor until he was tired, he left the stage for the stall and said: 'Now we'll begin all over again.' The actor, who no doubt was angry at being sent over the words so often and shown up before a large company, thought he would cross words with Mr Gilbert and save his face by picking a quarrel. He waited until he was told again it was all wrong for about the hundredth time, and then, stepping down to the footlights, he shouted to the man of a thousand Savoy delights: 'Mr Gilbert, I am not a very good-tempered man.' 'No,' said Gilbert, 'I'm not considered to have the temper of a saint either.' 'But I'd like you to understand, Mr Gilbert, that I am a very strong man.' 'Really?' said Gilbert. 'Well I stand six feet four in my stockinged feet, but if you want to know the difference between us, I am an extremely clever man.'

The brilliance of this rejoinder, its arrogance and its callousness, become more apparent the more it is studied. But it was not merely in rehearsals that Gilbert sought to wield power. His whole concept of the theatre was authoritarian, as the following letter shows. It was written on 11 December 1889 to a member of one of D'Oyly Carte's touring companies, then playing *The Mikado*:[11]

> I have just seen a telegram from the Stage Manager to the effect that on his remonstrating with you as to your performance of Ko-Ko, you defied *his authority*. I assure you, in your own interest, that such a course of action is

most prejudicial to your advancement. The principle of subordination must be maintained in a theatre as in a regiment. If an unreasonable order is given it must be acted upon, and its unreasonableness represented to a higher authority. This is the rule of the Savoy Theatre, and no one would be retained on its staff who hesitated to recognise it. I find on enquiry that Mr Carte's grievance does not refer to your altering the dialogue, but to the introduction of *inappropriate, exaggerated, and unauthorized* 'business'. I need hardly say that one is as much an infraction of discipline as the other, and no actor will ever find his way into our London Company who defies any authority in this respect.

Putting together the information gathered so far, we find that Hesketh Pearson's 'typical easy-going Englishman' was highly authoritarian, extremely sensitive to supposed insults, relentlessly determined to avenge those same insults, oblivious to the feelings of others, conceited enough to regard himself as greater than Shakespeare, jealous of other people's success, boastful of his victories (which included making women cry), repetitious, hysterical in anger, abrupt, boorish, and, when facing exposure, cringing. The point which so often has been evaded, must be pressed home: who are the Englishmen of whom such behaviour is typical? The Victorians, like the Elizabethans, were robust people, but Gilbert was unique among them. Manifestly he was *a*typical and *ab*normal. One wonders whether he ever in his life held a proper conversation, that is, a discourse in which two people exchange opinion and information simply for their mutual pleasure.

It is against this background of abnormality that Gilbert's interest in murder takes on a significance one might not otherwise ascribe to it. Murder, and attendance at murder trials, was a standard Victorian interest. The newspapers of the day, including *The Times*, gave proportionately much greater space to crime than is the case today. Gilbert shared this interest to the full, having a detailed knowledge of many murder cases. In 1875, while engaged in the composition of *Broken Hearts*, he posed as a 'practising lawyer' in order to gain admission to the trial of Henry Wainwright, a gentleman who had put three bullets into the brain of his mistress, and, having failed to destroy her body with lime—he used the wrong sort—had cut it into ten pieces in order to carry it across London to a safe place. [12] In about 1899 Gilbert called on the novelist Anthony Hope bringing with him an account of the murder of William Weare by John Thurtell. Thurtell was a sporting and gambling bully who had lost a great deal of money to Weare, a solicitor of Lincoln's Inn. Thurtell shot Weare and hid the body with the aid of two accomplices, Probert and Hunt. The accomplices turned King's Evidence, and Thurtell was hanged in January 1824. [13] Gilbert's reaction to the Ripper murders which coincided with the production of *The Yeomen of the Guard*, is not recorded, but he attended the trial of Crippen in October 1910, and exhibited great anxiety lest the culprit should be acquitted. [14] For the purposes of his last play, *The Hooligan*, he obtained permission to spend time in the condemned cell at Pentonville, where Crippen had been hanged only a few weeks before (23 November 1910). [15] Similarly, one of the sources of the *Grand Duke* libretto of

Illustration by W.S. Gilbert to his
father's *The Magic Mirror*

1896 is a press cutting about the electric chair (first used in 1888) which had been sent to Gilbert by an American correspondent.

To add to his interest in murder, Gilbert had at least a small collection of macabre objects. The famous sword which inspired *The Mikado* was a genuine executioner's sword, hung by Gilbert in his library. This sword, which had presumably drawn blood, was actually carried on stage. One of Gilbert's pieces of furniture was a large oak sideboard of 1631, the property of Sir Thomas Holt, who had murdered his own cook by splitting his head with a cleaver. Finally, when the stage properties of the Savoy Theatre were auctioned on 4 November 1891—the Gilbert and Sullivan partnership being then in abeyance—Gilbert bought the executioner's block from *The Yeomen of the Guard*. This block at least had not been used, but he might have purchased Jessie Bond's spinning wheel.

If we turn now from the evidence of Gilbert's life and character to that of his art, a very similar portrait emerges. We have seen that Mark Lemon rejected *The Yarn of the Nancy Bell* as 'too cannibalistic' for the readers of *Punch*. Lemon has generally been derided for taking a priggish attitude to a harmless bit of fun; yet the following lines from *Annie Protheroe* (1868) are positively devilish in their implication. An executioner, called Gilbert Clay, prepares his axe for use against his rival the following morning: [16]

> He chipped it with a hammer and he chopped it with a bill,
> He poured sulphuric acid on the edge of it, until
> This terrible avenger of the Majesty of Law
> Was far less like a hatchet than a dissipated saw.
>
> And ANNIE said, "O GILBERT dear, I do not understand,
> Why ever are you injuring that hatchet in your hand?"
> He said, "It is intended for to lacerate and flay
> The neck of that unmitigated villain PETER GRAY!"

These lines are accompanied by a drawing of the ragged axe. For an issue of *Fun* in 1864 Gilbert had provided a picture of 'a most wicked gentleman calmly holding a baby in a pair of tongs over a blazing fire'. [17] For the final page of his own father's *The Magic Mirror* (1866) he provided a drawing of a hanged man. The drawing shows not the inert corpse of the victim, but the contortions of the death struggle. A more familiar scene of torture is to be found in the second act of *Ruddigore*. It will be remembered that the Baronets of Ruddigore are compelled by an ancient family curse to commit a crime a day or perish in agony; the curse is administered by the family ghosts, who keep the living Baronet up to his work by occasional doses of torture. So much could well have been given in narration, but Gilbert chose to depict the moment of torture on stage. Having refused to commit his crime Robin Oakapple is surrounded by the ghosts, who make gestures towards him as he writhes with pain, 'It gets worse by degrees'. In performance the effect of the scene is usually mitigated by an unconvincing mime of agony from the actor playing Robin; our concern here is with the mind of the man who thought such a scene funny enough to include in a comic opera.

The subject of torture is inevitably associated with the Tower of London. In writing *The Yeomen of the Guard*, therefore, Gilbert was able to introduce it naturally by way of artistic verisimilitude. Wilfred Shabolt, Head Jailor and Assistant Tormentor, describes the fine points of thumbscrew operation:[18]

> Truly, I have seen great resolution give way under my persuasive methods (*working a small thumbscrew*). In the nice regulation of a thumbscrew—in the hundredth part of a single revolution lieth all the difference between stony reticence and a torrent of impulsive unbosoming that the pen can scarcely follow. Ha! Ha! I am a mad wag.

Torture as the theme is not found in Gilbert's work with Sullivan before *The Mikado* (1885), where it breaks forth with vigour. It is not unreasonable to speculate that the outburst, which never completely died down in later works, was a by-product of the emotions engendered by the first properly deadly quarrel with Sullivan (see p 185). In any case *The Mikado* is familiar to audiences worldwide as an opera whose libretto is concerned to no small extent with boiling oil, burial alive, execution, suicide, the extraction of teeth and, of course, the gentle art of self-decapitation, 'Even if you only succeeded in cutting it half off, that would be something.' Jokes about pain and punishment are so much part of the texture of this libretto that it is hard to find a single short excerpt. The following paean to the block is much admired:[19]

> To sit in solemn silence in a dull, dark dock,
> In a pestilential prison, with a life-long lock,
> Awaiting the sensation of a short, sharp shock,
> From a cheap and chippy chopper on a big black block!

Much less well known is a lyric in the second act of *The Gentleman In Black* (1870). We move from the invigorating discussion of sudden death to the altogether more arcane topic of flagellation. The wicked steward Grumpff enters cracking a whip. He informs us that his employer keeps him to flog the women and children, while the strong men are flogged by machinery. 'But don't you abuse my whip: I'm very fond of my whip—I always have it about me':[20]

> No giddy flirt is this good whip:
> If once it holds you in its grip,
> Of fickleness you can't complain,
> It comes again, again, again!   (*Cracking whip*)
> You can't forget it—if you do,
> Be sure it will remember *you*—
> Its warm attentions will not wane,
> 'Twill come again, again, again!   (*Cracking whip*)
> A heedless whip, it little recks
> Of beauty, figure, age or sex;
> If once it hold you in its rein
> It comes again, again, again!   (*Cracking whip*)
> A democrat—prepared to strike!
> The old, the sick, the weak alike!
> When once it's been, it's always fain
> To come again, again, again!   (*Cracking whip*)

Besides being a very good description of Gilbert's own methods of dealing with the world, this song hints at possibilities within his character for which no evidence otherwise survives. Is it possible, one wonders, that he actually satisfied a taste for flagellation at one of the specialist establishments of Victorian London? The question must be abandoned because it cannot be answered. Nevertheless the lyric reads very much as though it were an intruder from some normally concealed corner of the writer's mind.

The man who holds the whip is of course in a position of dominance, able to hurt and humiliate others by making them submit to his will. Several of Gilbert's libretti make their fun out of the humiliating situation of the characters. Best known is *Utopia Limited* in which King Paramount, though nominally an absolute despot, is in reality in thrall to two wise men who threaten to have him blown up by dynamite if he disobeys them. The wise men have used their power to make the King write and publish a scandal sheet in which his morals are impugned. They have also forced him to write a comic opera wherein his personal appearance is burlesqued and the tenor gives grotesque imitations of the Royal peculiarities. In other words the king is forced to humiliate himself on pain of death; the audience are invited to enjoy watching him squirm. Gilbert once mooted a libretto set in the time of the French King Henry III; the attraction for him could well have been the subjection of that monarch to the Duc de Guise.

If humiliation features as an element in the plot of *Utopia Limited*, it forms the mainspring of *His Excellency*. The chief character is one Governor Griffenfeld, a practical joker who has tricked a young sculptor and a young doctor into believing they have been given court appointments. Elated, the young men are anxious to propose to the Governor's daughters, who are party to the plot. The ladies encourage the men, knowing their ultimate downfall. In order to obtain more exquisite pleasure from his trick, Griffenfeld arranges for a strolling player to impersonate the country's Regent and hand out more bogus honours. In the event the player turns out to be the true Regent, and Griffenfeld himself is humiliated. It is a neatly worked plot, further enlivened by a corps of Dragoons, who are humiliated by being made to drill as ballet girls. The essence of it all is put in a trio:[21]

> Oh what a fund of joy jocund lies hid in harmless hoaxes!
>> What keen enjoyment springs
>> From cheap and simple things!
> What deep delight from sources trite inventive humour coaxes,
>> That pain and trouble brew
>> For everyone but you!

Gilbert enjoyed practical joking in private life, having a distinct talent for humiliating or embarrassing his friends. Hesketh Pearson tell the following story of Gilbert's time as Government clerk:[22]

> ... [Gilbert threw out mysterious hints] to his fellow-clerks that he exercised considerable influence in the world of the theatre. One of the latter, much impressed, approached him with a request:
> 'Could you write me an order for the play, Mr Gilbert?'

'Of course I could. What shall I write it for – stalls or a box?'

'A box, if you please.'

Gilbert promptly wrote the order.

Next day the clerk approached him with a different expression on his face and a different sort of request. He had taken his wife and family to the theatre, had presented Gilbert's order, had been mortified by the laughter with which it was received, and wanted to know what Gilbert meant by it?

'I did precisely what you asked me to do,' Gilbert replied. 'You asked me whether I could write you an order for the play. I replied that I could, and in fact I did; but I never said that it would be of the least use to you.'

At this point the case may well rest. Was Gilbert or was he not a 'typical easy-going Englishman'? Apart from Mark Lemon the only critic to come straight out with a negative answer has been Sir Arthur Quiller-Couch. In a passage that has been much derided for its lack of humour, Couch wrote as follows:[23]

> But Gilbert had a baddish streak in him; and one in particular which was not only baddish but so thoroughly caddish that no critic can ignore or, in my belief, extenuate it. The man, to summarize, was essentially cruel, and delighted in cruelty. I lay no heavy stress on his addiction . . .to finding fun in every form of torture and capital punishment. This indeed persists in his work from *The Bab Ballads* right through the plays.

These remarks carry with them a certain tone of moral condemnation. Whether Gilbert should be condemned in the moral sense is a matter of opinion. What is surely not open to doubt is the reality of the cruel streak in him, which was not confined to his art, but manifested itself in many ways in his treatment of other people. In this respect both life and art can only be regarded as expressions of the same quality.

But what, precisely, *is* the quality of Gilbert's cruelty? In standard Freudian theory sadism is said to be a combination of sexual drive or libido with the death instinct, aggressively directed outwards towards other people. In effect this means that the sadist derives pleasure from practices—sexual or social—which hurt, humiliate or destroy those who fall into his power. By this account Gilbert was clearly a sadist. He sought power not merely in order to achieve a particular end, but because he enjoyed being the master of other people's fate. He deliberately sought to destroy all those who opposed his will, and boasted about it afterwards; he was fascinated by violent death, and once put a scene of torture on stage for a joke.

And yet Gilbert does not seem to be sadistic in the full sense. The full sadist has an intense relationship with his victim; he lingers over the pain he causes, and is anxious to witness its minutest effect. If the victim cannot feel, the sadist has lost his pleasure. Gilbert, by contrast, behaved as if he were totally oblivious to the feelings of those he hurt. His chief concern always seems to have been with himself and with his own feelings. If his wishes were thwarted in any way he raged mercilessly and relentlessly until his power was restored, whereupon he would continue placidly as if nothing has happened. He treated his actors not as persons but as puppets, without independent will or even existence; he bullied them, but did not care whether they laughed or cried as a result. In all his many quarrels, lawsuits, witticisms and persecutions it is the absence of relationship which differentiates them from sadism proper. To him dominance was merely the just order of the universe, intensely satisfying, at any cost in pain to those other people whose disobedience provoked his wrath. Of sexual pleasure, except in the special Freudian sense that all pleasure is erotic, there is no trace.

Only one kind of sadist has no relationship with his victims—the baby. The consciousness of the baby has none of the sympathetic qualities we prefer to associate with the adult mind. The baby is entirely self-centred; he sits enthroned at the topmost point of his egocentric universe, and is aware of others only as appendages to his own needs and wishes. The idea that other people might have an independent existence does not occur to him; if they thwart him, he rages at them for failing to obey his imperious ego; when they obey he is content, for they are mere instruments to him. Omnipotence is the key to his character; it is the source both of his anger and of his peace.

Both in life and in art the cruelty of Gilbert appears to derive precisely from an omnipotent infantile ego. It will be remembered that he was placid—indeed patient—until some untoward event threatened his power, whereupon he would erupt and not cease to rage, either in person or through law, until the status quo was resumed. The case of the Comtesse de Brémont is interesting in this respect, partly because it shows the cycle in complete form, partly because it shows that Gilbert—like the baby—was oblivious of the sex of the person who had offended him. The first mistake of the countess was to be a woman of a certain repute; she offended Gilbert by offering to write his obituary for nothing, but he did not administer a private rebuke; instead he howled publicly in letters to the national press, and when she worsened her crime by issuing a writ, the response was literally a worldwide gathering of retaliatory material. Again this material was not communicated privately to the countess—she would certainly have withdrawn the writ—but was used for a public 'vivisection' of the culprit, who was then expected to be good in future. For his part Gilbert ceased to bear ill will as soon as he had won. The basic mechanisms of this process may be observed in any pram or pushchair in the High Street; central to it is the omnipotence of the infantile ego which recognises nothing as valid outside itself. Gilbert was unusual only inasmuch as he remained in the condition of a baby throughout his long life.

Having established Gilbert's identity as a baby in the literal sense, we are now in a position to see clearly into a number of aspects of his life and work which have seemed odd or inexplicable, or merely part of his originality. First, and most obviously, the name *Bab*, which Gilbert first bestowed on himself at the age of thirty. *Bab* is short for 'babby' or 'baby', and is the name used for Gilbert by his family when a child. In re-employing it in 1866 as a pen name Gilbert appears to have been giving subconscious acknowledgement to his own infantilism. James Ellis, the editor of the *Bab Ballads*, has recognised the fundamental baby quality in them:[24]

... the truth is that the 'Babs' are addressed to the child in each of us—to that ineradicable part of us that delights in being selfishly asocial, in having its own way at all costs, in being spiteful and vengeful, in letting chaos come again—the child we try to outgrow or at least disguise. Hovering as it does between the naive and the diabolic, it is a quality which causes some to laugh and others to wince. The bizarre little creatures in the Bab Ballads . . . are mentally and temperamentally children, masquerading as knights, bishops, generals and sea dogs. . . . Children can get away with murder, so to speak—the sort of social murder Gilbert often wanted to commit.

Ellis assumes that the infantilism of the Bab Ballads is a mask deliberately worn by Gilbert rather than a direct expression of his personality. However we have seen too much of Bab in action to accept this. The flavour of the Bab Ballads is not easy to capture in a single brief quotation. Highly pertinent to the present discussion is The Story of Gentle Archibald (1866), a tale in which a little lad is turned by an obliging fairy into a miniature harlequin:[25]

Some dreadful power unseen, but near,
Still urged him on his wild career,
And made him burn, and steal, and kill,
Against his gentlemanly will.
The change had really turned his brain;
He boiled his little sister JANE;
He painted blue his aged mother;
Sat down upon his little brother;
Tripped up his cousins with his hoop;
Put pussy in his father's soup;
Placed beetles in his uncle's shoe;
Cut a policeman right in two;
Spread devastation round, - and ah,
He red-hot-pokered his papa!

Gilbert, it will be recalled, was aged thirty when he wrote these words; it is part of his childishness that his physical age, right up to the time of his death, hardly seems a subject for comment. The rather similar lines in Patience were written at forty-five.

Thus far the name of Freud has not intruded much into our discussions. It is not necessary to invoke Freud in order to establish Gilbert's infantilism or to describe the nature of his cruelty. However, we may now perhaps turn to the sage of Vienna for uesful light on what might be termed the dynamic working of Gilbert's personality. The following passage is taken from the second of the Three Essays On Sexuality (1905):[26]

The cruel component of the sexual instinct develops in childhood even more independently of the sexual activities that are attached to erotogenic zones. Cruelty in general comes easily to the childish nature, since the obstacle that brings the instinct for mastery to halt at another person's pain—namely a capacity for pity—is developed relatively late.... It may be assumed that the impulse of cruelty arises from the instinct for mastery and appears at a period of the sexual life at which the genitals have not yet taken over their later role. It then dominates a phase of sexual life which we shall later describe as pre-genital organization.

These words describe Gilbert at any time of his life. As we have seen, it is *Bab's* failure to develop a relationship with his victims which prevents him being classed with the adult sadists; Freud separates out the directly sexual component of childhood cruelty, while suggesting that the child is not restrained by a capacity for pity. The pre-genital organisation referred to by Freud relates to the child as he is before the age of about five. This organisation has two or perhaps three stages: the oral stage; the anal-sadistic stage; ambivalence—predominantly anal-sadistic. [27]

According to Freud, these stages represent a time in the life of a child when sexual energy has not yet found its proper outlet through the sexual organs—the energy fixes itself instead first on the mouth then on the anus. A true genital stage is reached at about the age of five, but there is then a period of latency until puberty proper. The oral stage is of interest to the student of *Bab* inasmuch as Freud says it is cannibalistic, being 'derived from the apparatus for obtaining mastery'. [28] That is to say, the mouth is the oldest and most primitive of the means for satisfying the great instinctive needs.

It would not do to make too much of the cannibalism of *The Yarn of the Nancy Bell* in this connection, though we are entitled to note it as consistent with Gilbert's infantilism. Much more interesting and significant is Gilbert's extreme oral aggression, which had the effect of consuming those against whom it was directed. Hesketh Pearson, who reports Gilbert as being able to swear non-stop for five minutes without repeating himself, describes an occasion in 1909 when the librettist attacked the scene painter Joseph Harker for failing to carry out his (altered) wishes. 'I have seldom heard more violent abuse hurled at anyone than that with which Gilbert assailed me on this occasion,' said Harker. Fortunately for himself, Harker was independent of Gilbert's patronage, but *Bab* later took the opportunity to make a public announcement of the scene painter's non-cooperation. In wit it was much the same story; Gilbert used his verbal facility almost literally to bite the head off those who annoyed him. As might have been expected, he dominated dinner table conversation, and Seymour Hicks has recorded the egocentric obsession of his ordinary talk. In other words, Gilbert fully exemplifies Freud's description of the mouth in the oral stage as an 'apparatus for obtaining mastery'.

As its name implies, the anal-sadistic stage is a period in which sexual pleasure is derived from the exercise, or deliberate non-exercise, of the anal function; in its 'ambivalent' form, this period may, in Freud's view, last throughout life, 'The predominance in it of sadism and the cloacal part played by the anal zone give it a quite peculiarly archaic colouring'. [29]

No evidence survives to enable one to judge Gilbert's status in cloacal matters directly, though we are entitled to surmise that he was, *par excellence*, one of those babies who refuses to do as he is bidden on the pot. He did, however, show to a marked degree the traits of what Freud called the anal-erotic character. In his essay *Character And Anal Erotism* (1908) Freud says it is a fact of clinical experience that neurotic people who as children have refused to empty their bowels when placed on the pot will show in later life certain characteristics:[30]

> The people I am about to describe are noteworthy for a regular combination of the three following characteristics. They are especially *orderly*, *parsimonious* and *obstinate*. Each of these words actually covers a small group or series of inter-related character traits. 'Orderly' covers the notion of bodily cleanliness, as well as conscientiousness in carrying out small duties and trustworthiness. Its opposite would be 'untidy' and 'neglectful'. Parsimony may appear in the exaggerated form of avarice; and obstinacy can go over into defiance, to which rage and revengefulness are easily joined.

According to Freud the orderliness, parsimoniousness and obstinacy are sublimations of an original anal erotism. Gilbert's neuroticism is self-evident; he was also orderly, parsimonious and obstinate. Taking the characteristics in turn, we find orderliness as a leading principle of his life. As we have seen, he reacted strenuously to any and every disturbance of the order of his egocentric universe; when arranging the contents of that universe he insisted on order throughout. Thus his actors were drilled like soldiers to a pre-ordained pattern, and his choruses were arranged in neat lines and semicircles. When other methods of coercion failed, he regularly resorted to the written code of the social order, the law, to win his way. His written work carries orderliness and regularity to great lengths, not merely in the rigid patterns of the verse, but in the generally neat shape of the libretti. Even the scenery and costumes of his works were subject to careful control; it was his standard practice to ensure the accuracy of all uniforms worn on stage, while the rigging of *H.M.S. Pinafore* was as nautically correct as he could make it. We do not read that his private life was arranged by the clock, like Kant's, but he certainly expected punctiliousness in his guests. In business affairs no detail of a contract or controversy was too small to receive his attention. Unlike Sullivan, he was never late with his work.

As far as the surviving records go, Gilbert was not parsimonious. Provided his omnipotence had not been disturbed he was capable of almost generous acts of charity; nor did he live meanly—quite the reverse. Nevertheless a very strong concern with money is evidenced in all his business dealings, and in such remarks as the confession that he had never written any verse—especially not love verse—for which he had not been well paid. The comment on the £7000 made from the failure of *Ruddigore* which Seymour Hicks reports was made several times. Insofar as it lay in his power he always presented himself to the world as a businessman rather than artist, and the Carpet Quarrel owed at least part of its ferocity to his discovery of Carte's dubious methods of accountancy.

A clear example of parsimony at work in Gilbert's imagination is to be found in *The Grand Duke*, where the character of Rudolf exhibits orderliness and parsimony in equal measure. Rudolf is immensely wealthy, but he deliberately lives a mean life while surrounding himself with cheap ceremonial which is strictly maintained. His opening song manages to combine parsimony and orderliness in unmistakable form within the space of a few lines:[31]

> I weigh out tea and sugar with precision mathematical—
> Instead of beer, a penny each—my orders are emphatical—
> (Extravagance unpardonable, any more than that I call),
> But on the other hand, my Ducal dignity to keep—
> All Courtly ceremonial—to put it comprehensively—
> I rigidly insist upon (but not, I hope, offensively)
> Whenever ceremonial can be practised inexpensively—
> And, when you come to think of it, it's really very cheap!

Like the torture scene in *Ruddigore* this material appears to proceed straight from *Bab's* subconscious mind; it assumes an interest on the part of a public audience in something which is in fact peculiar and private. Later in the opera Rudolf and his bride Caroline von Krakenfeldt sing a duet celebrating the joys of a mean marriage. In Freud's terms they are celebrating the joys not of conjugal love but of fecal retention, the connection between gold and faeces being well established.[32] The life the couple hope to lead is described as 'a most beautiful and touching picture of connubial bliss in its highest and most rarefied development':[33]

> CAR: As o'er our penny roll we sing,
>   It is not reprehensive
>   To think what joys our wealth would bring
>   Were we disposed to do the thing
>   Upon a scale extensive.
>   There's rich mock-turtle—thick and clear—
> RUD: Perhaps we'll have it once a year!
> CAR: You *are* an open-handed dear!
> RUD: Though, mind you, it's expensive.
> CAR: No doubt it *is* expensive.

Obstinacy, the third of Freud's anal-erotic characteristics, belonged to Gilbert in no small measure. Almost any incident from his life exhibits it to some extent, but perhaps the most conspicuous example concerns the Lozenge Plot. As will be remembered, Sullivan consistently made clear his refusal to set this plot. Even so, Gilbert brought it forward year after year, until his persistence with it began to threaten the very existence of the partnership. As soon as the events of the Carpet Quarrel permitted him to do so, he arranged to have the plot set by another composer. He was similarly determined to further the career of Nancy McIntosh, using every instrument in his power to thrust her in where no one else wanted her. There is in fact no recorded instance of him giving up a point when once he had fairly begun to pursue it.

Orderliness, parsimony, obstinacy, agression, anger, cruelty, egocentri-

city, omnipotence—these are the components of Gilbert's infantile sadistic character. As far as I am aware there is no evidence of any kind to suggest that he ever
advanced beyond the pregenital stage which Freud terminates at about five years.
Facts and features which make good sense in terms of this stage become bewilder-
ing if one tries to interpret them on the assumption that *Bab* was 'really' a normal
adult or a typical Englishman. He was neither, though if one must see him as
normal he might be called a typical obstreperous child who has yet to learn
that other people have exactly the same rights and feelings as himself.

To every sadism there is a corresponding masochism. We have concentrated
so far on the positively vindictive side of Gilbert's character in order to establish
its abnormality. On the passive side of his nature he was equally odd, though his
biographers have understandably put him forward as an uncomplicated lover of
home and beauty. The masochism of his work has been brushed aside as mere
literary feebleness, in spite of the obvious importance it held for him. Hesketh
Pearson is again a guilty party in this respect, for he regarded the blank verse
plays as meaningless excursions into sentimentality on the part of a man whose
true métier was wit. Before looking at these plays in detail we should perhaps
define masochism. Freud has it thus: [34]

> The term masochism comprises any passive attitude towards sexual life and
> the sexual object, the extreme instance of which appears to be that in which
> satisfaction is conditional upon suffering physical or mental pain at the hands
> of the sexual object. . . .It can often be shown that masochism is nothing
> more than an extension of sadism turned round upon the subject's own self,
> which thus, to begin with, takes the place of the sexual object.

In this passage Freud distinguishes two types of masochism: one a merely
passive sexual attitude, the other a positive turning of the destructive energies of
sadism against the self. Both types are to be found in Gilbert, the first
prominently displayed by his biographers as proof of his normalcy. Significantly
the third, most common type of masochism, in which suffering is inflicted by a
loved person, does not appear. This is so because Gilbert always remained
egocentric; he never attained relationships of the kind in which full sadism and
masochism become possible.

Gilbert's clearest expression of mere passivity is to be found in a short story
called *The Wicked World*, published in *Hood's Comic Annual* 1871. This story is the
basis of the blank verse play of the same name. In it Gilbert undertakes to describe
his version of an ideal fairyland; the resulting description is of an entirely passive
world, without conflict or tension of any kind: [35]

> The scene, then, is Fairyland. Not the Fairyland of the Pantomimes, but the
> Fairyland of My Own Vivid Imagination. A pleasant, dreamy land, with no
> bright colours in it—a land where it is always bright moonlight—a land with
> plenty of impalpable trees, through which you can walk, if you like, as easily
> as my pen can cleave the smoke that is curling from my cigar as I write—a land
> where there is nothing whatever to do but sit and chat with good pleasant-
> looking people, who like a joke, and can make one, too—a land where there is

no such thing as hunger, or sleep, or fatigue, or illness, or old age—a land where no collars or boots are worn—a land where there is no love-making, but plenty of innocent love ready-made.

There are no men in this Fairyland. I can't have a man in my Paradise—at least not at first. I know so much about men, being myself a man, that I would rather not think of them in connection with a place where all is calm, gentle, and tranquil and happy. I know so little about women that I propose to people this happy, dreamy, peaceful place with none but women. There must be no envy, hatred, malice or uncharitableness of any kind in my Fairyland. There must be nothing sordid, nothing worldly, nothing commonplace. Universal charity must reign in my Fairyland, and that, you see, is why I people it with women.

Much in this passage brings to mind the homoousian world of the infant, from the lack of collars and boots to the surrounding presence of women. It is a paradise of the omnipotent ego from which men, who might challenge that omnipotence, are strictly excluded. The bar on love-making indicates as specifically as possible that we are dealing with a pre-sexual fantasy in which love is both innocent and ready-made. All is peace and benevolence, as the undisturbed mood of the child may be peace and benevolence. We have seen how quickly, and in what way, this mood could be transformed.

If it stood alone, the *Wicked World* story might perhaps be considered a passing fancy, with no deep roots in the author's personality. However, as we have seen, Gilbert deliberately created a very similar idyll during his years at Grim's Dyke. Here, defended by spring guns, he lived out his fantasy of Fairyland. Here was an animal sanctuary in which *Bab* could tame robins and lead a fawn; here came the beautiful women with whom *Bab* conducted innocent relationships; here he danced and conjured and dined among friends—at ease because no one dared contradict him. Only the children's parties of earlier years were apparently missing, but *Bab* continued to pay particular attention to his child guests. At Grim's Dyke all disharmony was kept at bay, and *Bab* reigned supreme at the centre of his own universe.

Remoteness from the ordinary world of conflict and desire is one of the leading characateristics of Gilbert's blank verse plays. All are set in distant times and places, and all deal in one way or another with the disruptive effects of sexual love. Closest to Gilbert's affections was *Broken Hearts* (1875), which, he said, contained 'more of himself' than any other of his works. [36] The setting of this play is 'The Island of Broken Hearts' in about the years 1300-50. The scene is described in the following passive and melancholy terms: [37]

A tropical landscape. In the distance, a calm sea. A natural fountain—a mere thread of water—falls over a rock into a natural basin. An old sundial formed of the upper part of a broken pillar, round the shaft of which some creeping flowers are trained, stands on a small mound. The time is within half an hour of sunset.

The Island of Broken Hearts is inhabited by a number of beautiful but anaemic Burne-Jonesian maidens, who, following the death of their lovers, [38]

Bab Leads a Fawn

Have sought this isle far from the ken of man;
And having loved, and having lost our loves,
Stand pledged to love no living thing again.

The only man allowed on the island is Mousta, 'a deformed ill-favoured dwarf, hump-backed and one-eyed', who acts as the maidens' servant. He is in love with them, and it is tempting to interpret him as a figure symbolising *Bab's* attitude to sexual desire. The villain of the story, however, is one Prince Florian, who lands on the island from a boat. Unknown to himself Florian is loved by Hilda, one of the sequestered maidens. Believing him drowned she has fled to the island, and in accordance with her vow never to love any living thing again has given her affections to the fountain. Vavir, one of her companions, is in love with the sundial.

Happening to possess a scarf which renders the wearer invisible, Florian woos Vavir by pretending to be the voice of the sundial. Vavir, who had previously seemed to be dying, revives when he tells her that her devotion to the sundial is about to release from it a young man whose soul has been imprisoned there by a cruel magician.

Unfortunately for Vavir, Florian now sees Hilda. Hilda unwittingly reveals her love for him, and he reciprocates it. The upshot of the plot is that Florian is saved from the consequences of his own amorousness (he has also wooed a girl who loves a mirror) by the self-sacrificial death of Vavir:[39]

VAVIR: *(very feebly)*—Weep not; the bitterness of death is past.
Kiss me, my sister. Florian think of me—
I loved thee very much! Be good to her.
Dear sister, place my hand upon my dial.
Weep not for me; I have no pain indeed.
Kiss me again; my sun has set. Good night!
Good night!
Vavir dies; Hilda falling senseless on her body.

So ends the play which contains most of the 'real' Gilbert. It projects a passive, pining ideal of womanhood, placed far away from contact with the normal world. So far are the women from ordinary affection that they actually love inanimate objects, which anyone who wishes may interpret as sexual symbols. Florian, the intrusive representative of sexual love, causes havoc and death by his arrival. The emotional centre of the play is Vavir, who spends her entire time a-dying. It is hard not to interpret her as a Gilbertian *anima* who suffers and dies as a result of the masochistic inversion of the sexual instinct. Linguistically speaking the letters 'V' and 'B' are very close to each other. The name 'Vavir' is thus near to 'Babir' and would indeed be pronounced so in Spanish. We glimpse the 'true' Gilbert—a soul in masochistic retreat from sexual love.

The same theme, more elaborately worked out, informs *Gretchen* (1879). In this play—a version of the *Faust* story—Faustus is a monk who has fled from the world to the cloister because of an unhappy love affair. Mephisto tempts him to cure his cynicism in relation to women by the sight of Gretchen, an entirely pure and virtuous girl with a famous capacity to make saints of sinners. Faustus meets her in apparent sincerity, but soon falls in love with her and seduces her—we gather she becomes pregnant. Faustus talks rather vaguely of marriage, but as soon as she finds he is a priest, and so unable to marry, Gretchen rejects him and bids him seek forgiveness from Heaven. The text of the play makes it quite clear that from the moment she entered on sexual knowledge Gretchen had begun to die. Three months after the meeting of Faustus and Gretchen her three friends Bessie, Barbara, and Agatha talk together about her:[40]

> BESS: . . . But three months since, no happier maiden lived;
> And now—kind Heaven help us all!—they say
> She will not live to see her twentieth year!

Gretchen dies in the closing moments of the play with a speech on her lips which is very like that of Vavir. Both of these heroines are victims of the corrupting power of sex, which intrudes with literally murderous effect in to their placid lives.[41]

> GRETCHEN: I love thee, Faustus,
> Ah me! but it is meet that I should die,
> For I can turn my head, but not my heart—
> And I can close mine eyes, but not my heart—
> So, Faustus, it is meet that I should die!
> Weep not—
> I go from Death to Life—from Night to Day!
> Weep not—my heart is glad, and all my cares
> Fold their black wings and creep away abashed,
> As shrinks the night before the coming dawn.
> Farewell!
> The hand of death is heavy on my heart,
> The little lamp of life is dying out.
> It matters not—the dreary Night is past,
> And Daylight is at hand!
> *During* GRETCHEN'S *speech, the music of an organ is heard faintly;*
> *it swells into a loud peal as* GRETCHEN *dies.*

Gilbert put ten months' labour into *Gretchen*. The weakness of its language is part of the masochism of the concept. In *Bab's* other world Gretchen would have sought substantial damages via the best available solicitor; her language would then have been vigorous and to the point. Paradoxically, it is the very significance of the play which enfeebles it—the self-destructive power of Gretchen's masochism was at work also within Gilbert's imagination, reducing both character and author to impotence.

The stage version of *The Wicked World* (1873) differs in a number of ways from the original short story. On this occasion the scene is set on the top of a cloud, from which there is a view of a medieval city on the earth below. There is a rhymed prologue describing the purpose of the play; since Gilbert placed *The*

Wicked World at the head of his first printed collection of plays, the following words are the first any reader of his collected works would see: [42]

> The Author begs you'll kind attention pay
> While I explain the object of his play.
> You have been taught, no doubt, by those professing
> To understand the thing, that Love's a blessing:
> Well, *he* intends to teach you the reverse—
> That Love is not a blessing, but a curse!

The fairies who inhabit the cloud are ideally pure and innocent beings. They look in horror—and fascination—on the world below, 'all ghastly with the lurid light of sin'. All fairies have physically identical counterparts in the wicked world, and after some discussion the fairies decide to work an exchange: two mortal men are to be exchanged for two fairy men, who will take their place below. The exchange is made; the earthlings arrive fighting, and soon begin to spread the corrupting power of mortal, sexual, love. On this occasion the fairies do not die but expel the men; one of them, Selene, sums up her view of love thus: [43]

> It is a deadly snare—beware of it!
> Such love is for mankind and not for us;
> It is the very essence of the earth,
> A mortal emblem, bringing in its train
> The direst passions of its antitype.
> No, Ethais—we will not have this love;
> Let us glide through our immortality
> Upon the placid lake of sister-love,
> Nor tempt the angry billows of the sea,
> Which, though it carry us to unknown lands,
> Is so beset with rocks and hidden shoals,
> That we may perish ere our vessel reach
> The safe haven of its distant shore.
> No, Ethais—we will not have this love!

Lest there be any doubt about the nature of the love rejected by the fairies, the last words of the prologue spell it out. The 'he' referred to is the author, and the 'I' the speaker of the prologue: [44]

> But, let me ask you, had the world ne'er known
> Such love as you, and I, and he, must mean—
> Pray where would you, or I, or he, have been?

We are now in a position to understand why the fairies of *Iolanthe* consider it death to marry a mortal, and why Iolanthe, who did so, was condemned to die. Marriage brings with it the pollution of sexual knowledge, for which the masochistic punishment is death. Sexual knowledge 'strikes at the root of the whole fairy system', which exists to keep it at bay. In Freudian terms the fairies exist at the pre-genital stage of development—the childhood stage—and resist taking the normal next step even to the death.

The association of sexual knowledge with death in Gilbert's mind leads naturally and inevitably to the consideration of what Freud called the death instinct. In *Beyond The Pleasure Principle* (1920) Freud put forward the view that the fundamental destiny of all life is death. Adopting the views of Sandor Ferenczi, he thought of the basic tendency of all organic life as conservative inasmuch as the organism tries to maintain itself as it is, and changes only under external compulsion. The fundamental tendency of the instincts is therefore regressive, with death—the ultimate end of life—as their final goal. This drive towards the final organic necessity is the death instinct; it is opposed by the forces of libido, which drive towards life and change.

Freud also called the death instinct the Nirvana Principle, which is the desire for the complete discharge of all internal psychic tension, leading to a state of blissful contentment—the psychic equivalent of death. We have encountered Gilbert's Nirvana in the ideal description of Fairyland in the *Wicked World* story. It displays all the dissolution of tension, all the immobility sought by the death instinct. Its female inhabitants are explicitly in flight from life, and libido—the life force—is regarded as a menace. Short of a description of a tomb, one could hardly call for a more complete vision of the goal of the death instincts. And yet it was this vision that Gilbert realised in his years at Grim's Dyke. The 'real' Gilbert was not simply a masochist—he was a man saturated with the death instincts, perhaps even a man who was already dead.

The death instinct is not a universally accepted part of Freudian theory; some of his followers have rejected it altogether, and others have doubted its usefulness. In dealing with Gilbert, therefore, one cannot tread on quite such sure Freudian ground as in the case of his sadism, which is the death instinct turned against other people. Nevertheless, much of Gilbert's life and work stands illuminated if one sees him as a man in whom the death instinct was an active principle.

In the first place, although Gilbert was and is famous as a wit he was not, like say J.L. Toole, a funny man. As far as the present writer is aware, there is no occasion on which he is recorded as having laughed. One feels he must have laughed, if only when he saw someone embarrassed or humiliated—yet the evidence for it appears to be lacking. 'There was something a little grim beneath the vivacity of his conversational manner. The settled gravity of his countenance was almost menacing in the sense of slumbering hostility it conveyed'.[45] P.G. Wodehouse, who never forgot 'the glare of pure hatred' he once saw in Gilbert's eye, wrote of his face in these terms:[46]

> If you have seen photographs of Gilbert, you will be aware that even in repose his face was inclined to be formidable and his eye not the sort of eye you would willingly catch. And now his face was far from being in repose. His eyes, beneath their beetling brows, seared me like a flame.

Gilbert once played Harlequin for a charity matinee. By its very nature the part requires lighthearted tomfoolery but Gilbert, according to John Hollingshead, gave a good idea of what Oliver Cromwell might have made of the character.[47] Much the same tale is told by his method of making a joke. The words were preceded by a little grunt or cough and delivered without a smile or apparent awareness of humour—a formula he positively prescribed for the performance of his comedy *Engaged* (1877), 'It is absolutely essential to the success of this piece that it should be played with the most perfect earnestness and gravity throughout'.[48]

When it came, the Gilbertian witticism was normally unkind or acid, as when he said that he had not seen Henry Irving's *Faust* because he went to the pantomime only at Christmas. In all these things—the settled face, the grave manner, the absence of laughter, the mean-spirited content—it is possible to detect the operation of a single principle. If it is not a principle of death, it is certainly not a principle of life. The element of gaiety—unmistakable in such a wit as Wilde—is missing; in its place there is something cold, something unresponsive, something alien to pleasure—something dead. Incidentally, if a private gramophone recording apparently made in 1906 is to be trusted, Gilbert's speaking voice was a high tenor whine rather than the big manly bark one might expect.

Allardyce Nicholl remarks somewhere that Gilbert gives the impression of a man who is afraid of life. Fear might well be responsible for *Bab's* extreme sensitivity to any ostensibly hostile act on the part of others. Incapacity to deal with life in the ordinary way assuredly lay behind his readiness to use the impersonal and mechanical instrument of the law to deal with matters which other people would have settled over whiskey and soda. One recalls that in *The Gentleman In Black* the strong men were flogged by machinery. Sometimes it was the machinery of the law, sometimes the machinery of constant repetition of a sentence or bit of stage business.

All machinery is lifeless. The spirit of machinery permeates Gilbert's work, from the stereotyped plots to that magic lozenge which Sullivan so hated, whose effect was to turn people mechanically into the characters they were pretending to be. As a familiar example of the mechanicality of Gilbert's work one might take the dénouement of *H.M.S. Pinafore*. On the unsupported statement of Little Buttercup, Captain Corcoran and Able Seaman Ralph Rackstraw are found to be changelings. At once, and by a purely mechanical process, Captain and Sailor change places and take on each other's characteristics, even though in human terms a lifetime's experience separates them. Similarly the Captain is the father of Ralph's beloved, Josephine. If they are changelings he and Ralph must be the same age, but in the opera Ralph is a young man and Captain Corcoran an ageing one. No member of the audience objects to this transformation because the world of *H.M.S. Pinafore* is clearly artificial and mechanical, with no pretence to life of the organic kind. Our concern here is to detect the artificiality and this mechanicality and track them to their primary source in Gilbert's own lack in a certain kind of life.

One of the most entertaining features of the Savoy libretti is to be found in the little dances performed by the 'Grossmith' character, whether he be First Lord of the Admiralty (*H.M.S. Pinafore*) or Lord Chancellor (*Iolanthe*). All these dances make their effect by the same means. For most of the time the character conducts himself with the perfect earnestness and gravity of deportment proper to his official position. Thanks to Gilbert's meticulousness in such matters he invariably wears the correct costume for his function. Then, without warning, he breaks into mad capers in which the twitching of his legs plays a prominent part. The audience generally rolls in the aisles, and it is almost certainly true to say that without these dances the Savoy operas would not be as popular as they are. At first sight the death instinct seems far away—how can anything so funny be dead? Yet what is the nature of the life which animates the First Lord as he dances? He is not happy, for he never was human; nor is his behaviour an appropriate response to the stage situation. Physically the dances resemble those of puppets and it is in the galvanic life-without-life of the puppet that their nature lies. The same galvanism animates the mad manikins who cavort through the *Bab Ballads*. They move, but they do not live, any more than the Sea Lord lives. As a man in retreat from life Gilbert did not know how to make *any* of his characters live. Therefore their merriment is like his own—mechanical and arbitrary, and lacking a dimension; as expressive in one way of the 'real' Gilbert as *Broken Hearts* is in another.

The bright and witty façade of the Gilbertian libretti does, of course, conceal the inner void. Even so, from time to time a glimpse of the true state of affairs is to be had in the shape of an apparently incongruous intrusion of the death instincts. A well known example is the following lyric in *Princess Ida*, which has no precedent in Gilbert's Tennysonian source:[49]

> The world is but a broken toy,
> Its pleasure hollow - false its joy,
>   Unreal its loveliest hue,
>   Alas!
>   Its pains alone are true,
>   Alas!
>   Its pains alone are true.

Although rather more appropriate to the situation—Nanki Poo is to be beheaded—the madrigal from the second act of *The Mikado* similarly springs from Gilbert's own masochism:[50]

> Brightly dawns our wedding day;
>   Joyous hour we give thee greeting!
>   Whither, whither art thou fleeting?
> Fickle moment prithee stay!
>   What though mortal joys be hollow?
>   Pleasures come if sorrows follow:
> Though the tocsin sound, ere long,
>   Ding dong! Ding dong!
> Yet until the shadows fall
> Over one and over all,
> Sing a merry madrigal—
> Fa-la-fa-la!etc.   (*Ending in tears*)

Rather more debatable, but still consistent with Gilbert's personality, is the possibility that the great Carpet Quarrel itself was the product of a death wish. This extraordinary upheaval took place at a time when Sullivan and Carte together were laying plans for a future in which Gilbert—by his own choice be it said—had no part. If *Ivanhoe* had performed the miracle expected of it Sullivan might well have written no further comic operas. Gilbert at least must have feared as much. As a man who reacted with ferocity to every supposed affront, he was probably incapable of avoiding revenge on the perpetrators of *Ivanhoe*. Equally the revenge he took can be seen in retrospect as self-destructive, for he never afterwards wrote a line that lives in the public memory. The Carpet affair ripped up the Gilbert and Sullivan partnership by the roots, destroying in the process the confidence, the subliminal *savoir-faire*, without which no worthwhile work of art can be created. A close parallel would be the act of self-destruction by which Samson took his revenge on the Philistines. It is interesting, too, to note that the Carpet Quarrel coincided with the move to Grim's Dyke (September 1890); at the precise moment of his artistic Götterdämmerung Gilbert began to work out his personal version of the Nirvana Principle on Harrow Weald. In the nature of the case no proof can be forthcoming; yet the coincidence suggests a climacteric in Gilbert's career, leading to a dominance of the death instincts. Gilbert won the Carpet Quarrel in the legal sense, and indeed in the commercial sense, for he was found indispensable to the Savoy box office; yet the victory may have been Pyrrhic.

However one interprets the Carpet Quarrel, death was certainly in Gilbert's mind during the later part of his career. As we have seen, *The Grand Duke* is in part derived from the use of the electric chair. The plot actually turns on a curious legalistic death inflicted by playing cards. A duel is fought with playing cards; the drawer of the lowest card is considered legally dead, while the winner takes his place. Several characters are killed in this way during the course of the action, and one of them turns up as a ghost. The text has humorous references to disease, culminating in a song for Rudolph detailing his aches and pains. This lyric was written for *The Mountebanks*, where it was to have been sung by Pietro, 'dying by slow poison'; both Goring Thomas and Alfred Cellier set it before their respective deaths, but it is Sullivan's setting which—if that is the word—survives. Rudolph has been thrown into a fit of depression by the news that he is to be assassinated:[51]

> When you find you're broken down critter,
> Who is all of a trimmle and twitter,
> With your palate unpleasantly bitter,
>   As if you'd just eaten a pill—
> When your legs are as thin as dividers,
> And you're plagued with unruly insiders,
> And your spine is all creepy with spiders,
>   And you're highly gamboge in the gill—
> When you've got a beehive in your head,
>   And a sewing machine in each ear,
> And you feel that you've eaten your bed,
>   And you've got a bad headache *down here*—

> When such facts are about,
>   And such symptoms you find
>   In your body or crown—
> Well, you'd better look out,
>   You may make up your mind
>   You had better lie down!

Such is the material Gilbert thought fit for a comic opera in 1896. At first sight it is very unlike the vivacious work of the 80s, but the same principle connects both. In the earlier operas the brilliant surface disguises the underlying deadness of the mechanisms; in *The Grand Duke* disguise is missing, and the fundamental quality shows through. In passing we may remark that *The Mountebanks* is a libretto in which Hamlet and Ophelia are reduced to clockwork dummies wound up with keys, and the whole human race is suspected of working in the same way.

Finally we come to *The Hooligan* (1911), the play which Gilbert set in the death cell. If one were trying to invent a theoretical culmination for the Gilbertian death instinct it would be hard to find one more appropriate than this. A condemned convict named Solly muses on his last hours, and on 'wot it's goin' to be like when it comes'. In the event Solly dies of heart failure before the supreme moment arrives, much as Gilbert himself did in his lake at Grim's Dyke. A man of seventy-five may well be given to thoughts of death. However *The Hooligan* represents the final resting point of a longstanding tendency of Gilbert's work; under such circumstances we may well regard it as something more than a chance event, or the result of the preoccupation with death natural to an old man.

To sum up. The conventional view of Gilbert as a normal if obstreperous man is belied by the entire surviving body of evidence concerning his mind and personality. Neither the heartless persecution of the Comtesse de Brémont nor the conjuring tricks at children's parties can be adequately explained by calling him a kindly old buffer who just happened to like his own way, or even by treating him as a saint with a saint's bad temper. On the other hand, everything known about him can be accommodated within the assumption that the basis of his personal and artistic psychology was sadomasochistic at the infantile level. This single assumption accounts for such disparate and apparently unconnected features as the gyrations of the Lord Chancellor in *Iolanthe*, and the fairy laws of the same opera; it accounts for the rigid drilling of actors and chorus and the vision of a world populated entirely by women. If Gilbert's own testimony is to be trusted, he was in fact dominated by masochism and the death instincts rather than by the overt sadistic vigour of his public life and most popular work. Depending on point of view any sadistic act may be interpreted in a masochistic sense. Thus the torturing of Robin Oakapple in *Ruddigore* is intended to be enjoyed sadistically by the audience; but if Gilbert identified himself with Robin then the torture becomes masochistic punishment for crimes he has not committed. The sketch presented here by no means exhausts the possibilities for Freudian interpretation inherent in Gilbert. [52]

Freudian interpretations do not, of course, account for the whole achievement of any gifted man. There have been many sadomasochists—Gilbert was unique. Nevertheless the alternative to trying to understand his psychology is to ascribe to him an impossible degree of dissociated originality, as if his creative process had no connection with mere humanity. For too long his admirers, with Hesketh Pearson to the fore, have adopted precisely this unproductive approach.

3: The Princess Plot

As the possessor of an omnipotent ego, liable to instant judgements on the preposterousness of all things, Gilbert was necessarily relatively impervious to influences from the outside world. By the same token the mechanical mode of operation of his mind meant that those ideas and impressions which *did* find their way through his guard made a deep impact, and were likely to be repeated constantly. Before 1870 Gilbert's plays have no special characteristic shape; after 1870 they acquire a pattern derived from his adaptation of Tennyson's *Princess*, seen at the Olympic Theatre in the January of that year. Familiar to modern audiences from its appearance in *Princess Ida*, this pattern held vital significance for Gilbert.

As we have seen (p 28) Tennyson derived the plot of his poem from two oriental tales printed together in Henry Weber's *Tales of the East*. In his version the formidable princess of the folk stories has become an exotic bluestocking who has locked herself away in a remote but beautiful country house in order to devote herself to the education of women. She has gathered round her a group of 'sweet girl graduates' for the purpose, using the house as a university; men are forbidden to enter the university on pain of death.

The male heroes of the poem—an anonymous Prince and his two companions—set out to win the hand of the Princess, to whom the Prince had been betrothed at the age of eight. They visit her father, King Gama, who gives them letters of introduction, then disguise themselves as girls in order to gain access to the college. They don academic robes, but are soon recognised by Psyche and Melissa. Psyche has entered the college with her child, left with her after the death of her husband. The ladies promise not to expose the men, but the latter are found out rapidly when one of them sings a tavern song in the presence of the Princess.

Furious, the Princess flees on horseback, but falls into a stream while galloping over a bridge. She is rescued by the Prince but holds him prisoner, only to learn that his father has captured her father, holding him in ransom for the life of the Prince. The quarrelling parties decide to settle the issue by combat between the Prince and his two companions and the three brothers of the Princess. The Prince falls in the combat, but the Princess tends his wounds, and in the process grows to love him. At length she marries him willingly, leaving the university in the charge of Blanche, Melissa's mother, and already a considerable Gilbertian female, even in Tennyson.

In making his adaptation for the stage Gilbert followed Tennyson's outline fairly closely, though coarsening the jibes against women. He alters the betrothal at the age of eight to a betrothal in babyhood, and brings King Gama on stage early, as a visitor to the court of the Prince's father, named Hildebrand by him. The name Hilarion given to the Prince is Gilbert's also. Thereafter the plot follows Tennyson until the end, when in the stage version the Prince and his companions are made victors over the Princess's three brothers. The Princess now yields to Hilarion, and the dialogue runs thus: [1]

PRINCESS: You ridicule it now;
But if I carried out this glorious scheme,
At my exalted name Posterity
Would bow in gratitude!
HILDEBRAND: But pray reflect—
If you enlist all women in your cause,
And make them all abjure tyrannic Man,
The obvious question then arises, "How
Is this Posterity to be provided?"
PRINCESS: I never thought of that! . . . .
GAMA: Consider this, my love: if your mamma
Had looked on matter from your point of view
(I wish she had), why, where would you have been?

These words have a familiar ring; they are closely similar to the conclusion of the *Wicked World* prologue where the same question is asked, namely, 'How can the human race continue without sexual love?' The question, which also exercises the minds of contemporary lesbian feminists, appears to have preoccupied Gilbert throughout his career, for the plot theme associated with it is to be found in a number of his works. Reduced to its essentials the *Princess* plot is as follows:

1) A setting remote from the ordinary world.
2) A population of women who abjure men.
3) The incursion of a number of men from the outside.
4) Chaos and unpleasantness caused by the men.
5) A resolution—marriage in the case of *The Princess*.

We have already noticed the masochistic nature of this sequence of events: in a remote place a group of women are in retreat from the sexual life; when men make their appearance the result is pollution and, in extreme cases, death. Princess Ida, however, does not die; after great hesitation she makes a marriage, the only reason for her action provided by Gilbert being the need to propagate the species. The taboo on sexual life as such remains, but the species must continue. Though held by Gilbert for special reasons, it is a position not unlike the conventional Victorian attitude which placed women beyond and above the orbit of (male) lust. Just how special were Gilbert's reasons may be deduced from a passage in Freud's *The Economic Problem of Masochism* (1924):[2]

> But if one has an opportunity of studying cases in which the masochistic phantasies have been especially richly elaborated, one quickly discovers that they place the subject in a characteristically female situation; they signify, that is, being castrated, or copulated with, or giving birth to a baby. For this reason I have called this form of masochism ... the feminine form, although so many of its features point to infantile life.... Being castrated—or being blinded, which stands for it—often leaves a negative trace of itself in phantasies, in the condition that no injury is to occur precisely to the genitals or the eyes.

Freud's remarks refer primarily to the masochistic practices of men. However, they explain clearly why the centre of gravity in *The Princess*, and all Gilbert's blank verse plays, lies with the women, who live—or die—under the menace of copulation. Freud also points to the association of the feminine type of masochism with the infantile life, and it is here that one begins to think of *Bab*.

The Persian stories on which *The Princess* is based are fairly clearly folk tales on the topic of sexual initiation. The heroine resists the idea of men at first, indeed finds it repellent, but at length understands the true pleasure of love. Much the same idea is conveyed by such Western folk tales as *Beauty And The Beast* or *The Sleeping Beauty*. Now *Bab*, as we have suggested, remained permanently fixated at the anal-sadistic stage of development which precedes the genital phase; in other words he did not advance beyond a developmental age which Freud places at about five years. His blank verse plays show the masochistic dread with which he contemplated sexual initiation, and *The Princess* is, by origin, a folk tale on the very subject of sexual initiation. The importance of the *Princess* plot for *Bab* was that it dealt with the transition from his own pre-genital stage to the true genital stage. In *The Princess* the transition is actually made, if only because it is an unavoidable part of the source material, but in fact *Bab* never really made up his mind to it as his subsequent hesitations show. A glance through the works employing the *Princess* plot shows that the format of the plot does not vary, except in the dénouement, when a number of different solutions are tried.

Since it was produced in January 1870, *The Princess* must have been created substantially during 1869. The next work in order to share the same plot was *Thespis*, Gilbert's first collaboration with Sullivan, produced at the Gaiety on 26 December 1871. However in *Thespis* the subject matter is not fully worked out, probably because a Christmas entertainment was not the place for such a serious theme. The place of the remote retreat is taken by Mount Olympus, but the Gods who inhabit it are of both sexes. They are invaded by a group of human actors, who change places with them and cause chaos, but the underlying psychological point is not touched on. In the finale the errant humans are expelled, and Olympian life returns to its normal tenor.

Two years after *Thespis* Gilbert produced *The Wicked World* at the Haymarket. Here is a *Princess* plot proper, in which the setting is on top of a cloud, with the earth seen distantly below. The inhabitants of the cloud are a group of female fairies, who know nothing of human life and love except that both are very wicked. They send for a couple of mortal men, who arrive fighting and soon begin to play havoc with the fairies' hearts. To some extent the effect of the theme is veiled by facetiousness inasmuch as the fairies are not altogether unwilling to be corrupted. Nevertheless the play ends not in marriage but in the expuslion of the mortals and a return to fairy innocence; the shift into the genital phase is rejected.

In March 1875 Gilbert collaborated for a second time with Sullivan in *Trial by Jury*. The December of the same year saw *Broken Hearts* produced at the Court Theatre. We have already sufficiently examined the masochistic significance of this play. Its allegiance to the *Princess* plot is shown by the setting on a distant tropical island, and by the group of women who, like the Psyche of Tennyson's *Princess*, have sought isolation after the deaths of their lovers. The connection is continued by the arrival on the island of Florian, which is the name allotted by Tennyson to one of the companions of his unnamed Prince. Florian works deceitfully on the maidens' hearts, and though he eventually marries one of them, Vavir dies of this betrayal. Here we have both the marriage of *The Princess* proper, and masochistic love-death. The same process occurs in *Gretchen* (1879) where the heroine's world of innocence is shattered by Faustus, leading to her death. There is no hint in Gilbert of the redemption which both Goethe and Gounod allow to Marguerite.

An interesting variant on the *Princess* theme is to be found in *Pygmalion and Galatea* (Haymarket, 9 December 1871). In this play the problem of how to continue the race without sexual reproduction is solved by the magical expedient of bringing the statue of Galatea to life:[3]

> CHRYSOS: Who is your mother?
> GALATEA: Mother! what is that?
> I never had one. I'm Pygmalion's child;
> Have people usually mothers?
> CHRYSOS: That is the rule.
> GALATEA: But then Pygmalion
> Is cleverer than most men.

Pygmalion and his wife Cynisca have the power to blind each other if either proves unfaithful. When Cynisca learns of Pygmalion's association with Galatea—actually innocent on his side—she blinds him, an act which, according to Freud, is equivalent to castration. Faced with the unpleasant emotions her arrival has roused, Galatea returns to marble, after helping Pygmalion regain his sight. She is a representative of Gilbert's 'innocent love ready made' for whom the human actuality of love is altogether too much.

By the time he came to work in earnest with Sullivan, Gilbert seems to have made the *Princess* plot part of his ordinary methods of work. It can be traced in a number of the familiar libretti, not always with the significance attached to it in the blank verse plays. Nevertheless it is always the ending which varies; the main structure remains the same.

The Sorcerer (1877) is based on a short story first published in *The Graphic* for Christmas 1869.[4] The story must have been written at about the same time as *The Princess*, but it is the libretto which shows the influence of the *Princess* plot. The opera is set in the remote village of Ploverleigh, far from the wicked metropolis. The hero, Alexis, wishes to introduce love into the village on an egalitarian basis. He summons a magician for the purpose—a certain John Wellington Wells from London. By coming into the village from London Mr Wells serves the same function as the love-bearing intruders of the *Princess* plot. He administers his love potion to the villagers in a teapot, and they fall for each other in disastrously incongruous ways. The situation is resolved by sending Mr Wells down to Hell, much as Thespis and his crew are sent back down Mount Olympus, or the peccant mortals are expelled from the fairy cloud in *The Wicked World*. The resolution of the plot is a restoration of the status quo by the ejection of the intruder.

The leading idea of *H.M.S. Pinafore*, the notion that egalitarian love is absurd, is a reworking of the main theme of *The Sorcerer*; but the plot structure itself is not related to *The Princess*. *The Pirates of Penzance*, however, is set in a remote rocky cove on the coast of Cornwall. The pirates who have been carousing there leave it empty, whereupon Major General Stanley's daughters enter singing a chorus taken from the similar moment in *Thespis*. They are soon seized by the pirates for matrimonial purposes, allegedly against their wills. In the resolution the pirates, who are actually fallen noblemen, marry their victims. The apparent enthusiasm which Gilbert's women sometimes show for their fate should not be taken as an expression of approval on his part; his portrait of the sexual eagerness of women springs from disgust at the contrast between his own pre-genital ideal and his observations of real life. Both the sincerity and the irony in the following characteristic passage from *The Wicked World* spring from the same masochistic source:[5]

ZAYDA: Man is everything detestable—
    Base in his nature, base in thought and deed,
    Loathsome beyond all things that creep and crawl!
    Still, sister, I must own I've sometimes thought
    That we who shape the fortunes of mankind,
    And grant such wishes as are free from harm,
    Might possibly fulfil our generous task
    With surer satisfaction to himself
    Had we some notion what these wishes were!

The outlines of the *Princess* plot reappear in *Patience*. In this opera the initial remote setting is provided by the grounds of Castle Bunthorne, a variant of the Castle Adamant of *The Princess*. The close relationship between the two is indicated by the nature of the aestheticism satirised in *Patience*. Aestheticism was pre-eminently a cult of the drawing room; fresh air was its enemy, just as the hothouse was its friend; it flourished in London, yet Gilbert set his satire of it in the grounds of a country mansion. Clearly therefore the setting relates to Gilbert's own mind rather than to aestheticism as it was. The ladies' chorus, whom we meet in the first scene, are pale and weary from lovesickness, the object of their love being Reginald Bunthorne, himself the ultimate in world-weariness, whose poetry is 'the wail of the poet's heart on discovering that everything is commonplace'. The maidens' sickly idyll with Bunthorne is interrupted in no very subtle manner by the arrival of the Dragoon Guards from the healthy outside world, and in the dénouement it is the outside world which triumphs as the former aesthetic maidens become 'cheerily chattering every-day young girls'. Bunthorne, by contrast, remains true to himself, preferring to love a lily as Vavir of *Broken Hearts* loved a sundial.

The aesthetic subject matter of *Patience* was in fact particularly suited to Gilbert's temperament. He appears to have had little if any sympathy for aestheticism, but his own masochism, for different reasons, joined with it in rejecting the contemporary Victorian world. Aestheticism therefore provided a natural channel for the expression in *Patience* of what is really a personal vision. Swinburne dabbled in adult sadomasochism, but aestheticism was at bottom a form of life affirmation not, as Gilbert interprets it, a form of life denial. The aesthetes saw, as Gilbert saw, that the world is commonplace, but they strove always to burn with Pater's hard gem-like flame. [6] Gilbert never advanced beyond the initial perception.

In *Iolanthe*, which folowed *Patience* at the Savoy in 1882, the *Princess* plot is worked through in fairly specific terms. The setting is an Arcadian landscape, with river and rustic bridge. A band of fairies tell us of their close connection with love: [7]

> LEILA: If you ask us how we live,
> Lovers all essentials give—
> We can ride on lovers' sighs,
> Warm ourselves in lovers' eyes,
> Bathe ourselves in lovers' tears,
> Clothe ourselves with lovers' fears,
> Arm ourselves with lovers' darts,
> Hide ourselves in lovers' hearts.
> When you know us, you'll discover
> That we almost live on lover!

At first sight the love the fairies exist on appears to be the ordinary human kind. However, since they have a law which makes it death to marry a mortal—indulge in human love—it follows that what they really enjoy is Gilbert's own particular brand of 'innocent love-ready-made'. Iolanthe, one of the fairies, has actually committed the crime of marrying a mortal; she would have been executed for this breach of fairy law, but the Queen has 'commuted her sentence to penal servitude for life, on condition that she left her husband and never communicated with him again.' The sexual nature of Iolanthe's crime is made completely explicit when she is pardoned further, and introduces the fairies to her son, Strephon. Strephon, be it remembered, is mortal *below the waist*.

The scene of Arcadian reconciliation is now interrupted in the familiar way by the arrival of a number of men—in this case the entire House of Lords. When they meet, the fairies are at first antagonistic to the Peers, while being secretly attracted by them. For the second act Gilbert provides a neat reversal of roles when a scene in the very mundane yard of the Palace of Westminster is invaded by the fairy outsiders. At length attraction runs its course, and the fairies marry into the aristocracy. By a legal quibble the fairy law is amended to prescribe death for any fairy who fails to marry a mortal. It would seem that the whole basis of Gilbert's thought on this matter has been overturned, but the effect of the revised law is nullified when all the mortal partners sprout wings and become fairies. The marriages now belong to fairyland because the polluting human element has been taken away. Broken in the letter, the law is preserved in spirit.

Iolanthe was followed by *Princess Ida* in 1884. Comment on *Princess Ida* is almost superfluous here, as the opera is in all essentials the same as the stage play. Whatever one may say of the other libretti, the derivation of this work from the *Princess* plot can hardly be denied! *Princess Ida* was also the last work in which Sullivan allowed Gilbert a free choice of subject matter. From this time forward the composer began to resist the Gilbertian whims and mechanisms, insisting on a greater element of humanity from his collaborator. Whether this humanity was forthcoming is a topic we must discuss. In the meantime, the effect of Sullivan's rearguard action was to banish the *Princess* plot from the Savoy stage for almost ten years as Gilbert was compelled to provide different fare. He returned to it in *Utopia Limited* as soon as his victory in the Carpet Quarrel and the failure of the Royal English Opera had restored his authority within the triumvirate.

Utopia Limited (1893) is in essence a reworking of *The Happy Land* (1873), a burlesque of *The Wicked World* in which W.S. Gilbert collaborated with Gilbert à Beckett. However, the libretto also bears traces of Johnson's *Rasselas* (1759) which has sometimes been taken as one of the sources of Tennyson's *Princess*. In Gilbert's first draft of the *Utopia* libretto the work is called *The Happy Valley* [8]—the name given to the location of Rasselas' prison-palace. More significantly Gilbert has borrowed a name, Nekayah, from Johnson. In the twenty-eighth chapter of *Rasselas*, Prince Rasselas and Princess Nekayah debate the subject of marriage. Rasselas defends marriage as 'the dictate of nature'. Nekayah, however, takes a different view: [9]

> 'I know not', said the princess, 'whether marriage be more than one of the innumerable modes of human misery. When I see and reckon the various forms of connubial infelicity, the unexpected causes of lasting discord, the diversities of temper, the oppositions of opinion, the rude collisions of contrary desire where both are urged by violent impulses, the obstinate contests of disagreeing virtues, where both are supported by consciousness of good intention, I am sometimes disposed to think with the severer casuists of most nations, that marriage is rather permitted than approved, and that none, but by the instigation of a passion too much indulged, entangle themselves with indissoluble compacts'.

These words might almost constitute a programme for Gilbert's blank verse plays. In *Utopia Limited* we encounter first of all the familiar remote setting, on this occasion 'a picturesque and luxuriant landscape, with the sea in the distance'. Though in theory entirely innocent, the inhabitants of Utopia are fascinated by English *mores*, so much so that two of their princesses, Nekaya and Kalyba, have an English governess, who has taught them the prudish ways of the refined English Miss. The lotus-eating ways of Utopia are interrupted by the arrival of six 'Flowers of Progress' at the behest of Princess Zara, the eldest Utopian princess, who has just returned from an English education at Girton. The Flowers of Progress are Englishmen, representatives of the civic and military virtues of the Victorian *imperium*. They reform Utopia, causing chaos, and two of them woo the young Utopian princesses in the usual *Wicked World* fashion. However on this occasion expectations are reversed, for the maidens repel the invaders, only to be told that the proper behaviour for English girls is quite different. The English men in the following conversation are Lord Dramaleigh (Lord Chamberlain) and Mr Goldbury (a financier and Company Promoter):[10]

KAL: Oh, pray do not take advantage of our unprotected innocence.

GOLD: Pray be reassured—you are in no danger whatever.

LORD D: But may I ask—is this extreme delicacy—this shrinking sensitiveness—a general characteristic of Utopian young ladies?

NEK: Oh no; we are crack specimens....

GOLD: Are you really under the impression that English girls are so ridiculously demure? Why, an English girl of the highest type is the best, the most beautiful, the bravest, and the brightest creature that Heaven has conferred upon this world of ours. She is frank, open-hearted, and fearless, and never shows in so favourable a light as when she gives her own blameless impulses full play.

In the context of all we have seen of the *Princess* plot these exchanges are most surprising. No doubt it would be injudicious to place a modern liberal interpretation on the idea of giving blameless impulses full play, but nevertheless the tone is quite new in Gilbert's work, suggesting that he might have broken out of his pre-genital inhibitions at last. Moreover the other love relationships in the opera, between Princess Zara and Captain Fitzbattleaxe and King Paramount and Lady Sophy, are, by Gilbertian standards, conducted in normal terms. All these affairs culminate in the second act in what one can only describe as a Dance of Life. The stage direction reads thus:[11]

KING and LADY SOPHY dance gracefully. While this is going on LORD DRAMALEIGH enters unobserved with NEKAYA and Mr GOLDBURY with KALYBA. Then enter ZARA and CAPT. FITZBATTLEAXE. The two girls direct ZARA'S attention to the KING and LADY SOPHY, who are still dancing affectionately together. At this point the KING kisses LADY SOPHY, which causes the princesses to make an exclamation. The KING and LADY SOPHY are at first much confused at being detected, but eventually throw off all reserve, and the four couples break into a wild Tarantella, and at the end exeunt severally.

The spirit of this dance is far removed from the merely animated frolics of the Lord Chancellor in *Iolanthe*; it springs from a genuine inward impulse, and constitutes one of the reasons why *Utopia Limited* 'feels' different to the better known Gilbert and Sullivan operas. At the time of *Utopia* Gilbert was in the early stages of his relationship with Nancy McIntosh, the American singer who played Princess Zara in the first production. Conceivably in those heady days Gilbert's psychology underwent a sea-change of which the relationships of *Utopia* are the expression. All one can say for certain is that this work represents a new resolution of the *Princess* theme.

Except in *Fallen Fairies* (1909), which is the operatic version of *The Wicked World*, Gilbert did not again employ the *Princess* plot. However, he had it in mind in 1897, as the following letter shows. The 'difficulty' referred to is the problem of making an opera out of *The Wicked World*, where there is scope only for a female chorus:[12]

> It has occurred to me that the difficulty might be met by making the fairies *syrens* on a rock in the Mediterranean. They discourse of the evils that come from love, and consider that much good might be done if a shipful of mortals are lured to their island in order that they may be indoctrinated with the new theory. A shipful of classical warriors—Ulysses and his companions, say—are lured to their island by their songs, and as a consequence, the syrens, while preaching the horrors of love, fall hopelessly in love with the newcomers. Then all sorts of catastrophes result, the piece ending as *The Wicked World* ends, with the departure of the disgusted visitors in their ship and the restoration of peace and happiness to the syrens.

It is perhaps a matter of regret that Gilbert did not offer Sullivan his libretto on Ulysses and the Sirens in place of *Utopia Limited*. What the letter shows above all else is that he, like the Bourbons, had learned nothing and forgotten nothing. The new dawn apparently glimpsed in *Utopia* gives way here to the unchanged masochism of his early years. Equally, his clear exposition of the theme of *The Wicked World* shows that it must have been at least partly present to his conscious mind. If he had not employed the theme again after *Utopia* one would definitely think that he had worked it out of his system, emerging from the anal-sadistic stage at the ripe age of fifty-seven. As it is there is no discernible pattern in the sequence of resolutions; one ending after another is tried, but no conclusion is reached. In chronological order the works which employ the *Princess* plot end in the following ways:

The Princess (1870)	-	Reluctant marriage.
Thespis (1871)	-	Expulsion of the intruders.
The Wicked World (1873)	-	Expulsion of the intruders.
Broken Hearts (1875)	-	Death of the heroine.
The Sorcerer (1877)	-	Expulsion of the intruders.
Gretchen (1879	-	Death of the heroine.
The Pirates of Penzance (1819)	-	Willing marriage.
Patience (1881)	-	Marriage and rejection of marriage.
Iolanthe (1882)	-	Marriage in Fairyland.

Princess Ida (1884)	-	Reluctant marriage.
Utopia Limited (1893)	-	Normal marriage.
(Ulysses) (1897)	-	Expulsion of the intruders.
Fallen Fairies (1909)	-	Expulsion of the intruders.

Quite possibly the optimistic endings of the well known Gilbert and Sullivan operas are due to the need to end a comedy on a happy note. It would be too much to claim great profundity for Gilbert's treatment of his *Princess* plot, even though the theme was of personal importance to him. Nevertheless his dealings with it help to give his libretti a degree of substance and interest which is lacking from the work of more psychologically normal men. At the dramatic level the existence of two contrasting groups of invaders and invaded sets up simple but perceptible contrasts and tensions which are not present in conventional libretti where the chorus is made up of peasants or gypsies or whatever. Visually, too, the invasion technique tends to produce a contrast between the bold colours of the intruders and the pastel shades of the beleaguered maidens. These things are part of Gilbert's art, albeit springing from an infantile personality.

From the evidence of Gilbert's work we must now turn once again to his life. If he did indeed fail to make the Freudian transition to the genital stage the failure must have been expressed in his behaviour: did he or did he not behave as a sexually mature man? I believe the answer is almost certainly 'No', but before it can be given we must look a little further at *Bab*.

Bab was above all things a precocious little brat. A ballad entitled *The Precocious Baby* (1867) introduces us to the infant of a young mother and elderly father, who from the moment of his birth proved 'a horribly fast little cad'. The baby eventually dies 'an enfeebled old dotard at five', but on his way to a premature grave he manages a fairly full amorous career:[13]

> He'd chuck his nurse under the chin, and he'd say,
>   With his 'Fal, lal, lal'–
>   'Oo doosed fine gal!'
> This shocking precocity drove 'em away:
>   A month from today
>   Is as long as I'll stay–
> Then I'd wish, if you please, for to go, if I may.'

This ballad is described as 'A very true tale'. Clearly a story in which a baby runs through an entire lifetime in five years cannot be literally true; but what if there is a grain of truth in it? What if *Bab* himself had known love as a baby? The thing is neither impossible nor particularly unusual. In England the classic exponent of 'infant joy' is William Blake; the following description of love at the age of four comes from the German dramatist Friedrich Hebbel (1813-63):[14]

> It was in Susanna's dull schoolroom also, that I learned the meaning of love; it was, indeed, in the very hour when I first entered it, at the age of four.... her name was Emily, and she was the daughter of the parish clerk. A passionate trembling seized me, the blood rushed to my heart; but a

sentiment of shame also intermingled with my first sensations, and I lowered my eyes to the ground once more, as rapidly as if I had caught sight of something horrible. From that moment Emily was ever in my thoughts; and the school, so greatly dreaded in anticipation, became a great joy to me because it was there only that I could see her.

No such outpouring is to be found in the works of W.S. Gilbert, but something very like it is recorded by Gilbert's father. To read the works of the elder Gilbert can be an eerie experience for the student of the son—one ends by wondering which of them was more indebted to the other. The father's account of childhood love is given in the quasi-autobiographical *Memoirs Of A Cynic* (1880) which is an expanded version of a chapter of *Shirley Hall Asylum* (1863): [15]

> I managed in some manner to fall desperately in love with a little girl about my own age, the daughter of the matron of the workhouse, and a very stiff, prim, severe woman she was. How her daughter first came under my notice I know not. Certainly it was not in the general manner these affections start up in the breasts of schoolboys, by seeing the beloved object in church, for her mother was a rigid Dissenter, and we, of course, from our more genteel position in society, attended the parish church. I never spoke one word to her in my life; but it was no matter, my affection surpassed the bounds of reason. My love grew so strong I could conceal it no longer, and I determined to address her. [He writes, but is discovered and caned for his impertinence]. I can conscientiously state that it would be difficult for a youth to sustain a more cruel affliction than that of being caned in the presence of the object of his affections.

It would be injudicious to take this passage *au pied de la lettre* as a straight-forward account of an event in William Gilbert's life, but neither is it the kind of episode that would occur casually to the imagination. All one can legitimately do is point to its existence while remarking on the very strong psychological similarities between the Gilberts, father and son. At the same time, baby love is one of the familiar features of the Savoy libretti: [16]

> PATIENCE: Long years ago—fourteen maybe—
>   When but a tiny babe of four,
>   Another baby played with me,
>   My elder by a year or more;
>   A little child of beauty rare,
>   With marvellous eyes and wondrous hair,
>   Who, in my child-eyes, seemed to me
>   All that a little child should be!
>   Ah, how we loved, that child and I!
>   How pure our baby joy!
>   How true our love—and, by the by,
>   *He* was a little boy!

A few lines later, Patience stresses the non-sexual nature of the relationship by saying 'He was a *little* boy'. Almost as well known is the babyhood love of

Prince Hilarion for Princess Ida:[17]

> HILARION: I think I see her now....
> In my mind's eye, I mean—a blushing bride,
> All bib and tucker, frill and furbelow!
> How exquisite she looked as she was borne,
> Recumbent, in her foster-mother's arms!
> How the bride wept—nor would be comforted
> Until the hireling mother-for-the-nonce
> Administered refreshment in the vestry.
> And I remember feeling much annoyed
> That she should weep at marrying with me.
> But then I thought, 'These brides are all alike.
> You cry at marrying me? How much more cause
> You'd have to cry if it were broken off!'
> These were my thoughts; I kept them to myself,
> For at that age I had not learned to speak.

Given the well-established fact that childhood love is possible, and that it is explicitly described by the elder Gilbert, it is hardly extravagant or implausible to regard descriptions of the same thing in the works of the son as based on experience: at some time during his infancy *Bab* was in love with a little girl. This is no cause for surprise or alarm; it happened to Goethe, Alfred de Musset, Dante, Canova, Byron, and Napoleon among celebrated men.[18]

If Flaubert is to be trusted, the next stage after the love of a little girl is the love of a 'buxom, full-necked woman'. Certainly this appears to have been the experience of Gilbert's father, for in *The Memoirs Of A Cynic* he describes his development thus:

> During the time I was at Clapham I suffered another attack of the tender passion, but this time of a totally different description to the last. Instead of falling in love with a girl as young as myself (I may here add that since my adventure with the daughter of the matron of the workhouse I cordially detested all little girls), the present object of my affections had been fifty, but how many years before it would be difficult to say. She occupied the honourable position of laundrymaid to the establishment, and with her I desperately fell in love. It would be base flattery to say she was handsome; on the contrary, beyond a good-natured expression of countenance, there was but one attraction about her; but that, in my eyes, compensated for any other defects, assuming there to have been any—she was much older than myself. I seemed to hold it as a chivalrous feat to captivate the affections of a woman so much my senior; it made me feel more manly, and more on an equality with her. I will not exactly say she encouraged me, for that might be doing her an injustice; but certainly she did not discourage my attentions, and received graciously the buns and other delicacies I purchased for her. If, however, I became at all too demonstrative, she used to threaten to tell the Doctor [ie *Head of the School*] but, to do her justice, she never kept her word. This innocent flirtation continued till I left school, when, on parting with her in the laundry, I clasped her in my arms and kissed her affectionately.[19]

Many of the early writings of *Bab* contain an autobiographical element, though it is impossible to distinguish reliably between what is fact in them and what is fiction. One of the most curious of these pieces is a ballad entitled *Haunted* (1866). Decsribed as being written by 'Our depressed Contributor', the poem describes the miseries of a schoolboy's life, and then continues:[20]

> I pass to critical seventeen:
> The ghost of that terrible wedding scene,
> When an elderly colonel stole my queen,
>   And woke my dream of heaven:
> No school-girl decked in her nursery curls
> Was my gushing innocent queen of pearls;
> If she wasn't a girl of a thousand girls,
>   She was one of forty-seven!

These lines may of course be purely fanciful, having no connection either with Gilbert's life or his character. If that is the case there is no more to be said, except perhaps to marvel at the reconditeness of an imagination which could conjure up such things *ex nihilo*. If, on the other hand, they describe a real experience, then a number of interesting consequences follow and one of the greatest mysteries of Gilbert's work is cleared up. Let us adopt the second alternative.

Gilbert tells us that, like his father–and like Frederic in *The Pirates of Penzance*–he loved an older woman. We may conjecture that he wove an idyllic fantasy round the relationship, as his father did, while she simply permitted him to do so. There cannot have been true reciprocity, for Gilbert appears to have been caught unawares by her wedding. This wedding was not merely surprising–it was traumatic, for Gilbert says it woke his dream of heaven.

One of the signs of the immaturity of Gilbert's mind is the ease with which he became disillusioned, and the callowness of the resulting cynicism. In *The Memoirs of a Cynic* the elder Gilbert sets out to describe the stages by which he became cynical, one of which was seeing one of his stage heroines in the street as an old granny with a basket on her arm.[21] Gilbert *fils* describes an exactly similar experience in a ballad called *Disillusioned* (1867); it is one of the coincidences which leads one to wonder whether *The Memoirs of a Cynic* is not in part a description by the father of the son:[22]

> My favourite actor, who at will,
> With mimic woe my eyes could fill
>   With unaccustomed brine:
> A being who appeared to me
> (Before I knew him well) to be
>   A song incarnadine;
>
> I found a coarse unpleasant man
> With speckled chin–unhealthy, wan–
>   Of self-importance full:
> Existing in an atmosphere
> That reeked of gin and pipes and beer–
>   Conceited, fractious, dull.

If the sight of a drunken actor could disillusion Gilbert, and a similar experience with an actress could help turn his father into a cynic, what must have been the effect of the 'terrible wedding scene' which shattered another dream? The answer has already been provided by Gilbert senior, 'I may here add that since my adventure with the daughter of the matron of the workhouse I cordially detested all little girls'.

Cordial detestation. The response of the Gilbertian mind to many things was cordial detestation. In the case of the 'queen' of forty-seven, disillusionment and detestation must have gone hand in hand. But is not Gilbert famous all over the world for his hatred of elderly women?

Although one speaks for convenience of Gilbert's harsh treatment of the ageing female, his rage was not actually directed at age as such. The true aim was perceived by Sullivan when he objected to Gilbert's proposed treatment of the Lady Sophy in *Utopia Limited*:[23]

> The part of Lady Sophy, as it is to be treated in the second act, is in my opinion a blot on an otherwise brilliant picture, and to me personally unsympathetic and distasteful. If there is to be an old or middle-aged woman in the piece at all, is it necessary that she should be very old, ugly, raddled, and perhaps grotesque, and still more is it necessary that she should be seething with love and passion (requited or unrequited) and other feelings not usually associated with old age? I thought that 'Katisha' was to be the last example of that type.

Age apart, the characteristic of all Gilbert's elderly females is that in one way or another they are seething with love and passion. One thinks of the desperation with which Ruth clings to Frederic in *The Pirates of Penzance*, of Katisha's frenzied search for Nanki-Poo, and the dogged devotion of Lady Jane to Bunthorne in *Patience*. Lady Sophy herself was conceived by Gilbert in these explicit terms:[24]

> ...beneath her cold and self-contained exterior there lurks a spirit of wild and passionate devilry. She is compelled for professional and prudential reasons to keep this under the strictest control, but the effort is tremendous and unless she allowed herself now and then to 'break out' she would go mad. As she is alone and unobserved, this is a good opportunity to do so. Thereupon she has a desperate and extravagantly dramatic scena in which she describes, in the wildest terms, her consuming passion for the king.... This ends in a wildly melodramatic dance.

The frame of mind in which a man sits down to conceive a character like this is not easy to imagine—all we know is that Gilbert did so, not once but repeatedly. Yet what must have disgusted him as much in the marriage of his 'queen' as the betrayal of his own innocent love was the sexual desire shown by the elderly contracting parties. He, Gilbert, loved purely; she, the queen of forty-seven, loved carnally. The cordial detestation of *Bab* was turned not merely against elderly women, but against elderly women *in love*. Thus the marriage of a woman who perhaps did not even know of *Bab's* feelings for her has had its repercussions for the gaiety of nations. No man of normal mentality would react in this way to such an experience, but Gilbert's response is entirely consistent with the five-year level of development at which we have supposed him to have been fixed.

Hatred of sexual love may also have lain behind Gilbert's vicious treatment of the Comtesse de Brémont. She was not particularly elderly; on the other hand she obviously had a reputation for unconventional behaviour which would have been quite sufficient for Gilbert to mark her down for the full *Bab* treatment. Given the relatively slack morals of the theatre it is possible that those actresses against whom Gilbert acted with particular virulence had committed some kind of sexual peccadillo, real or imaginary.

Up to and including his supposed traumatic experience with an older woman, Gilbert's sexual development may be said to have been normal enough. However, the rejection of his love appears to have resulted in what Freud would have called a regression of libido or regression-in-aim, that is to say, a return to 'a lower, non-genital form of psychosexual satisfaction.'[25] When this happens, according to Freud, it is possible for 'the love-impulses to transform themselves into impulses of aggression against the object'.[26] In plain terms the lover develops a cordial detestation of what he formerly loved, but does so from the vantage point of a return to an earlier stage of development. The motive power behind this regression is none other than the death instinct, whose whole purpose is 'to lead organic life back into the inanimate state',[27] thereby restoring a previous state of affairs. Freud associated the pure state of the death instinct with the compulsion to repeat which is such a feature of Gilbert's work. In plain terms again, Gilbert retreated to the pre-genital stage and stayed there for the rest of his life. The text of *Broken Hearts* puts the process into blank verse:[28]

> We, broken hearts,
> Knit by the sympathy of kindred woe,
> Have sought this isle far from the ken of man;
> And having loved, and having lost our loves,
> Stand pledged to love no living thing again.

Turning now to what is known of Gilbert's sexual behaviour during his adult life, we find a pattern entirely consistent with fixation at the pre-genital stage. As we have seen, he loved to surround himself with attractive women. His biographers print a number of letters written to these ladies over many years, and mention the existence of others (now lost) written to children. All these letters share the same characteristics: they are friendly, even affectionate, jolly, and full of news; but they contain no hint of anything further. One written to Mrs Mary Talbot in 1902 may stand for them all. Mrs Talbot, nicknamed Cousin Mary, corresponded occasionally with Gilbert from 1894 to the year of his death. This letter was written on 19 November 1902:[29]

> My Dear Cousin Mary,
>
> Thank you very much for your good wishes. It is a great lark being sixty-six—you try it. It is so delightful to have attained a time of life

when one can feel that there is not the remotest chance of one's being a snake on another man's hearth. One feels *so* safe and (involuntarily) good. I am slowly getting stronger, but I am still rather Richardy (I hate the slang expression "Dickey") in the knees. If my left knee were as good as my right knee, all would be well. It would even be well if my right knee were as bad as my left knee, because they would at any rate be pairs. However, I can walk five miles at a pinch. My steam-car is going strong, and I hope I shall be able to give you a good spin when you come here. (Song for a lady motor-driver, "La donna e auto-mobile")....

Your aff.

Cousin Bill.

Gilbert's biographers, who censored everything else, occasionally allowed a mild sexual innuendo to slip through. In this letter Gilbert congratulates himself on being placed by age beyond temptation. The tone is jocular, and we need not place a weighty interpretation on it; nevertheless, we may remark that Gilbert *welcomed* sexual decay, where regret would be the usual course.

A consistent picture emerges from what is known of his relationships with actresses. A man with Gilbert's position and power in the theatre could have philandered on the grand scale had he been so inclined. No scrap of evidence is known to suggest that he did so. At Grim's Dyke he kept a small upper room called The Flirtorium which he used for the private extra tuition of actresses; even here no breath of scandal survives to bring the blush of shame to the cheek of posterity, though Lillian Russell refused to grace its predecessor in 1884. No doubt she found the idea too good to be true.

Gilbert's regulation of the morals of the Savoy Theatre is well known. Actors and actresses had dressing rooms on either side of the stage, and mixing was allowed only in the Green Room. When Jessie Bond, playing in *Patience*, received a billet-doux from some young men in the audience, Gilbert asked to see the note, became extremely angry, and went to deal with the culprits:[31]

> There are three ways of dealing with you, and you can take your choice. I will go before the curtain, if you like, explain what has happened, and say that Miss Bond refuses to continue whilst you are here, or you can go of your own accord, or I can send a couple of commissionaires to carry you.

The young men left the theatre, which promptly became known as the Savoy Boarding School. What is significant is the altogether unreasonable ferocity of Gilbert's reaction. Jessie Bond was one of his favourites—he was angry and ungenerous when she married—but he was not her keeper. His behaviour makes sense only if we are dealing with a case of *Bab*-in-the-manger: unable for very painful reasons to send a billet-doux to Miss Bond himself, *Bab* turned in fury on those who would pollute her and make her unworthy of his pre-genital ideal. When she voluntarily embarked on the sexual life by marrying he called her a little fool and refused to send her a present. No doubt a similar mechanism underlay his omnipotent attempts to control the morality of the theatre as a whole. What we may securely deduce from them is that Gilbert did not do himself the things he forbade to others; if he had been capable of philandering Miss Bond might have received her note in peace.

Gilbert married in 1866, when he was thirty and his wife seventeen. It is hard to assess the marriage. Gilbert's letters to his wife are indistinguishable in style and content from those to his lady correspondents; nothing she wrote to him has survived, nor were there any children. We may conclude from the lack of evidence that Mrs Gilbert was not a dominating personality, but this need not mean she was simply the complementary negative to his positive. *Bab's* marriage cannot have been so straightforward as that.

We have seen how Gilbert's relationships with women other than his wife were playful and rooted in the pre-genital fairy love of his deepest imagination; we have also seen how furiously he repelled the real world of sexual relationships whenever it came to his attention. A wife of seventeen—at least in 1866—is above all things innocent and virginal. Given the nature of his ideals Gilbert must have married his wife for her possession of these qualities. But the question then arises, 'How, given her purity and his cordial detestation of animal passion, was the marriage consummated?' This question exercised the mind of Freud, who regarded it as a fundamental one of civilised life. In *The Tendency To Debasement In Love* (1912) he drew attention to two currents in love, one affectionate, the other sensual. [32]

The affectionate current is the older of the two. It springs from the earliest years of childhood, and relates to members of the family 'and those who look after the child'. (One recalls that *Bab's* Precocious Baby loved his nurse, and wished to marry her.) At puberty the sensual current makes its appearance, seeking the satisfaction its nature demands. However the sensual current cannot act straightforwardly because of the prohibitions set up by the earlier experiences. As a result one of two things happens: either the sensual current seeks an outlet by association with debased, socially inferior, women against whom the prohibitions do not apply, or there is a stalemate—impotence, in fact—when the woman in question is loved and esteemed. To judge from his obscure mistresses, Sullivan followed the first course. But what of Gilbert? As we have seen, he did not use his Flirtorium for its right true end. A strong suspicion of impotence would follow from this circumstance alone; his idealistic love would not permit him to look upon his wife as a sexual object. Freud says that impotence is, after anxiety, the commonest reason why people seek psychiatric help. The preconditions for impotence were highly developed in Gilbert—it seems reasonable to conclude that he did not escape their consequences. Impotent men do not of course suffer lack of *desire*.

Impotence on the part of her husband may explain why Mrs Gilbert was apparently prepared to tolerate his Flirtorium and his women friends. If her own marriage was unconsummated she would have no reason to fear his infidelity. By the same token he would feel no fear of 'being a snake on another man's hearth'. Hesketh Pearson records an odd sentence used by Gilbert in 1879 to the manager E.A. Sothern. The sentence runs thus, 'I am afraid that in dealing with a widow one must accept the fact that if she is still a virgin it is her husband's fault rather than her own.' [33] Pearson does not quote the context in which this remark was made. It may mean little, or nothing. Or in the context of Gilbert's own life it may mean much.

There remain a couple of possibilities for Gilbert's sexual life, both of which might have left him impotent with his wife. The first would be a completely clandestine sexual life in the sophisticated brothels of Victorian London. Madame Rachel's, for instance, which he mentions in his burlesque *Dulcamara* (1866), had a *maison de rendezvous* in the back premises. In the nature of the case no evidence for such a career would survive. Secondly, given his masochistic tendencies, he might have found satisfaction through a masochistic ritual or game. The masochist, says Freud, wants to be treated like a small and helpless child.[34] *Bab*, one would think, would have been ready enough to play the tiny child for the right kind of attention. The most likely game would be one in which he dressed in nappies and was punished by his wife for naughtiness.

Impotence on the part of Gilbert would of course account for his childlessness. If the language of his *Dan'l Druce* (1876) means anything in the personal sense Gilbert must certainly have longed for a child. Druce is a man obsessed with the desire for a child, which he describes as *'some one thing of my creating'* (Gilbert's italics).[35] Druce is also a miser, who hoards gold in a hole in the floor. It happens that a Royalist Colonel named Sir Jasper Combe is fleeing from the Parliamentary forces with a baby (the play is set after the battle of Worcester). Combe enters Druce's hut, and by a bit of melodramatic jiggery-pokery flees with the gold, leaving the baby behind in exchange. Hailing the child as a miracle, Druce ceases to be a misanthropic miser and returns to his former trade of blacksmith. After fourteen years Sir Jasper returns and threatens to take the child, called Dorothy, away. However it transpires that Druce is her real father, his wife having been enticed away by Sir Jasper some time before the birth of the baby. Sir Jasper confesses his guilt, and Dorothy remains with her true father.

Apart from an opening which puts one strongly in mind of *Peter Grimes* the play is not distinguished. However it brings together with almost naive precision certain features which Freud says belong to the anal-erotic character. In his paper *On Transformations of Instinct as Exemplified in Anal Erotism* (1917) Freud says this:[36]

> As a starting point for this discussion we may take the fact that it appears as if in the products of the unconscious—spontaneous ideas, phantasies and symptoms—the concepts *faeces* (money, gift), *baby* and *penis* are ill-distinguishable from one antother and are easily interchangeable.

Dan'l Druce is in no doubt about the connection between babies and money:[37]

> I love my gold as other men love their bairns; it's of my making, and I love it! A mean sordid love, maybe, but hard, and bad, and base as thou thinkest me, I've prayed a thousand times that my gold might take a living form, that the one harmless hope of my wrecked life might come true.

The connection between money and babies is emphasised again at some length in a speech which follows this. For our purpose we may note the emphasis on making, and the prayer for gold to be turned into living form. We have encountered the same process in *Pygmalion and Galatea*, where the statue comes to life at Pygmalion's prayer; it would appear that Galatea was, in a very special sense, Pygmalion's daughter. However, Gilbert himself was addicted to a particular form of making in his lifelong attempts to coach novice actresses into stardom:[38]

> Probably one of the strongest tenets of Gilbert's creed was the faith that the imitative art of acting can be perfected by instruction without inspiration....
> He was prodigal of advice and help whenever he saw—or believed he saw—talent, nor was his lavish assistance confined to his own companies. More than one popular actress owe their [*sic*] fame and fortune entirely to Gilbert's tuition.

When the actresses he coached proved ungrateful Gilbert was annoyed. In fact he must have been rather more deeply hurt, for it would seem that by his coaching he was *making daughters*. The daughters thus made were treated in a purely mechanical way, much as Pygmalion shaped the inanimate stone or Dan'l Druce added to his gold. The final element of the fantasy appears when Dan'l Druce, against all probability, turns out to be a true father after all.

It is against this background that we must see Gilbert's relationship with Nancy McIntosh. Once he had come upon her in 1892 he did more than everything in his power to create a successful career for her. She evidently possessed a fine voice, but no effort from Gilbert could make her a successful actress. However he became so involved with her that he persuaded her to come and live with him and his wife at Grim's Dyke, eventually adopting her as his daughter and heir. With any other man one would suspect—nay be certain of—a sexual liaison carried on with the complicity of the wife. With Gilbert the case was different. Mrs Gilbert seems to have understood, for she and Nancy remained friends and companions after Gilbert's death and up to hers, in 1936. Most regrettably neither of them left an account of life with *Bab*. But *Bab* did, at last, in his own fashion, produce a daughter. This was how his posterity was to be provided.

So far in our discussions we have avoided all mention of the most famous of Freud's postulations, the Oedipus Complex. There is good reason, for Gilbert, so prodigal with self-revelation in other respects, has left little material by which one might interpret his relations with his parents. Indeed, the absence of anything obviously Oedipal has been a major reason for regarding him as normal, as though psychology began and ended with Oedipus' adventures. Before embarking on this risky subject it may perhaps be as well to summarise Freud's writings about it.

At a very early age a little boy develops an 'object-cathexis' (love or desire) for his mother. This love derives ultimately from the breast, and is accompanied by the boy's identification with his father. For a time there is no conflict of

Rosina Brandram as Katisha
(*Illustrated Sporting and Dramatic News*, 27 June 1885)

interest, but at length the boy's love for his mother becomes so strong that his father is seen as an obstacle or rival. The boy now wishes to get rid of his father, in order to take the father's place with the mother; consequently the boy's attitude to his father becomes ambivalent. This is the simple Oedipus complex, which in practice is usually modified by a compensating feminine and affectionate attitude to the father, with a certain hostility to the mother. [39]

Eventually the Oedipus complex must disappear because its wishes cannot be fulfilled, but Freud holds that the chief agent of its disappearance is the threat of castration—if the little boy shows any kind of sexual interest he is threatened with castration, as often as not by his nursemaid. If he should decide to seek the affection of his father in a feminine way, then of course he must undergo castration in order to become a girl. Faced with this dilemma, the boy generally gives up his Oedipus complex; his surrender merges with the period of sexual latency beginning at about the age of five. However, the child now begins to identify with his parents, and their authority begins to internalise itself in him, leading to the eventual formation of the super-ego or conscience. [40] The power of other figures of authority such as teachers is now added to the receding memory of parental authority, building up in the end to a sense of destiny or fate, and finally of death. [41]

All we know directly of Gilbert's attitude to his parents is that when they separated in 1876 he took his father's side, writing to his mother in distinctly cool and formal terms. [42] Gilbert was then forty, his father over seventy. Clearly one cannot base a full-blown theory on such information. However we have in *The Mikado* a vigorous and colourful Oedipal drama, which illuminates the mind of *Bab* even if it tells us nothing reliable about his parents.

It is, I take it, self-evident that the parent figures in *The Mikado* are the Mikado himself and Katisha. They are the right age, and are extremely authoritarian. She is in love with the Mikado's *son*, and he has decreed beheading as the punishment for flirting: [43]

> Our great Mikado, virtuous man,
> When he to rule our land began,
>   Resolved to try
>   A plan whereby
>   Young men might best be steadied.
> So he decreed in words succint,
> That all who flirted, leered or winked
> (Unless connubially linked),
>   Should forthwith be beheaded.

From beheading to castration is a short enough step and flirting, in Oedipal terms, may be taken as a general expression for sexual desire. The Mikado, therefore, is the father who threatens the son with castration for sexual interest. In the play the Mikado's son is Nanki-Poo, but it is Ko-Ko who has actually been condemned to death for flirting. It follows that the hero of the Oedipal drama, the true son of the Mikado, is Ko-Ko. As the play unfolds we learn that the

Mikado is coming to see that his wishes with regard to the execution/castration of Ko-Ko have been carried out. Ko-Ko is panic-stricken, but soon hits on an idea: Nanki-Poo, the Mikado's son, shall be executed as a substitute. And by means of an affidavit the execution is duly carried out—it is described to the Mikado 'with most affecting particulars'. With the substitute son duly punished, Ko-Ko is now free to woo Katisha, the mother figure. This he does in a well-known scene, and, as he does so, she loses her formidable qualities and turns into 'a silly little goose', albeit a slightly bloodthirsty one. Oedipally speaking the mother figure loses her prohibitive character as soon as the deception has been worked on the father. Furthermore the father himself ceases to be a threat once the union with the mother is accomplished. In the final scene the deception is revealed, but the Mikado simply remarks imperturbably, 'Nothing could possibly be more satisfactory.'

The Mikado is of course a work of art—and a comic one at that—over and above any Oedipal meaning it may have. On stage Gilbert could not possibly have represented Ko-Ko as marrying his mother; nor could Nanki-Poo have been really executed. Yum-Yum, Ko-Ko's ward and Nanki-Poo's bride, is part of the stage plot rather than the Oedipal plot. However, the death with which she is threatened—burial alive—may be of interest in connection with Gilbert's general attitude to sex. It will be remembered that according to the Mikado's laws when a married man is beheaded his wife must be buried alive. The law has never been put into effect because married men never flirt. Now burial alive is not a Japanese punishment; it is the death which the Romans visited on the Vestal Virgins for unchastity. But why, in *The Mikado*, should the wife be given the punishment of an unchaste woman when her husband flirts? Only one explanation fits the bill: the flirting which is being punished is sexual congress between man and wife; the husband is to be beheaded/castrated, and the wife is to receive the death of a woman who has broken her vows of chastity. The fate of Gretchen comes into view from an unanticipated perspective. Husbands who *never* flirt are, of course, impotent. As we have seen, Gilbert himself may well have been such a man.

There is no reason either in art or in psychology why an image or figure which stands for one thing may not also stand for another. Katisha's part in the Oedipal drama of *The Mikado* is undoubtedly that of mother, but in other ways she is treated as the ardent woman of forty-seven who betrayed *Bab*. Given *Bab's* predilection for nursemaids it is possible that even her Oedipal role may be that of mother surrogate. Foster mothers are familiar characters in Gilbert, and it may be that in sober truth it was one of his nurses who betrayed him. Certainly one senses some acute crisis of affection behind the following verses included in *The Baby's Vengeance* (1869). The lines, it must be stressed, were written by a man of thirty-three:[44]

> 'Tis now some thirty-seven years ago
> Since first began the plot that I'm revealing.
> A fine young woman, wed ten years or so,

Lived with her husband down in Drum Lane, Ealing,
Herself by means of mangling reimbursing,
And now and then (at intervals) wet-nursing.

Two little babes dwelt in her humble cot:
    One was her own—the other only lent to her:
Her own she slighted. Tempted by a lot
    Of gold and silver regularly sent to her,
She ministered unto the little other
In the capacity of foster-mother.

I was her own. Oh! how I lay and sobbed
    In my poor cradle—deeply, deeply cursing
The rich man's pampered bantling, who had robbed
    My only birthright—an attentive nursing!
Sometimes, in hatred of my foster-brother,
I gnashed my gums—which terrified my mother.

One darksome day (I should have mentioned that
    We were alike in dress and baby feature)
I *in* MY cradle having placed the brat,
    Crept into his—the pampered little creature!
It was imprudent—well, disgraceful maybe,
For, oh! I was a bad, black-hearted baby!

So great a luxury was food, I think
    There was no wickedness I wouldn't try for it.
Now if I wanted anything to drink
    At any time I only had to cry for it!
Once, if I dared to weep, the bottle lacking,
My blubbering involved a serious smacking!

The obvious way to interpret this poem would be in terms of sibling rivalry. However Gilbert had no known brothers, only sisters, whereas the theme of baby-swapping in his works always involves two boys. In view of the close connection between gold and faeces it is possible that the baby who received maternal love obliged with his pot whereas *Bab* did not. All one can say with certainty is that whenever Gilbert used the baby-swapping motif it is always the rejected and apparently inferior baby who becomes victor in the end. Thus in *H.M.S. Pinafore* the lowly seaman Ralph Rackstraw becomes Captain, and in *The Gondoliers* Luiz the drummer-boy becomes King. Unfortunately the clue which would make possible a precise interpretation is missing.

Finally we may turn to a matter which has remained in the background of Gilbert studies for many years. This is the obscene play supposedly written by Gilbert and circulated secretly in typescript form. Hesketh Pearson, who had seen this typescript, says the play was as witty as any of Gilbert's libretti, but declined to identify him positively as the author. [45] In his book *Obscenity And The Law* Norman St John Stevas says that Gilbert and Sullivan wrote an obscene opera, *The Sod's Opera*, a copy of which was kept in the guard room at St James's Palace. [46]

It is generally agreed among students of erotica that *The Sod's Opera* is identical with an obscene pantomime, *Harlequin Prince Cherrytop*, first printed privately in July 1879, and reprinted in 1895. Only one copy of the first edition is known to exist, [47] but the 1895 edition is said to be 'By the late G.A.S. (Author of "The Mysteries of Verbena House")'. Popular opinion, followed by Norman St John Stevas, seems to have taken the initials G.A.S. to stand for *G*ilbert *A*nd *S*ullivan, but others have regarded them as standing for *G*eorge *A*ugustus *S*ala (1828-95), a well known journalist and, privately, an author of erotic literature. [48]

On the face of it the case is a simple one: Gilbert's supposed obscene opera is in fact the work of Sala, who was, incidentally, a colleague of his on the staff of *Fun*. However there are just sufficient hints of Gilbert in the text of the pantomime to raise at least a shadow of suspicion about its authorship. For instance, at one point a fairy is mistaken for a commercial traveller, much as the Fairy Queen in *Iolanthe* is mistaken for the head of a girls' school; one of the lyrics is set to the tune of *The Tight Little Island*, which inspired 'Happily coupled are we' in the second act of *Ruddigore*; a couplet near the beginning has a familiar ring:

> His father, mother, sisters, aunts and cousins,
> Courtiers and maids of honour by the dozens.

Similarly a couplet near the end carries overtones of *Trial by Jury*:

> Oh mighty potentate! Oh, cove most regal!
> Ain't you aware that bigamy's illegal?

Such similarities as these do not in any way amount to proof of Gilbertian authorship. Equally Sala's speciality lay in flagellation and sadism/masochism, both of which are absent from the text of *Harlequin*, which is, so to speak, normally obscene. Is there, then, any possibility of Gilbertian involvement?

According to Hesketh Pearson, Gilbert's smoking-room conversation was 'strongly Rabelaisian' and 'unprintable'. [49] His official biographers, so prone to censorship in other respects, print a surprising amount of mild sexual innuendo, including the following limericks:

> There was a young lady of Pinner,
> Who was a society sinner.
>   She went off, they say,
>   To Paris one day—
> And the rest—shall be told after dinner. [50]

> When I asked a young girl of Portrush,
> 'What book do you read?' she said, 'Hush!
>   I have happened by chance
>   On a novel from France,
> And I hope it will cause me to blush.' [51]

This last limerick was sent in a letter to Cousin Mary (p. 98). If he could write in this way to a woman we are entitled to think him capable of something more forceful in male company. There is, moreover, an odd suggestion of real obscenity in *Ages Ago*. In this work two of the portraits who come to life are called Dame Cherry Maybud and Lord Carnaby Poppytop.[52] Ordinarily one would think nothing of such names, but with *Harlequin* in mind their possible sexual connotation is obvious enough. If such a connotation is admitted, then we may legitimately ask whether these names have not strayed from a generally concealed acquaintance with obscene literature. The flagellation lyric from *The Gentleman In Black* (p 64) also adds its moiety to the suspicion that Gilbert and Sala may have had more in common than their joint work on *Fun*.[53]

Unfortunately Hesketh Pearson does not say how he came by his copy of the obscene play, nor how he knew of Gilbert's Rabelaisian talk. In the absence of documentary proof it would be rash to believe positively either that Gilbert wrote an obscene work or that he had an interest in erotica. Nevertheless there is just sufficient evidence to make one wonder whether Pearson's sources were not well informed after all. The essence of pornography is the reification of human beings and human behaviour: it tends towards abstraction and fantasy, and ultimately towards nonsense. It is infantile, egocentric, and often mechanical.[54] In all these respects Gilbert was fully qualified to excel. We may conclude that if he ever *did* turn his hand to pornography he was probably rather good at it. There is by the way no question of Sullivan having written music for the work of G.A.S. All the lyrics are identified as having been written to existing tunes, after the accepted pantomime convention.

4: The Death of Jack Point

According to the final stage direction of *The Yoemen of the Guard* Jack Point falls 'senseless' at the feet of Colonel Fairfax and Elsie Maynard as they embrace in marriage. The precise interpretation of the word *senseless* has been the subject of considerable discussion: does Point simply faint away or does he, as many think, actually die? George Grossmith, the original performer of the part of Point, gave a light interpretation because he thought no audience would take him seriously. Gilbert, however, seems to have intended a death, and refrained from making his instructions specific only because he feared the possibly adverse affect on the box office of death in a comic opera. Once *The Yeomen of the Guard* was safely launched to success he felt free to sanction the sombre ending, and said so to Henry Lytton, who had adopted the practice of kissing the hem of Elsie's dress before he collapsed as Point: [1]

> Gilbert and I, when we had become close friends, often had long talks about this opera, and in particular about my interpretation of the lovable Merryman. I told him what had led me to attempt this conception, and asked him whether he wished me to continue it, or whether it should be modified in any way. 'No,' was his reply; 'keep on like that. It is just what I want. *Jack Point* should die and the end of the opera should be a tragedy.'

Within the context of *The Yeomen of the Guard* the death of Jack Point is an effect without cause inasmuch as no reason is offered as to why a young man should drop dead at the feet of his beloved. Point and Elsie are a pair of strolling players who at the beginning of the opera are tacitly engaged to each other. Elsie contracts an empty marriage with Colonel Fairfax in order to earn money to buy medicines for her sick mother. However she falls in love with him in earnest when, having escaped execution, he woos her in his disguise as Leonard Meryll.

Point's death is his reaction to losing Elsie in this way.

That Gilbert attached great importance to Jack Point cannot be doubted, for he counted *The Yeomen of the Guard* among those works in which he laid bare his soul. Hesketh Pearson reports his belief in this matter, while characteristically denying its truth, 'He put a great deal of what he thought was his essential self into the character of Jack Point, and regarded his idealised Gilbert as a greater creation than any of Shakespeare's jesters.'[2]

In making this judgement Pearson was misled both by his own unshakable devotion to Gilbert's normality and by the rather obvious literary inferiority of Jack Point to the fool in *King Lear*. However, the death of Point follows the same masochistic pattern as those of Vavir and Gretchen in the blank verse plays which, Gilbert insisted, expressed more of his 'real self' than any other works. In each case death supervenes in an apparently healthy person after a disappointment in love. If Gilbert, who was in a position to know, regarded Jack Point as an expression of himself, then we are surely entitled to take him at his word.

The *Yeomen* is not in fact Gilbert's first play to describe a man suffering from a disappointment in love. The Faustus of *Gretchen* (1879) is also a broken lover. Gilbert avowed that Goethe's (call it Gounod's) *Faust* was the starting point for *Gretchen*, but he ignored the well-known character of Faust as a symbol of human aspiration in order to represent him as unhappy in love. The alteration can hardly be a matter of chance:[3]

> How shall I speak to such a one as thou
> Of an intense and all-believing love,
> Betrayed, abandoned, trampled underfoot?
> Of pure and simple faith in one fair woman—
> Unswerving faith—faith, absolute and whole—
> And of the deadly agony that came
> Of finding that well-trusted woman false?
> All the more false for the divine truth-promise
> That played upon her fair and placid brow;
> All the more false for the hot passion-vows
> That leaped, in hurried whispers, from her lips!
> I gave her all the wealth of my rich heart—
> I lived upon her love—I fed my life
> With the sweet poison of her lying lips
> In utter trust. God help me!—one dark day
> In the high noon of all my happiness,
> My heart upraised to heaven, in gratitude
> For the fair promise of our coming life,
> She left me, for a man whose proferred love
> Had formed the theme of many an idle jest.
> But he was rich—and so—she went to him!
> At once the open volume of her life
> Lay plain before me, and I read therein
> That she was—womankind!
> Mad with the frenzy of a shipwrecked heart,
> And with the old fond test-words of our love
> Ringing a mocking echo through my brain,
> I cursed the world and all the women in it,
> And here sought sanctuary.

The territory staked out in this speech is already familiar to us—the innocent and trusting love wholly shattered by an unexpected marriage by the beloved. So too is the irrational scope of the disillusionment, which is extended to all women. If, as *The Baby's Vengeance* (p 105) suggests, Gilbert considered himself deprived of maternal affection, then one would expect his subsequent love to be both abnormally intense and abnormally vulnerable in the event of failure. Faustus flees to a monastery as the ladies of *Broken Hearts* have fled to an island, as Gilbert himself fled to the pre-genital stage of development.

On the basis of passages in his own works and those of his father, we have speculated that Gilbert also underwent the experience of childhood love. Given the general lack of information about his early years one would not expect to be able to identify the other party to this affair, even if it were not simply unilateral on his part. However a chance remark in one of Gilbert's published fragments of autobiography suggests that the other child may have been the later famous singer Euphrosyne Parepa (1836-74). Gilbert is describing his first literary excursion in 1857, when he was twenty-one:[4]

> Madame Parepa-Rosa (at that time Mddle. Parepa), whom I had known from babyhood, had made a singular success at those concerts [Alfred Mellon's Promenade Concerts] with the laughing song from *Manon Lescaut* [Auber], and she asked me to do a translation of the song for Alfred Mellon's play-bill. I did it; it was duly printed in the bill. I remember that I went night after night to those concerts to enjoy the intense gratification of standing at the elbow of any promenader who might be reading my translation and wondering to myself what the promenader would say if he knew that the gifted creature who had written the very words he was reading was at that moment standing within a yard of him. The secret satisfaction of knowing that I possessed the power to thrill him with this information was enough, and I preserved my incognito.

Clearly one would not expect a frank statement of childhood love from Gilbert, even if Euphrosyne Parepa was involved; he did, however, consider the babyhood association significant enough to include in what is a very concise summary of his career. His words suggest that he never altogether lost contact with the singer, and he assuredly knew her well enough in 1857 for her to ask him to do a translation for her. From her own point of view Euphrosyne may well have thought of Gilbert simply as an old family friend, a clever young man who hoped to be called to the bar. But what of *Bab*? *Bab* might have thought many things; *Bab* might, as he later put it, have construed her customary affability into expressions of affection. *Bab* might have suffered a shock when in 1863 she married a Captain H. de Wolfe Carvell. No incontrovertible evidence survives to reinforce this supposition, but several of the *Bab Ballads* suggest interest on Gilbert's part.

Captain Carvell died at Lima on 26 April 1865. Euphrosyne was therefore left a widow at the age of twenty-nine—Gilbert was still unmarried. On 23 December 1865 the following short poem by Gilbert appeared in the pages of *Fun*:[5]

TO EUPHROSYNE
With My Carte de Visite

I've heard EUPHROSYNE declare
That handsome men, both dark and fair,
Are dear at three a penny.
I've searched the world, and this I know,
That nowhere, at a price so low,
Could I discover any.

Men ridiculed my folly when
I asked the price of handsome men,
And christened me a ninny.
Till PHOCAS KAMMERER I tried,
And found the article supplied
At twenty-four a guinea!

The name PHOCAS KAMMERER is a pun on 'Focus Camera'; the poem refers to the Victorian habit of collecting photographs of famous men. Gilbert's meaning—unusually—is not completely clear. Euphrosyne seems to be plentifully supplied with handsome men, but Gilbert fails to find them. He then sends her a photographic *carte de visite* of himself, with the implication that it is handsome. The use of the name Euphrosyne may be adventitious, and the poem may be a bit of insignificant fancy taken from thin air. On the other hand the only possible *meaning* it can have is that Gilbert had sent Euphrosyne Parepa, recently widowed, a photograph of himself as a handsome man, indeed the only available handsome man.

On 9 June 1866 Gilbert published a ballad in *Fun* under the title 'To My Bride'. This poem describes Gilbert's then circumstances accurately, and proceeds to ask his prospective bride to declare herself:[6]

Oh! bride of mine—tall, dumpy, dark or fair!
Oh!—widow—wife, maybe, or blushing maiden,
I've told *your* fortune: solved the gravest care
With which *your* mind has hitherto been laden.
I've prophesied correctly, never doubt it;
                    Now tell me mine—and please be quick about it!
You—only you—can tell me, and you will,
To whom I'm destined shortly to be mated,
Will she run up a heavy *modiste's* bill?
If so, I want to hear her income stated.
(This is a point which interests me greatly),
                    To quote the bard, 'Oh! have I seen her lately?'
Say, must I wait till husband number one
Is comfortably stowed away at Woking?
How is her hair most usually done?
And tell me, please, will she object to smoking?
The colour of her eyes, too, you may mention:
Come, Sybil, prophesy—I'm all attention.

Several references in these lines suggest they may have been written with

Euphrosyne Parepa in mind. The first status Gilbert ascribes to his bride is widowhood. Euphrosyne was a widow, and young men do not usually imagine themselves marrying widows. The reference in the third verse to husband number one being comfortably stowed away at Woking also has to do with widowhood, for Woking was a major London cemetary. Finally the words 'Oh, have I seen her lately?' are taken from a comic song by Charles Merion which runs as follows: [7]

She went away a month today,
Her absence grieves me greatly,
She'd a strawberry mark upon her arm,
Oh! have you seen her lately?

In June 1866 Euphrosyne Parepa was on a concert tour of the United States with Carl Rosa. By quoting from the song Gilbert suggests both that she is away and that he is grieved by her absence. The flippancy of tone with which he writes does not of course prove him indifferent.

Euphrosyne Parepa married Carl Rosa in the United States in February 1867. Gilbert does not seem to have responded directly in the *Bab Ballads*, though he did express a world-weary mood in *Disillusioned*, a ballad published a month before his own wedding, which took place on 6 August 1867. Gilbert is said to have proposed to his wife after the success of *Dulcamara* in December 1866; news of his failure in the case of Euphrosyne may have had something to do with it, as may her strong physical resemblance to the singer.

Gilbert's final known connection with Euphrosyne was *Trial by Jury*. This libretto, featuring a breach of promise case, was written originally for Carl Roşa, Euphrosyne's husband. Rosa was to write the music, and Euphrosyne was to appear as Angelina, the plaintiff. *Trial by Jury* was set by Sullivan only because Euphrosyne died on 21 January 1874. Gilbert attended her funeral on 26 January. He *may* have been completely indifferent to her, yet he knew her all her life, wrote lyrics for her, sent her his picture, and wrote a libretto for her. Under these circumstances some kind of attachment, at least on his part, can hardly be thought improbable.

The main source of the *Yeomen of the Guard* libretto is Harrison Ainsworth's novel *The Tower of London* (1840). This work has a grand historical plot concerned with Lady Jane Grey, and a sub-plot, used by Gilbert, of life below stairs. Before discussing the sub-plot we may perhaps pause to look at an interesting detail of the main plot.

One of the minor mysteries of the *Yeomen of the Guard* libretto is the identity of the queen who in the song 'When our gallant Norman foes' is described as suing at the Tower to save her head. No queen is known to have done this, but the general vote has gone to one or other of the executed wives of Henry VIII—Anne Boleyn or Catherine Howard. Ainsworth's novel, however, offers a more likely candidate in the shape of Lady Jane Grey, the Nine Days' Queen. One of the illustrations in the novel, by George Cruikshank, depicts Lady Jane Grey, recently deposed, kneeling at the feet of Mary Tudor *in the Tower*. Jane is actually

Euphrosyne Parepa 1836-1874

Gibert's wife, Lucy Agnes Turner 1849-1936

George Cruickshank - Jane imploring Mary to save her husband's life
(Illustration to Harrison Ainsworth's *The Tower of London*)

pleading for the life of her husband, Lord Guildford Dudley, but a glance at the illustration, plus an imperfect memory of the text, which was not directly part of the *Yeomen* libretto, might easily have led Gilbert to think of her as pleading for her own life.

Gilbert's borrowings from the *Tower of London* sub-plot extend beyond definable detail to the whole historical-romantic atmosphere of *The Yeomen of the Guard*; the recognisable detail is taken mostly from the first part of the book. Briefly, Cuthbert Cholmondeley, a devoted follower of Lord Guildford Dudley, falls in love at first sight with Cicely, 'The Rose of the Tower'. Cicely requites his passion but is loved in her turn by Master Lawrence Nightgall, the chief jailor at the Tower. Nightgall, a dark Satanic man, jealous of the love of Cuthbert and Cicely, contrives to lock Cuthbert in a dungeon. Cicely promises to marry Nightgall in order to save the life of Cuthbert, and the rest of the story is occupied by the hair's-breadth 'scapes through which justice is finally done. Nighgall's keys are stolen twice in the book, and on two occasions a prisoner makes his escape across the moat while being shot at from the walls. Gilbert's Dame Carruthers has her prototype in Dame Potentia Trusbut, 'a stout buxom personage, a little on the wrong side of fifty, but not without some remains of comeliness'. Three of Gilbert's characters, however, are not found in *The Tower of London*. These are Jack Point, Elise Maynard and Colonel Fairfax. Two of them evidently owe something to Vincent Wallace's *Maritana* (1845), libretto by Edward Fitzball.

In Wallace's opera Maritana, a gypsy singer, is married seceretly to Don Caesar, who is to be shot in two hours' time. Maritana is veiled for the marriage ceremony; consequently when Don Caesar is saved—because the bullets have been 'withdrawn from the arquebuses' by one Lazarillo—the bride and groom do not recognise each other. Don Caesar, whose royal pardon has been concealed by the scheming Don José, eventually finds his bride, kills Don José, and is appointed Governor of Valentia by the King. A somewhat similar arrangement of plot and characters is to be found in Offenbach's *La Périchole* (1868) which Gilbert must have known because it accompanied the first performance of *Trial by Jury*. However the resemblence to *Maritana* is much closer.

If these incidents are placed together with those from *The Tower of London*, it will be apparent that most of the plot of *The Yeomen of the Guard* is accounted for. What is new in Gilbert's libretto is the character of Jack Point, his pathetic devotion to Elsie Maynard, and the action of Fairfax in carrying off Elsie from under his nose. This sequence of events is exactly the same as the one described in Faustus' speech—and it might easily be a reflection of the events surrounding the marriage of Euphrosyne Parepa, as Gilbert perceived them. Euphrosyne was a travelling singer and Gilbert, though not a singer, was a merryman, albeit a 'moping mum' masochistic one. There was no formal understanding between the two, but Gilbert had convinced himself of her intention to marry him. He was shocked and amazed when Captain Carvell performed the function of Colonel Fairfax in carrying off Euphrosyne. The singer married the soldier, and *Bab* learned a lesson in the ways of the world:[8]

When a jester
Is outwitted,
Feelings fester,
    Heart is lead!
Food for fishes
    Only fitted,
Jester wishes
    He was dead!

We have suggested that the trauma which drove Gilbert back to the pre-genital stage of emotional development involved an older woman (p 98). In the absence of precise dating it is impossible to be sure when this event took place. One would expect the involvement with the older woman to follow *Bab's* childhood affair with Euphrosyne, but precede any feelings he may have had for her in 1857, the year of the *Manon Lescaut* translation. Gilbert himself says he was seventeen (1853) when he lost his elderly queen. Now, it may be fortuitous, but Don Caesar, who is Colonel Fairfax' prototype in *Maritana*, actually makes jokes about marrying an elderly ugly female. Fitzball's dialogue runs as follows:

DON JOSE: Your must marry—
DON CAESAR: Marry? I? What, for an hour and threequarters? You are
               jesting.
DON JOSE: No! Quite the contrary.
DON CAESAR: Ah, then I see it's my name you require.
DON JOSE: Perhaps—
DON CAESAR: To elevate some antique maiden, who sighs to become a
               countess—fifty years of age, no doubt.
DON JOSE: It is immaterial to you.
DON CAESAR: And ugly as a gorgon, eh?
DON JOSE: You will never behold her.
DON CAESAR: How? Am I to marry an invisible woman?
DON JOSE: Her features will be rendered invisible to you by a thick veil,
               which will also prevent her seeing you; but you must give
               your honour not even to demand her name. Will you consent
               to take such a woman for thy wedded wife?

These exchanges reveal the source of one of the flaws in the dramaturgy of *The Yeomen of the Guard*, namely, how is it possible for a man to marry a woman without hearing her speak her name? This however is a small matter compared with the link they seem to provide between the *Yeomen* libretto and Gilbert's experience with an older woman. Here, once again, is the relevant stanza of the ballad *Haunted*:

I pass to critical seventeen:
The ghost of that terrible wedding scene,
When an elderly colonel stole my queen,
    And woke my dream of heaven:
No school-girl decked in her nursery curls
Was my gushing innocent queen of pearls;
If she wasn't a girl of a thousand girls,
    She was one of forty-seven!

It is, of course, *Colonel* Fairfax who robs Jack Point of Elsie. In terms of the supposedly Henrican times in which *The Yeomen of the Guard* is set the rank of colonel is an anachronism—it belongs to a later stage in the development of the Tudor army. Yet Gilbert, who was meticulous in such matters, allowed the error to stand. What is more, the climax of *the Yeomen of the Guard* is a *wedding scene*—the same wedding scene in which Jack Point falls dead at Elsie's feet. To make assurance doubly sure Elsie actually enters in her wedding dress, shortly followed by the shattered Point. It is an example *par excellence* of the power of the death instinct to dominate and destroy.

We can now see Elsie Maynard, the agent of Jack Point's woe, as a dual figure. In the first part of the opera she is Euphrosyne Parepa, the travelling singer; in the second she is also the older woman who shocked Gilbert by marrying a colonel. The husband is a military man in both cases, but Gilbert could not credibly have represented the heroine of his opera as a middle-aged woman. Gilbert is Point, as he is Faustus and Gretchen and Vavir—a soul killed by rejection. If the fact is doubted we are left with no explanation for his reiterated statements that in the blank verse plays and in the character of Jack Point he had revealed his true self. The account offered here may be incorrect in its reconstruction of events inasmuch as the actual source of Gilbert's trauma lay elsewhere. But the general outline is too clear and too consistent to be mistaken, or ignored. As a final shot we may perhaps notice the marked interest in opera singers exhibited by Gilbert's father in his *Memoirs Of A Cynic*. At the very least the operatic prepossessions of the father must have introduced the son to a world in which the love of singers was deemed respectable.

The *Yeomen of the Guard* libretto may have struck Gilbert as a seal set on his own past. The work absorbed him thoroughly, and he always regarded it as his best libretto. Since the story ends with the death of Jack Point one would not think any further developments were possible. However, in 1892 Gilbert met Nancy McIntosh, a young *singer*. Before long Jack Point was out of his grave and appearing with Miss McIntosh in *His Excellency* (1894).

As we have seen the main plot of *His Excellency* is concerned with the practical jokes of Governor George Griffenfeld and his daughters. There is also a bye-plot involving Christina, a wandering ballad singer, played in the first production by Nancy McIntosh. Christina enters the town of Elsinore to ply her trade, but finds herself fascinated by the statue of the Regent which the citizens have erected in the market place. She conducts an imaginary conversation with the statue, playing both parts herself:[9]

STATUE: ... What hast thou given, and to whom?
CHRISTINA: My heart, my Lord Prince, and to your Highness, for look you, I love you passing well—even I, who never loved a living man!

The conversation is overheard by the real-life subject of the statue, the Prince Regent, who is in Elsinore disguised as a strolling player. The two are instantly attracted and while Christina goes off to sing on the Castle Green the

Regent declares his intention of meeting her again. They do meet in the finale to the second act, when the Regent declares his love, and she replies with 'Sir, I am your Highness's handmaid!'

Hesketh Pearson says that *His Excellency* is an old libretto patched up. [10] If this is so the patching clearly involved the insertion of the part of Christina for Nancy McIntosh. The play is complete without Christina, whose small part is rather awkwardly fitted in. Whereas everyone else in the play speaks in Gilbert's characteristic prose, Christina speaks throughout in the Wardour Street style of *The Yeomen of the Guard*. In performance the contrast between the two is quite marked. With Gilbert Wardour Street spelt sincerity; his purpose was evidently to provide Nancy with a serious romantic part, though he denied her a love duet. The result is that in this opera the association between the strolling ballad singer and the strolling player has a happy ending. As in *Pygmalion And Galatea* a statue is loved and comes to life. Here however the statue was doubly dead—firstly in the capacity as stone and secondly in its capacity as the avatar of the dead Jack Point. To some extent Gilbert's choices were restricted by the need to accommodate Miss McIntosh in an already-written text. Nevertheless the method he chose had the effect of reversing the effeçts of the *Yeomen* dénouement. [11]

In terms of Gilbert's personal life it seems reasonable to regard Miss McIntosh, the singer, as a substitute for the lost singer Euphrosyne Parepa. She thus functioned both as a daughter and as a dream-wife—the longed-for satisfaction of an old ambition. Gilbert always disclaimed any knowledge of music—no man was more intrinsically unlikely to adopt a singer as his daughter. The relationship of Jack Point and Elsie Maynard in *The Yeomen of the Guard* and that between Christina and the Regent in *His Excellency* explain precisely why he did so.

5: The Theatrical Background

The true originality of Gilbert's work, and the fact of its sole survival from the output of the mid-Victorian theatre, tend to make it seem even more unusual than it is. To a modern audience his libretti must seem almost freakishly original—absolute creations without any relationship whatever to works by other writers. Yet every artist must have roots, and Gilbert is no exception. His work is made up of a number of clearly identifiable strands, each of which made its contribution to the qualities we call Gilbertian. At the beginning of his career he was hardly Gilbertian at all; at the end he was Gilbertian and very little else. We have seen that the basis of all his endeavour was a highly abnormal infantile psychology; on this foundation he built, by a largely mechanical process, the *tour de force* of eccentricity and whimsy with which the world is familiar. But he began with the theatre as it existed at the outset of his career in the 1860s.

The nature of Victorian theatre was profoundly affected by three forces: the official censorship administered by the Lord Chamberlain, the need to cater for popular audiences, and the shadow of Shakespeare. To take the last first, the example of Shakespeare acted as a lure to any poet with dramatic ambitions. However the phenomenal powers of Shakespeare are not given to men who otherwise possess genius. As a result those literary minds which attended to the theatre at all wasted themselves in the vain endeavour to write something Shakespearean. The less ambitious but more viable plays they might have achieved went unwritten. Gilbert, by contrast, possessed a great advantage in that he had superb powers as a versifier but none whatever as a poet; he was never tempted into the Shakespearean trap, if only because he regarded himself as a better dramatist than Shakespeare.

The official censorship was concerned to ensure the inoffensiveness of all plays in matters of sex, religion and politics. Various devices were used to circumvent the regulations, but the overall effect was to drive intelligent discussion of any topic out of the theatre. Gilbert brushed with the censor once over the caricature of three prominent politicians in *The Happy Land* (1873), but his achievement was to write intelligently within the confines set by the censorship; his oddity and originality permitted him to bypass restraints that might have baffled a comparably gifted dramatist with a more normal turn of mind.

In the absence of modern electronic means of entertainment a much wider cross-section of the Victorian public attended the theatre than is the case today. By the same token the entertainment on offer had to cater for the avid but unsophisticated tastes of people who today would be afraid to enter a theatre. Gilbert responded by writing works which he described as 'rump steak and onions', that is 'a palatable concoction of satisfying and seasoning ingredients which is good enough to please the man of refinement in the stalls, and not too refined for the butcher boy in the gallery'. [1] It is as 'rump steak and onions' that Gilbert's libretti survive to this day. They continue to reach audiences that other operas cannot reach, while giving pleasure and satisfaction to intelligent people. It is notable that Gilbert instantly cut out any material which seemed likely to reduce the drawing capacity of his work. He evidently wished to revive all the ancestors at the end of *Ruddigore*, but the boos of the first night audience were quite sufficient to make him change his mind.

Although he eventually wrote works in most of the genres available to the Victorian playwright, Gilbert was led by the nature of his personality and gifts to associate himself particularly with the three forms that allowed for the expression of fantasy; these were the Pantomime, the Burlesque, and the Extravaganza.

The pantomime, having its roots in the eighteenth century, was divided into two parts: the opening and the harlequinade. In the opening a traditional plot, usually based on folk lore or an exotic imported tale such as Aladdin, was set on foot; the characters were then changed by a fairy into the creatures of the harlequinade before being restored at the end in a grand finale celebrating love and reconciliation. The opening was relatively elevated in tone, using rhymed couplets or blank verse; the harlequinade was a series of low comedy episodes of chase, trickery and knockabout—the staged equivalent of the modern cartoon film. Both parts relied heavily on visual splendour and scenes of transformation, with plentiful music imported from popular opera and operetta or the music hall.

Gilbert never ceased to take an interest in pantomime, having been the author or co-author of several in the early part of his career. The obstreperous spirit of the harlequinade is never far away in the *Bab Ballds*, but the famous libretti are more closely related to to the extravaganza, which differed from the pantomime mainly in having no harlequinade. The master of the extravaganza form was J.R. Planché (1796-1880), who is remembered today as the librettist of Weber's *Oberon* and as a pioneer of historically accurate costumes on the Victorian stage. As practised by Planché extravaganza was divided into two types, the classicl and the Fairy. Classical extravaganza involved the reduction of classical myth to familiar domestic terms after the manner of Offenbach's *Orpheus In The Underworld* and *La Belle Hélène*;

Gilbert's *Thespis* was a horse from the same stable. Fairy extravaganza combined a fantastic tale with domesticity and topicality in splendid settings; it was essentially a pantomime opening written at full length. The dialogue, written in rhymed couplets, was given over largely to the pun. In the following speech, taken from Planché's *Fortunio* (1843), the fairy queen speaks to her band after they have danced a quadrille with words adapted to a French tune:[2]

> FAIRY QUEEN: Break off! My fairy nose a mortal smells!
> Creep into acorn cups and cowslip-bells!
> Make yourselves scarce!
> *Music. Fairies disperse and vanish into flowers &c—one sticks fast.*
> How now, you clumsy lout!
> Is that the way you pull a flower about?
> A pretty fairy 'pon my word. Pray who
> D'ye think's to sleep in that rose after you?
> Crumpling the leaves in this untidy way!
> *Putting them to rights.*
> Now get you in, you naughty fay!
> *Beating him.*
> And here—whose wing is this? Pray fold it up!
> You can't be cramped for room sure in that cup!
> I'm quite asham'd of you I do declare;
> You're not a morsel like the elves you were;
> But that you dress from common habits varies,
> No soul on earth could fancy you were fairies!
> As I'm your queen, by my stop watch I've reckon'd
> You've ta'en to vanish more than half a second!
> Who is't that comes? A girl in male attire!
> She needs my aid—does she deserv't? I'll try her.

Much in this passage calls to mind *Iolanthe*; Gilbert quite probably knew it, for *Fortunio* was a well remembered work; yet there is a world of difference between Planché's pedestrian fantasy and the irony of the passage in which Gilbert's huge fairy queen speaks of curling herself up inside a buttercup. We may note also several other ways in which Gilbert's work sets itself apart. Planché's fairies are of the conventional bottom-of-the-garden type; those of Gilbert are young women in fairy frocks. Planché naturally includes male elves among his fays—Gilbert deliberately excludes men. Similarly girls in male attire were barred from Gilbert's mature works. Nevertheless by establishing the fairy extravaganza as an accepted form Planché opened the way for Gilbert's own very different fairies, who might not otherwise have found acceptance. In fact Planché welcomed Gilbert's extravaganzas as examples of the kind of comedy he had been trying to introduce. We may note in passing that if Shakespeare had lived during the nineteenth century the extravaganza would have permitted him to write works every bit as worthy of him as *A Midsummer Night's Dream*.[3]

Burlesque shared many of the features of extravaganza, but at an altogether more raucous level. The formal difference was that whereas extravaganza might have an original story, burlesque was a mockery of some existing story or work.

The form permitted anything to be burlesqued, provided only it were familiar enough for the audience to understand the point of the parody.

The normal technique of burlesque was not to make its subject absurd by exaggeration but to deflate it by reducing it to vulgar, not to say Cockney, terms. Red noses, huge wigs, comic or music hall songs, cellar flap breakdowns, short skirts, transvestism, and low necklines were *de rigeur*. In performance, half the succes of the show seems to have been due to the energy of the actors, and the rest to the enormity of the puns. Contemporary critics, one of whom was Gilbert, were united in their condemnation of burlesque and of its writers. The following classic passage from *The Field of the Cloth of Gold* (1868) by William Brough encapsulates many of the features of the form: [4]

> *Music. Enter TETE DE VEAU, carrying a written address, and followed by BLOC and CITIZENS; at the same time the Royal State Barge comes to quay L. KING HENRY and QUEEN CATHERINE, both very ill from the voyage, descend from the barge, followed by the DUKE OF SUFFOLK, ANNE BOLEYN, SIR GUY THE CRIPPLE, and GUARDS. CITIZENS shout.*
> *Concerted music.*
> *Air - 'La Femme à Barbe'*
> DE VEAU: *(coming forward)* - Your Majesty, I've an address to read.
> HENRY: I'm much too ill to hear it, sir, indeed;
> I'll read when I am better—give it me.
> DE VEAU: *(reading)*—May't please—dear me, hum, hum, 'your Majesty'—
> HENRY: Don't—don't! Where's Suffolk?
> SUFFOLK: Here, my liege, in waiting.
> HENRY: My loving *Suffolk*, I feel *suffoc-ating*.
> I am so ill.
> SUFFOLK: Nay, sire, cheer up, I pray,
> You were so brave and jolly yesterday.
> HENRY: Yesterday all was fair—a glorious Sunday,
> But this *sick transit* spoils the *glory o' Monday*.

In spite of his dislike of it, Gilbert absorbed much of the spirit of burlesque. Though it sometimes—often—degenerated into routine, burlesque was a form of criticism, and Gilbert was nothing if not critical. Both *The Pirates of Penzance* and *Ruddigore* are burlesques in motive, though the method has been refined according to Gilbert's own canons of taste. In his burlesque of *Hamlet*, entitled *Rosencrantz and Guildenstern* (1891), he stated his views clearly: [5]

> I pray you, let there be no huge red roses, nor extravagant monstrous wigs, nor coarse men garbed as women, in this comi-tragedy; for such things are as much as to say, 'I am a comick [*sic*] fellow—I pray you laugh at me, and hold what I say to be cleverly ridiculous.' Such labelling of humour is an impertinence to your audience, for it seemeth to imply that they are unable to recognise a joke unless it be pointed out to them. I pray you avoid it.

Closely related to extravaganza and burlesque, which had their continental counterparts, was the imported French *opéra-bouffe*. The works of Meilhac and Halévy with Offenbach's music raised the level of intelligence in these pieces, even when they were apparently silly. [6] In *La Grande Duchesse de Gerolstein* (1867) they set new standards of political satire for the English stage, and in 1873 Gilbert paid them the compliment of basing his *Realm of Joy* on their *Le Roi Candaule*. In 1871 he translated their libretto of *Les Brigands* (Offenbach 1869), gaining on the way a hint for *The Pirates of Penzance* and part of the plot of *The Mountebanks*. *The Brigands* might even be called Gilbert's first mature libretto, for it exhibits a more sophisticated musical organisation than anything he had contemplated in his own work at that time. Ultimately the salacious *tic douloureux* of Offenbach's works, and their topical political thrust, formed no part of Gilbert's method, but the stylistic affinities of Savoy opera are clearly Parisian, not Viennese.

For a man who was destined to achieve so much Gilbert began his career in literature both late and without obvious signs of genius. He spent his youth scribbling plays for home performance, and at eighteen wrote a burlesque in eighteen scenes, but when he first emerged in print his style was still immature, not to say unremarkable. His first *Fun* poem (February 1862) is an essay in the nonsense manner of Edward Lear; another early poem (March 1864), called *The Baron Klopfzetterheim*, is a not-very-felicitous imitation of *The Ingoldsby Legends*:[7]

> Near the town of St Goar,
>   On the bleak Rhenish shore,
> Dwelt a terrible Baron–a certain KLOPFZETTERHEIM.
>   I've not got it pat,
>   But it sounded like that,
> Though whether it's properly spelt to the letter, I'm
>   Not at all sure; I
>   Confess for this story
> To memory (second rate) only a debtor I'm.
>   Indulgence I claim,
>   It's a high-sounding name,
> And a name, too, to which one can easily set a rhyme.

Much the same tale is told by the early theatrical pieces. If it really is his, *Uncle Baby* (1863) must have been written under the dominating influence of his father's style and opinions on the evils of alcohol. The operatic burlesques are not intrinsically superior to those of other operators in the field, but they do show Gilbert beginning to create the pool of ideas from which the great libretti are tapped. A charming example occurs in *The Merry Zingara* (1868) his burlesque of *The Bohemian Girl*. We meet a crowd of robbers and retainers who wickedly carouse on tea–an idea which was used again for the tea cup brindisi in *The Sorcerer*. The tune is 'Sound now the trumpet fearlessly' from *I Puritani*:

> Brown now the crumpet fearlessly!
> Circulate the muffins and the brown bread!
> Toast now the tea-cake peerlessly!
> Sally Lunn, the Sally Lunn, Sally Lunn.
>   Quaff unadulterated tea,
>   Bohea–bohea–bohea!
>   Toast now the tea-cake fearlessly,
> Sally Lunn, the Sally Lunn, Sally Lunn.

These lines expose one of the techniques Gilbert learned from extravaganza, namely the reduction of the grand and heroic to the domestic and familiar. One would expect banditti to carouse at least on cocoa, but Gilbert has allotted them the homeliest of all drinks. The trick permeates the Savoy libretti in various guises, a conspicuous example occurring in *The Gondoliers*, where Inez, awaiting examination in the torture chamber, is described as having 'all the illustrated papers'. From the same opera one might cite the song 'Rising early in the morning', wherein the two kings are described as going about menial chores. Gilbert also reversed the process from time to time by treating the prosaic in fantastic terms. The most notable instance of this practice is *Trial by Jury*, an apparently sober and realistic legal battle which introduces us to all sorts of improbable people and events, including an entire chorus of bridesmaids and a plaintiff in her wedding dress. In the same spirit the deadly serious Sir Joseph Porter teaches Captain Corcoran to dance a hornpipe on the cabin table (*H.M.S. Pinafore*) and the sober Palace Yard at Westminster is invaded by fairies. The insane little dances performed by the 'Grossmith' characters are also part of this process.

At some point during the 1860s Gilbert discovered the inversion of normal expectations as a conscious principle. His discovery is generally given the name topsyturvydom; it first received deliberate expression in a *Bab Ballad* entitled 'My Dream' (1870):[8]

> The other night, from cares exempt,
> I slept—and what d'you think I dreamt?
> I dreamt that somehow I had come
> To dwell in Topsy-Turveydom!—[sic]
>
> Whère vice is virtue—virtue, vice:
> Where nice is nasty—nasty, nice:
> Where right is wrong and wrong is right—
> Where white is black and black is white.

Topsyturvydom is a notion well suited to mechanical treatment, besides bearing a distinct resemblance to real life, and Gilbert did not fail to exploit it to the full. The following notes were written for his play *Topsyturvydom*, which opened the Criterion Theatre in 1874:[9]

> Poverty is honoured—wealth despised. Ignorance is honoured—learning despised.
> Children are born learned, gradually forget everything until, as old men, they are utterly ignorant. Women are bold, men bashful. Vice is rewarded. Virtue punished. Judges administer injustice. Dishonesty is rewarded. Cowards are honoured. Brave men elbowed aside. Therefore the most ignorant, the most vicious, the most lazy man is made ruler. Women hate their husbands. Thieves are employed to arrest honest men.

No particular attitude is expressed by these words. Their inverted purpose is not to point a moral but to adorn a joke, which is infantile at bottom because it belongs to the moment when the child discovers that things may go backwards, or that he may look at them through his legs. In its elementary form topsyturvy-dom is neither particularly clever nor particularly interesting. However Gilbert's simplest use of it is found mostly in the pieces written for the Gallery of Illustration. Among the familiar operas it is really prominent only in *The Pirates of Penzance*, where the pirates are inverted villains who cry at the mention of orphanhood, and the policemen are inverted heroes who tremble at the approach of danger. The Duke of Plaza-Toro (*Gondoliers*) who leads his regiment from behind may be considered an inverted leader, as perhaps may Sir Joseph Porter, who tells the sailors of the *Pinafore* that they are every man's equal, excepting his. For the most part, however, unexpectedness in the operas is achieved by a subtle blending of the prosaic and the preposterous:[10]

> POOH-BAH: I am, in point of fact, a particularly haughty and exclusive person, of Pre-Adamite ancestral descent. You will understand this when I tell you that I can trace my ancestry back to a protoplasmal primordial atomic globule. Consequently my family pride is something inconceivable. I can't help it. I was born sneering.

The effect of Gilbert's preposterousness is enhanced by his peculiar use of logic. There is nothing intrinsically sane or rational about logic; given mad premisses, logic will drive to a mad conclusion without any break or flaw in the argument. Gilbert managed to have the best of all worlds by developing apparently sane premisses to mad conclusions simply by taking them at their face value. The best known example of his technique in this respect is *The Pirates of Penzance*, but it is found in a less marked degree in several other libretti.

The germ of *The Pirates of Penzance* seems to lie in the phrase 'O hard when love and duty clash', which Gilbert would have found in Tennyson's *Princess* when he was working on the stage version of the poem. The idea of duty has become meaningless in the twentieth century, but in its derivation from Kant's Categorical Imperative it was one of the central tenets of the Victorian age, adhered to both by Christian believers and by avowed non-believers like George Eliot. For his part Gilbert treated duty not as the stern daughter of the voice of God but in homely terms as an obligation incurred by Frederic when apprenticed accidentally to a band of pirates. Already we see the techniques of extravaganza at work. However Gilbert now proceeded to display Frederic's sense of duty in an absurd light by interpreting it with pedantic literalness in unlikely situations. Thus when he is legally freed from the terms of his apprenticeship Frederic's duty to his pirate friends ceases. Because he was always an honest fellow who went a-pirating only because the terms of his indentures bound him to it, it now becomes Frederic's duty as a citizen to exterminate the pirates. When he finds himself still bound by his indentures because of a legal technicality, he instantly reverts to his old comrades. The changes are mechanical, but also amusing, because they generate the sense of incongruity which lies at the heart of all jokes.

The Pirates of Penzance is the most thoroughgoing of Gilbert's essays in

Richard Temple as the Pirate King
(*Illustrated Sporting and Dramatic News*, 20 June 1880)

Scenes from *The Pirates of Penzance*
(*Illustrated Sporting and Dramatic News*, 1 May 1880)

absurd logic. However it appears as an element in several other libretti. In *H.M.S. Pinafore* it is the sentimental literary idea that love levels all ranks; in *Patience* it is the idea of love as necessarily unselfish. Patience the dairymaid loves Archibald Grosvenor until she realises he is perfect. Since there can be nothing unselfish in loving a perfect man she renounces him as the logical consequence of her own premiss. On the other hand he is free to love her because she is imperfect; the issue is resolved only when he decides to become a common man, so rendering himself imperfect and fit to be loved. The theme is not so prominently or so convincingly treated as in *The Pirates of Penzance*, but the underlying method is the same.

For *Ruddigore* Gilbert found a potentially magnificent theme for logical treatment in the shape of Rose Maybud's book of etiquette, written 'by no less an authority than the wife of a Lord Mayor'. Rose begins well, guiding all her actions by the book, but in the second act the idea simply disappears. In this way one of the forces of cohesion which makes the *Pirates* satisfying was lost. Much the same thing happens in *Utopia Limited*, where the idea for logical treatment is the rather technical financial one of limited liability. Gilbert had already touched on this theme in *The Gondoliers*, in which the Duke of Plaza-Toro turns himself into a limited company. In the later opera an entire nation becomes a limited company under a Board of Directors. Unhappily ingenuity ceased at this point. Apart from an hilarious Board Meeting conducted in terms of a Christy Minstrel show Gilbert conjured nothing from an apparently promising concept. Perhaps the material was not really as potentially fruitful as it seemed.

Apart from its use as a motive force in the plot, Gilbert regularly employed logic to resolve the complicated situations he had created by the end of the second act. A highly improbable announcement is made by someone whose word carries no outside authority, yet the statement is accepted literally at its face value and the logical consequences are immediately acted on. The classic instance is the dénouement of *H.M.S. Pinafore*, in which the Captain and Ralph Rackstraw change places on the unsupported statement of Little Buttercup that they have been changed at birth. The same thing happens at the end of *The Gondoliers*, when the rightful king is declared and accepted on the flimsiest of evidence. *Iolanthe*, *Ruddigore* and *The Mikado* end on a legal quibble by which a mere form of words is deemed to have real effects. In *The Grand Duke* a playing-card duel causes legal death, which is taken literally when the 'dead' people turn up as ghosts.

The final ingredient in the mixture of Gilbertianism must be counted as the extremely slow and laborious means by which the enduring libretti were evolved. In the course of composition all these works were taken through numerous prose drafts, but more important than this they represent the distillation of many previous plays and poems written over a number of years. A comprehensive account of the origins and transformations of all the ideas in the Savoy operas would require either the services of a computer or the lucubrations of an American scholar. We have noticed in passing the sources of many of the operas, but it may be useful to summarise them here as a way of emphasising the length and difficulty of Gilbert's path to originality.[11]

OPERA	SOURCES
THESPIS 1871	*The Princess*; classical burlesque.
TRIAL BY JURY 1875	Poem published in *Fun* 11 April 1868.
THE SORCERER 1877	Short story *An Elixir Of Love* 1869.
H.M.S. PINAFORE 1878	*Bab Ballads*: 'Joe Golightly' 1867; 'Captain Reece' 1868; 'The Bumboat Woman's Story' 1870
PIRATES OF PENZANCE 1880	*Our Island Home* 1870.
PATIENCE 1881	*Bab Ballad*: 'The Rival Curates' 1867; *Punch*.
IOLANTHE 1882	*Bab Ballad*: 'The Fairy Curate' 1870; *The Wicked World* 1873.
PRINCESS IDA 1884	*The Princess* 1870
THE MIKADO 1885	No known literary source.
RUDDIGORE 1887	*Ages Ago* 1869; burlesque tradition.
YEOMEN OF THE GUARD 1888	*The Tower of London* 1840; *Maritana* 1845; *Bab Ballad*: 'Haunted' 1866.
THE GONDOLIERS 1889	*Le Pont des Soupirs* (Offenbach) 1861.
UTOPIA LIMITED 1893	*The Happy Land* 1873.
THE GRAND DUKE 1896	*The Prima Donna* (Tito Mattei) 1889; *The Duke's Dilemma* 1853.

These sources do not of course include the many places in his own and other men's works from which Gilbert took ideas and phrases. Nevertheless they are sufficient to enable one to come to terms with his originality, and see it as the achievement of a mortal man rather than that of of a *deus ex machina*. If we now add the components previously discussed it becomes possible to understand at least part of the process by which he became himself. The attribution to him of an infantile personality does not imply that his mental powers were other than those of a gifted adult; on the other hand his infantalism determined which of the many influences available to him were to operate and was perhaps responsible for the very slow maturation of his art. The list is as follows:

1) A personality fixated at about the five-year level.
2) An involvement with the death instincts leading to sadomasochism, mechanicality and rigidity.
3) Traumatic experiences in love, which may well be respnsible for 1 & 2.
4) The extravaganza/burlesque/pantomime tradition.
5) The imported French operetta.
6) The pedantic treatment of the ridiculous, and *vice versa*.
7) Topsyturvydom.
8) Logic applied in a literal but absurd way.
9) Constant reworking and re-use of old material.

All these things combine to make the quality we call Gilbertian. They are not equally present in everything he wrote, but he wrote little from which they are completely absent, and nothing in which they are transcended. What is more they are not simply a matter of the words. The logic of the plot development and the mechanical quality of the fantasy have their counterpart in the carefully stylised production technique and manner of delivery invented by Gilbert for his work. A Savoy libretto is a total work of art whose integrity was described by G.K. Chesterton in this way:[12]

> He would not permit anything really to mar the complete congruity of his own incongruity. He stopped all gags so despotically that one can only say that he gagged the gaggers. He would not allow a word of contemporary political or social allusion, beyond the few which he touched upon very lightly himself. His whole conception, right or wrong, was to make a compact artistic unity of his poetical play; and the fact that it was also a nonsensical play was not a reason, in his eyes, for anything being thrown into it; because its very frivolity was fragility. It was not a potato sack into which the clown could poke anything with a poker; it was a coloured soap-bubble which would burst if tickled with a straw.

In refusing a grant to the D'Oyly Carte Opera Company the Arts Council of Great Britain made much play with the old-fashioned and dull nature of the Company's productions. Genuine dullness is indefensible but to demand, as the Arts Council seemed to, mere novelty and sophistication in Gilbert's works is a mistake. A Savoy libretto is something like a noh play, having rules and conventions proper to itself which it is a gross impropriety to violate. It is probably true that in the end the D'Oyly Carte Company was killed by the death instinct in Gilbert; the rigidities he created lasted long after his personal departure and, becoming institutionalised, obstructed change when change was necessary to survival. To this extent the new vogue in Gilbert and Sullivan production begun by the New York *Pirates of Penzance* (1980) is both inevitable and welcome. Nevertheless, any producer should understand as part of his professionalism that a Gilbert libretto is not, like *Orpheus In The Underworld* or *The Tales of Hoffmann*, a producer's paradise in which ingenuity can do no wrong. Gilbert's entire career was a struggle against the *olla podrida* of burlesque—as represented by *Orpheus*—and any new production of his works should at least be self-consistent in style.

In his palmy days Gilbert showed a fastidiousness of taste remarkable in a man who had fought his way to the front in the Victorian comic theatre. His work has often been called Aristophanic, a misnomer if comparison with the Athenian's earthy gusto and open political partisanship is implied. On the other hand it may be that his refinement does indeed owe something to Greek theory and practice.

As a boy at school Gilbert translated Sophocles and other Greek dramatists. Memories of his early classical studies emerge from time to time in the libretti, for instance in the reference to *The Frogs* in *The Pirates of Penzance*. More significantly, Gilbert's imaginative world was not altogether unlike Aristophanes' Cloudcuckooland. In his essay on Aristophanic comedy (1820) Hookham Frere describes the early comedy of Europe as 'a fancy portrait of the society of the time'. He then compares it with the Old Comedy:[13]

But the ancient Aristophanic comedy proceeded upon a principle of compensation totally different. In this species of composition, the utter extravagance and impossibility of the supposed action is an indispensable requisite; the portion of truth and reality, which is admitted as a counterpoise, consists wholly in the character and language. It is a grave, humorous, impossible, GREAT LIE, related with an accurate mimicry of the language and manner of the person introduced, and great exactness of circumstance in the inferior details.

Gilbertian opera is just such a *Great Lie* as Frere describes. However preposterous the events on stage the characters remain imperturbable, their language matter-of-fact. Before, and after, they break out into a mad little dance their deportment is always soberly suitable to their rank in life. The same care to clothe unreality with the guise of reality was manifest in Gilbert's production methods. *H.M.S. Pinafore* was rigged like a real ship, and he would have liked a real clock for the Palace Yard in *Iolanthe*. Uniforms were always meticulously accurate; in *Patience* the dress materials came from Libertys, the aesthetic suppliers, and in *The Mikado* some of the costumes were genuinely Japanese. Even Gilbert's definition of comedy (derived from Planché) approximates to the Aristophanic practice, 'All humour, properly so called, is based upon a grave and quasi-respectful treatment of the ridiculous and absurd.'[14]

Comparison of Gilbert with Aristophanes should not be pressed further than it will go. In respect of topicality, gusto, political partisanship and sexual frankness the libretti of Meilhac and Halévy come closer to the practice of Aristophanes than Gilbert cared to. Perhaps the most judicious statement of the position has been made by Maurice Baring:

The Gilbert of the operas has been compared to Aristophanes;[15] and the comparison has been said to be a wild one. To place Gilbert in the same rank as Aristophanes, it is said, would mean he should have written lyrics as beautiful as those of Shakespeare. But to compare Gilbert and Sullivan with Aristophanes is not, I think, a wild comparison, for the lyrical beauty which is to be found in the choruses of the Greek poet, is supplied, and plentifully, by the music of Sullivan.[16]

Gilbert jokingly conceded that in making his Sophoclean translations he always gave due credit for the result to Sophocles himself. The specific reference to Sophocles raises the interesting possibility that one of the finest points of Gilbert's art as a librettist—his use of the chorus—may have been derived from Sophocles. As is well known, Sophocles differs from both Aeschylus and Euripides in making his chorus both a participator in the events of the play and a commentator upon those events; his choruses are generally characterised, as Elders of Colonus or Theban Elders, and are able to conduct a dialogue with the main protagonists, besides singing lengthy passages in their own right.[17]

In any operetta other than those of Gilbert the chorus is likely to be a vapid dummy, strolling aimlessly on stage to provide a refrain for the soloist and breaking into dance at the merest hint of a pretext. Gilbert's choruses do not behave like this; they take part in a significant way in the action, sometimes even carrying it themselves, and always commenting on it. Thus in *Trial by Jury* the chorus, on hearing of the Defendant's amorous escapades, functions both as a commentator and as a character:[18]

> Oh, I was like that when a lad!
>   A shocking young scamp of a rover,
> I behaved like a regular cad;
>   But that sort of thing is all over.
> I'm now a respectable chap
>   And shine with a virtue resplendent,
> And therefore I haven't a scrap
>   Of sympathy with the defendant!

The high point of Gilbert's dramatic use of the chorus is in *Iolanthe* where, in the second act, the male and female choruses are allotted a scene to themselves, without principals. Thereafter, perhaps because of the very perfection he had reached in *Iolanthe*, his practice became more uncertain. A low point is reached in *Utopia Limited*, where the male chorus as such hardly exists and the ladies, after the opening number, fade into anonymity. Gilbert once knew better than that, and it is reasonable to suppose that what he knew he learned from Sophocles.

Failing direct observation from the plays of Sophocles, Gilbert might have found a clear statement of the best way to treat a chorus in Aristotle's *Poetics*, 'The chorus too should be regarded as one of the actors; it should be an integral part of the whole, and take a share in the action—that which it has in Sophocles rather than in Euripides.[19]

In notes prefacing his blank verse plays Gilbert takes the trouble to remark that they obey the unity of time, being supposed to take place within the course of twenty four hours. Strictly speaking the unities are not classical at all, but it is apparent that Gilbert did his best to abide by them. *H.M.S. Pinafore*, for instance, obeys all three unities of time, place, and action. Most of the other operas obey one or more of the unities, and often the change of place is only for the sake of fresh scenery, not because the scene has moved significantly from one place to another. This being so, it is hard to believe that Gilbert had not read and absorbed Aristotle's remarks in the *Poetics* concerning the unity of plot:[20]

> The truth is that, just as in the other imitative arts one imitation is always of one thing, so in poetry the story, as an imitation of an action, a complete whole, with its several incidents so closely connected that the transposal or withdrawal of any of them will disjoin and dislocate the whole. For that which makes no perceptable difference by its presence or absence is no real part of the whole.

Here lies the principle of Gilbert's objection to the incongruities of contemporary burlesque, and the secret of the graceful self-consistency of his own work at its best. It is true that the rigid structure of his mind helped him to exclude irrelevancies that might have tempted other men, but his achievement is also the product of a positive aesthetic. Many men have read Aristotle; few have profitted by the experience. Gilbert deserves to be recognised as one of those few. It is even possible that if he could have known both, Aristotle would have preferred Gilbert to Aristophanes as more consistently fastidious.

6: *Gilbert's Satire*

To be a satirist in any age it is necessary to have insights into the nature of society which are not held in society at large. Satirists do not often become rich or spend their lives unmolested by their victims. Aristophanes suffered a mauling at the hands of Cleon, Juvenal was banished to Egypt by Domitian, and Voltaire, though he made himself rich by other means, was thrown into the Bastille on more than one occasion; Pope owed his wealth to his translation of Homer, not to his satires. For his part Gilbert both became extremely rich and suffered surprisingly little retaliation from his contemporaries. The reason is clear: while his tongue often gave great offence at the purely personal level, his pen was not directed with true seriousness of satirical purpose at any particular target. Like his father he was quick to diagnose someone else's behaviour as abominable or detestable, but if he had written something likely to displease his audience—and so hurt his pocket—he withdrew it at once. As a result his closest approaches to satirical sharpness are found today in those parts of his libretti which have survived in spite of being cut from performance. A man who is willing to withdraw potentially unpopular work for pecuniary reasons can hardly be said to care passionately about what he has written. For all his fury and intransigence there is nothing to suggest that Gilbert's satire sprang from anything like the savage indignation of Swift or the equally savage disappointment of Juvenal.

The basis of Gilbert's world-outlook was rooted in that masochistic part of him— the 'real' part—which shrank from life, and in particular from sex. As he looked out from the centre of his ideal fairyland he saw that the world was a pig of a place, and did his best to give expression to his vision through his blank verse plays. Because he himself was *Bab*, an infant, that vision was not a particularly penetrative or compelling one. It finds its clearest expression in *The Wicked World*:[1]

DARINE: And what are sins?
SELENE: Evils of which we hardly know the names.
                There's vanity—a quaint fantastic vice,
                Whereby a mortal takes much credit for
                The beauty of his face and form, and claims
                As much applause for loveliness as though
                He had designed himself! Then jealousy—
                A universal passion—one that claims
                An absolute monopoly of love,
                Based on the reasonable principle
                That no one merits other poeple's love
                So much as—every soul on earth by turns!
                Envy—that grieves at other men's success,
                As though success, however placed, were not
                A contribution to one common fund!
                Ambition, too, the vice of clever men
                Who seek to rise at other's cost; nor heed
                Whose wings they cripple, so that they may soar.
                Malice—the helpless vice of helpless fools,
                Who, as they cannot rise, hold others down,
                That they, by contrast, may appear to soar.
                Hatred and avarice, untruthfulness,
                Murder and rapine, theft, profanity—
                Sins so incredible, so mean, so vast,
                Our nature stands appalled when it attempts
                To grasp their terrible significance.
                Such are the vices of that wicked world!

As a criticism of life these words are callow enough. They express the shock of childhood on discovering that the world is not what it seems from the nursery window, and in this respect stand as fitting companions to the ballad *Disillusioned* quoted on page 96. In his personal life Gilbert dealt with the wicked world either by imposing on it his own strict discipline or—it amounts to the same thing—by imposing on it the strict letter of the law through litigation. If in his art he had never risen above passages like the one quoted he would certainly be as forgotten today as the *Punch* wits of his youth, or indeed those of any subsequent generation. He saved himself from this oblivion not by deepening his vision but by transmuting it into Gilbertian gold.

The shattering of a callow ideal leads to an equally callow cynicism. We have seen the mechanism at work in both the Gilberts, father and son, though the son appears to have been the more thoroughgoing case. He, the son, was aware that in the wicked world people do in fact profess to be moved by ideals and noble feelings; but since they are really moved by envy, malice, avarice and the rest it follows as the night the day that they must be hypocrites. How else can a cynic explain the difference between profession and performance? The analysis is characteristically jejune, but Gilbert never found reason to alter it, as the following passage from *The Mountebanks* (1892) bears witness. The words are found on the label of a bottle containing a magic drink:[2]

Man is a hypocrite, and invariably affects to be better and wiser than he really is. This liquid, which should be freely diluted, has the effect of making everyone who drinks it exactly what he pretends to be. The hypocrite becomes a man of piety, the swindler a man of honour; the quack, a man of learning, and the braggart, a man of war.

This drink is none other than the lozenge which Gilbert pressed on Sullivan with such determination; his devotion to it reveals how much it meant to him, though by 1892 he seems to have forgotten how to handle it, as we shall see. In the early part of his career he had no special way of expressing his concept of hypocrisy, but on 19 November 1870 he produced *The Palace of Truth* at the Haymarket Theatre. This play provided him with a lifelong technique for the exposure of hypocrisy, just as *The Princess* had furnished a plot structure earlier in the year. *The Palace of Truth* is founded on a story by Madame de Genlis (1746-1830), though Gilbert says it is as old as *The Arabian Nights*.

The court of King Phanor are accomplished hypocrites. They give extravagant praise to the royal poetry though one of them, Aristaeus, poses as a blunt man who hates it. Another, Zoram, pretends to a musical knowledge he does not possess, while Princess Zeolide assumes a posture of coldness towards her suitor Philamir. Philamir is ostensibly intense in his devotion to Zeolide, while the lady Mirza seems to be unselfish in her loyalty. The king, however, possesses an enchanted palace:[3]

Every one

Who enters there is bound to speak the truth—
The simple unadulterated truth.
To every question that is put to him
He must return the unaffected truth.
And, strange to say, while publishing the truth
He's no idea that he is doing so;
And while he lets innumerable cats
Out of unnumbered bags, he quite believes
That all the while he's tightening the strings
That keep them from a too censorious world.

The king and queen decide to test each other and the courtiers by visiting the Palace of Truth, as the enchanted palace is known. As soon as they arrive the magic begins to work its effects, turning everyone into the opposite of his or her apparent self. Thus the cold Princess Zeolide gushes with love for Philamir, while he reveals himself as a heartless adventurer; the musician is exposed as an ignoramus, while the bluff Aristaeus becomes a merry old soul. All are now giving expression to their true feelings, especially the scheming traitress Mirza; at the same time everyone thinks he or she is maintaining the accustomed pretence and behaves accordingly. After due complications the power of the palace is shattered and previous relationships are restored, all the sounder for the admixture of a little honesty. The following extract gives the flavour of the whole:[4]

ALTEMIRA, ZEOLIDE, CHRYSAL, ZORAM.

ALTEMIRA: And here are author and composer, too—
And critic, teeming with humanity.
Come let us hear it.
Zeolide sings a song. At its conclusion Chrysal & Zoram applaud.
CHRYSAL: *(Coming forwards with all the action of a man who is expressing*
extreme approval)
Oh, I protest, my ears have never heard
A goodly song more miserably sung.
Clapping hands.
Oh, very poor indeed—oh, very weak;
No voice—no execution, out of tune—
Pretentious too—oh, very poor!
Applauding as if in ecstasies.
ALTEMIRA: *Amused*—Indeed! I think I've often heard you say
No voice could rival Princess Zeolide's?
CHRYSAL: *Enthusiastically*—I've often said so—I have praised her voice
Because I am a courtier—paid to praise.
I never meant one word of what I said;
I have the worst opinion of her voice,
And so has Zoram.
ZORAM: I? Oh, dear me, no!
I can form no opinion on the point,
I am no judge of music.

Like the *Princess* plot, the magic trick of *The Palace of Truth* sank deep into Gilbert's mind, for its use became habitual with him in later years. This much was already apparent to William Archer in 1881. Writing on Gilbert in *English Dramatists of Today*, Archer recognised the change that had come about in his methods after *The Palace of Truth*: [5]

But first a few words as to "The Palace of Truth". In this play, the keynote of Mr Gilbert's peculiar talent is struck, his style of satire is epitomized. His most successful works have all for their scene an imaginary Palace of Truth, where people naively reveal their inmost thoughts, unconscious of their egotism, vanity, baseness, or cruelty. Touches of this peculiar mannerism are apparent in earlier works such as the two fantastic farces "Creatures of Impulse" and "The Gentleman in Black"; but it was first consciously adopted in "The palace of Truth".... since he discovered "The Palace of Truth", he has hardly ever succeeded in freeing himself from its enchantment.

Both in its praise and in its blame Archer's remains one of the few really penetrative essays ever written on Gilbert. He, Archer, was aware of the unfocused nature of Gilbertian cynicism, and diagnosed one of the important reasons for its ineffectiveness. Writing of *Engaged* (1877) and *Tom Cobb* (1875) which are Gilbert's most consistent excursions into the realms of *The Palace of Truth*, Archer had this to say: [6]

The characters are presented, as it were, with their moral skins off, for the satire very seldom gets more than skin deep. They are divested of the

wrappings and integuments which generally shield our vanities and meannesses from the common gaze. I say our vanities and meannesses, for it is to
be noted that in no single instance, unless it be that of Zeolide in "The Palace
of Truth" itself, does Mr Gilbert's flaying process reveal any unexpected
nobleness or generosity. It is this which, in a sense, takes the sting from his
cynicism. It is so unrelieved that we recognise it as a mere trick or mannerism, and not the result of genuine insight. The jester who railed at everyone
from king to scullion, offended no one.

As we have seen, Gilbert's cynicism was not simply a mannerism or trick
but sprang from the central core of his experience. Nevertheless his expressions of
it fail in their intended effect precisely because their application is universal. *Bab*,
the infantile egotist, faced the world with no concepts more sophisticated than a
sense of his own righteousness and a corresponding sense of the *un*righteousness of
everyone else. By the exercise of his formidable powers of dominance, temper,
and repartee *Bab* was able to protect himself in this position throughout his life;
he preserved his ego, but by the same token his art never acquired the qualities of
light and shade that would have made it a true scourge of human weakness.

Before looking at the use of the *Palace of Truth* technique in the Savoy
libretti, it is perhaps worth recording the curious use of it in *The Mountebanks*.
This work was obviously important to Gilbert. He risked the destruction of his
collaboration with Sullivan in his attempts to force the composer to set it, and
took steps to produce it with another man's music as soon as opportunity offerred.
The magic drink which causes a person to become in reality that which he is
pretending to be is clearly another form of the magic palace which causes its
inhabitants to speak the truth. Since Gilbert prefaces his description of the drink
with an announcement of man's hypocrisy one would expect *The Mountebanks* to
be a reworking of *The Palace of Truth* or *Engaged*—a sustained exposure of humbug,
perhaps embodying an incident from Gilbert's personal suffering at the hands of
hypocrites. Instead the treatment is purely material and mechanical. During the
first act for various reasons the characters pretend to be monks, clockwork
dummies of Hamlet and Ophelia [*sic*], an old woman, a girl mad for love, and a
man dying of poison. The magic potion is drunk, and in the course of the second
act all these people enter successively as the reality of their former pretence. That
is all. Structurally the work is identical to *The Sorcerer*, where the oddly assorted
couples enter under the influence of the love philtre, but here there is no element
even of surprise because we have already seen the characters pretending in the first
act. Of the *Palace of Truth* exposure of hypocrisy there is no trace; at best there is
only the sadistic pleasure of laughing at people who have been turned into
helpless puppets by forces outside their control. Only at one point does Gilbert
give expression to what must have once been in his mind. This is in the duet
between the clockwork Hamlet and Ophelia in the second act. The words deserve
to be quoted in full as representing the *ultima Thule* both of Gilbert's view of the
world and of the mechanical operation of his mind:[7]

If our action's stiff and crude,
Do not laugh because it's rude.

Hamlet and Ophelia as clockwork dummies,
The Mountebanks 1892
(*Illustrated Sporting and Dramatic News*, 9 January 1892)

If our gestures promise larks,
Do not make unkind remarks.
Clockwork figures may be found
Everywhere and all around.
Ten to one, if we but knew,
You are clockwork figures too.
And the motto of the lot,
'Put a penny in the slot!'

Usurer, for money lent,
Making out his cent. per cent.—
Widow plump or maiden rare,
Deaf and dumb to suitor's prayer—
Tax collectors, whom in vain
You implore to 'call again'—
Cautious voter, whom you find
Slow in making up his mind.
If you'd move them on the spot,
Put a penny in the slot!

Bland reporters in the courts
Who suppress police reports—
Sheriff's yeoman, pen in fist,
Making out a jury list—
Stern policemen, tall and spare,
Acting all 'upon the square'—
(Which in words that plainer fall
Means that you can square them all)—
If you want to move the lot,
Put a penny in the slot!

In the familiar libretti, and indeed in his work generally, Gilbert dispensed with the formal apparatus of the Palace of Truth; the characters simply speak and behave as if they were under the influence of the Palace, even though their circumstances are outwardly normal. *Trial by Jury* well exemplifies the method, for almost all the people in this work are humbugs of one sort or another.

The Palace of Truth on this occasion has been transformed into a court of justice; we are about to witness a trial for breach of promise of marriage. The usher warns the jury to beware of bias, but then, at the prompting of the magic palace, reveals that the whole case is to be rigged against the defendant:[8]

And when amid the plaintiff's shrieks,
The ruffianly defendant speaks—
    Upon the other side;
What *he* may say you needn't mind—
From bias free of every kind
    This trial must be tried!

The defendant, when he enters, makes no bones about the fact that he has thrown over one lady for another, whereupon the jurymen admit their own youthful backslidings in the chorus quoted on page 134. As soon as this little confession of hypocrisy is out of the way the learned judge enters. In the first of many songs of a similar type he informs us that he married the elderly ugly daughter of a rich attorney in order to obtain money and work, but, having become rich himself, has now renounced her. His whole career is a piece of shameless jobbery, enthusiastically endorsed by the chorus. The plaintiff, who soon enters, has a confession of her own;[9]

> Fairest days are sun and shade:
> I am no unhappy maid!

Speeches for the prosecution and defence are perhaps licensed exercises in hypocrisy, but it is sufficiently apparent that the plaintiff is a hard-headed gold-digger—Gilbert's standard feminine type—who is out for all she can get. When the judge finally elects to marry her himself one feels they are worthy of each other.

Trial by Jury is a masterpiece, arguably the finest work of Gilbert and Sullivan; it represents the most consistent and concentrated use of the Palace of Truth technique in the operas. The technique is not much present in *The Sorcerer*, perhaps because the story on which *The Sorcerer* is based was written in 1869—before the composition of *The Palace of Truth*. The self-revelations of Sir Joseph Porter in *H.M.S. Pinafore* are a subject to which we must return, but *The Pirates of Penzance* furnishes a typical example of the Palace of Truth at work in the shape of Major General Stanley's patter song. The General enters with a flourish, and at once proceeds to advertise his own incompetence:[10]

> In fact, when I know what is meant by mamelon and ravelin,
> When I can tell at sight a chassepôt rifle from a javelin,
> When such affairs as sorties and surprises I'm more wary at,
> And when I know precisely what is meant by commissariat,
> When I have learnt what progress has been made in modern gunnery,
> When I know more of tactics than a novice in a nunnery,
> In short, when I've a smattering of elemental strategy—
> You'll say a better major-general has never sat a gee.

Later in the opera the General candidly says he has lied to the pirates in order to save his own and his daughters' lives, while the policemen make no bones about their fear of the pirates. Frank hypocrisy crops up in *Patience*, in Bunthorne's soliloquy:[11]

> Am I alone,
>   And unobserved? I am!
> Then let me own
>   I'm an aesthetic sham!

The confessions of the Lord Chancellor in *Iolanthe* differ from those of his predecessors inasmuch as he blurts out not incompetence and dishonesty but their opposites:[12]

> Ere I go into court I will read my brief through,
> (Said I to myself–said I),
> And I'll never take work I'm unable to do,
> (Said I to myself–said I).
> My learned profession I'll never disgrace
> By taking a fee with a grin on my face,
> When I haven't been there to attend to the case,
> (Said I to myself–said I!)

The satirical thrust in these lines is perhaps directed not at the Lord Chancellor himself but at the unworthiness of the legal profession generally. However the Chancellor has earlier told us of his amorous attachment to his wards, so he too must be accounted a dweller in the Palace of Truth. He is joined there by the 'disagreeable man', King Gama of *Princess Ida*: [13]

> If you give me your attention, I will tell you what I am:
> I'm a genuine philanthropist–all other kinds are sham.
> Each little fault of temper and each social defect
> In my erring fellow creatures I endeavour to correct.
> To all their little weaknesses I open people's eyes;
> And little plans to snub the self-sufficient I devise;
> I love my fellow-creatures–I do all the good I can–
> Yet everybody says I'm such a disagreeable man!
> And I can't think why!

After *Princess Ida* Gilbert made less use of the Palace of Truth, presumably because the opposition of Sullivan had forced him to seek out new material. The most notable instance of its use in *The Mikado* is Ko-Ko's shameless acknowledgement of his base reasons for yielding his bride Yum-Yum to Nanki-Poo: [14]

> He yields his life if I Yum-Yum surrender.
> Now I adore that girl with passion tender,
> And could not yield her with a ready will,
> Or her allot,
> If I did not
> Adore myself with passion tenderer still!

Baser than Ko-Ko's attempt to save his own life is the behaviour of Richard Dauntless, the sailor-hero of *Ruddigore*, who betrays his foster-brother Robin Oakapple in order to gain the hand of Rose Maybud. The sailor's brisk treachery well exemplifies the Gilbertian view of human nature, besides showing the Palace of Truth at work in behaviour as well as speech. One might also call Richard's action topsyturvy inasmuch as it is the opposite of what one expects from an honest British sailor. In the mature Gilbertian style all the component elements mix to reinforce each other.

As a serious work *The Yeomen of the Guard* does not call for the exposure of humbug, though Colonel Fairfax–as befits the man who steals Elsie from Point–is made thoroughly unlikeable. However the Duke of Plaza-Toro in *The Gondoliers* is true to the succession; in his case the theme is cowardice: [15]

In enterprise of martial kind,
   When there was any fighting,
He led his regiment from behind—
   He found it less exciting.
But when away his regiment ran,
   His place was at the fore, O,—
      That celebrated,
      Cultivated
      Underrated
        Nobleman,
The Duke of Plaza-Toro!

When Gilbert and Sullivan began to collaborate again after the Carpet Quarrel the partnership was no longer on an instinctively sound footing. One of the many ways in which the libretto of *Utopia Limited* differs for the worse from its forebears lies in Gilbert's failure to employ the Palace of Truth technique when it might be expected from the context. The entrance song of King Paramount looks as if it should be a new instance of the old trick, but what the king confesses is actually his own humiliation, liable as he is to be blown up by dynamite if he offends his two wise men:[16]

But as it is our Royal whim
Our Royal sails to set and trim
   To suit whatever wind may blow—
What buffets contradiction deals
And how a thwarted monarch feels
   We probably shall never know.

Here is something darker than satire, for the lines can be construed as amusing only if it is funny for a man to spend his life under the threat of death. The reverse side of the coin is seen when the wise men enter, exulting in their power:[17]

If ever a trick he tries
   That savours of rascality,
At our decree he dies
   Without the least formality.

No member of an audience witnessing a performance of *Utopia Limited* can consciously discern the way in which these lines differ from the familiar *Palace of Truth* outpourings, but the difference nevertheless registers as a sense of something amiss in *Utopia Limited*, something not as 'good' as the previous operas. Suspicion becomes certainty in the finale to the first act, wherein a number of Establishment figures enter in succession, each wearing his appointed uniform. By all Gilbertian precedent people wearing uniform are incompetent and good for nothing, basely motivated and unworthy—they all tell us so. However the similar people in *Utopia Limited*—the 'Flowers of Progress'—are none of these things; they are dull, virtuous and capable, as the Lord Chamberlain tells us:[18]

> Court reputations I revise,
> And presentations scrutinize,
> New plays I read with jealous eyes,
>   And purify the stage.

The satirical nullity of such verse as this—which Gilbert thought a stroke of genius—helps to throw into relief the value of the *Palace of Truth* technique in the earlier works. Though the satire cannot be taken seriously as satire, because of its automatic and universal application, it is nevertheless altogether more interesting and intelligent than the witless small-talk of the characters in a conventional operetta. Furthermore, the very lack of satirical focus has probably aided the survival of Gilbert's work. If he had concentrated with genuine venom on specific contemporary targets his libretti would by necessity have been more rooted in time and place than they have turned out to be. Gilbert undoubtedly took his own cynicism for the last word on human nature; but unlike his father, who became a crusader for specific causes, he eventually learned how to express it as an artist and not as a thumper of tubs. We return to the idea of rump steak and onions: Gilbertian satire is distinctive enough to entertain an intelligent person, but not sharp enough to alienate anybody—hence the long succession of Judges, Generals, Chancellors, and Admirals who have taken pleasure in it.

Thus Gilbert takes his place as a member of that peculiar British fraternity, the satirists who offend no one. Another such was Thackeray, whose bourgeois characteristics have led in modern times to the neglect of most of his work. For the Victorians, however, Thackeray was a living force, not merely through the popularity of *Vanity Fair* but through the entire corpus of his writings. Gilbert was just beginning to make his way in journalism at the time of Thackeray's death in 1863. He confessed to an admiration for Thackeray, owned a small statue of him, and emulated him by illustrating his own work. Given these circumstances it would hardly be surprising if Gilbert were to show the influence of Thackeray to some extent. In fact as a social satirist Gilbert is entirely derivative from Thackeray; his two main themes, snobbery and the House of Lords, are, *par excellence*, the subjects which Thackeray himself treated. Gilbert's mind was not nearly so copious as Thackeray's, nor was his style so sensitive. Nevertheless, the resemblances are too clear to be mistaken. Let us look at some examples.

George, the hero of Thackeray's *George de Barnwell*, a burlesque of Bulwer Lytton, is a grocer's assistant of a topsyturvy kind. He is reading Greek at the counter when Miss Millwood enters for 'six penn'orth of tea dust'. For her trouble the fair maiden is treated to the following harangue by the egregious George: [19]

> I was born, lady, to grapple with the lofty and the Ideal. My soul yearns for the Visionary. I stand behind the counter, it is true; but I ponder here upon the deeds of heroes, and muse over the thoughts of sages. What is grocery for one who has ambition? What sweetness hath Muscovado to him who has tasted of poesy? The Ideal, lady, I often think it is the true Real, and the actual but a visionary hallucination. But pardon me; with what may I serve thee?

In this passage we encounter the amusingly incongruous mixing of the rarefied with the mundane which is one of the fundamental characteristics of Gilbertism; at the same time the passage is topsyturvy because we do not expect a grocer's assistant to talk like a Platonic philosopher. There is a hint in the language of Bunthorne's aesthetic confrontation with the multiplication table in *Patience*, but the real parallel is with *H.M.S. Pinafore*. In *H.M.S. Pinafore* Ralph, the humble foremast hand, reveals that he has read, if not Platonic philosophy, at least *George de Barnwell*, for he addresses Josephine in these terms: [20]

> I am poor in the essence of happiness, lady—rich only in never-ending unrest. In me there meet a combination of antithetical elements which are at eternal war with one another. Driven hither by objective influences—thither by subjective emotions—wafted one moment into blazing day, by mocking hope—plunged the next into the Cimmerian darkness of tangible despair, I am but a living ganglion of irreconcilable antagonisms. I hope I make myself clear, lady?

These two passages might be taken for parts of the same work, so close is the similarity of mood and style. The opening chapter of Thackeray's *Book of Snobs* (1846/7) is entitled 'The Snob Playfully Dealt With'. Posing as a snob himself, Thackeray describes how he has been forced to cut the acquaintance of George Marrowfat because the fellow ate pease with a knife. In a passage which seems to have inspired Gilbert's Bab Ballad *Etiquette* (1869) he describes how the breach was necessary even though the two men had met in the crater of Mount Vesuvius and George had saved his life. However, a reconciliation takes place when Marrowfat, who has been refined by a stay on the continent, eats his pease properly with a fork: [21]

> What was my astonishment, what my delight, when I saw him use his fork like any other Christian! He did not administer the cold steel once. Old times rushed back upon me—the remembrance of old services—his rescuing me from the brigands—his gallant conduct in the affair with the Countess Dei Spinachi—his lending me the £1700. I almost burst into tears with joy—my voice trembled with emotion. 'George, my boy!' I exclaimed, 'George Marrowfat, my dear fellow!' a glass of wine!' Blushing—deeply moved—almost as tremulous as I was myself, George answered, 'Frank, shall it be Hock or Madeira?' I could have hugged him to my heart but for the presence of the company.

For the purposes of *Etiquette* [22] Gilbert borrowed from the relationship of George and Frank the absurd idea that two men who are bound together by all sorts of shared experiences may be parted by a social nicety. For *Iolanthe* he borrowed the idea that the British address each other by their Christian names only in moments of acute crisis. It will be remembered that Lords Tolloller and Mountararat are both in love with Phyllis. They become very emotional as they try to decide which shall surrender her to the other: [23]

TOLLOLLER: ... if you rob me of the girl of my heart, we must fight, and

> one of us must die. It's a family tradition that I have sworn to
> respect. It's a painful position, for I have a very strong regard
> for you, George.
> MOUNTARARAT: (*Much affected*) - My dear Thomas!
> TOLLOLLER: You are very dear to me, George. We were boys together—
> at least *I* was. If I were to survive you my existence would
> be hopelessly embittered.
> MOUNTARARAT: Then, my dear Thomas, you must not do it.

The kind of observation on which Thackeray based his account of George's
relationship with Frank did not come naturally to Gilbert. To notice and record
human behaviour one must be a little detached, and always cool. Gilbert noticed
other people only when they got in his way and then it was not to comment on
them with pleasure. For this reason the apparent closeness of observation displayed in the exchange between Tolloller and Mountararat could only have come
to him through a literary source; he was not of course blind to the world around
him, but his characteristic reaction to it was a snort rather than a mental note.

The setting of the second act of *Ruddigore* in a gallery whose portraits step
down from their frames is well known to derive from *Ages Ago*, which Gilbert
wrote with Fred Clay in 1869. Most of the pictures in *Ages Ago* can walk but one
of them, Brown, cannot leave his frame because he is only a half length.[24] Here
now is the same incident from Thackeray's burlesque *A Legend of the Rhine*.
Wolfgang the archer has followed the ghastly White Lady of Windeck into her
chamber; she feasts him, and then leads him to a deadly tryst at the altar:[25]

> She held out her hand—Wolfgang took it. It was cold, damp—deadly cold;
> and on they went to the chapel.
>   As they passed out, the two pictures over the wall, of a gentleman and a
> lady, tripped lightly out of their frames, skipped noiselessly down to the
> ground, and making the retreating couple a profound curtsey and bow, took
> the places which they had left at table.
>   ... As they came along, all the portraits on the wall stepped out of their
> frames to follow them. One ancestor, of whom there was only a bust,
> frowned in the greatest rage, because, having no legs, his pedestal would not
> move; and several sticking-plaster profiles of the former Lords of Windeck
> looked quite black at being, for similar reasons, compelled to keep their
> place.

Thackeray's story does not develop like *Ages Ago* or *Ruddigore*, though the
Gothic setting is the same; nevertheless the source of all Gilbert's walking
pictures is clear enough—clinched by the joke about the half-portrait. This joke
could usefully be revived in modern productions.

One of the best known songs in all Gilbert and Sullivan is 'The Policeman's
Lot' (*The Pirates of Penzance*). The burden of the lyric is to the effect that outside
his professional occupation with crime the criminal is like any other member of
society:[26]

> When a felon's not engaged in his employment,
> Or maturing his felonious little plans,

His capacity for innocent enjoyment
Is just as great as any honest man's.

Verbally Gilbert's lyric is not Thackerayan, but the underlying thought appears to have been taken from 'On A Pear Tree', one of the *Roundabout Papers* (1860/3). Thackeray begins by remarking on the way some criminals seem to rob with impunity, while the honest man who is tempted is caught at once; many of the undetected rascals are 'in Clubs and on 'Change, at church or the balls and routs of the nobility and gentry'. Thackeray then continues in the following way; the passage will have caught Gilbert's eye for its references to prominent criminals, one of whom we have already met:[27]

> What is the difference between you and a galley-slave? Is yonder poor wretch at the hulks not a man and a brother too? Have you ever forged, my dear sir? Have you ever cheated your neighbour? Have you ever ridden to Hounslow Heath and robbed the mail? Have you ever entered a first-class railway carriage, where an old gentleman sat alone in a sweet sleep, daintily murdered him, taken his pocket-book, and got out at the next station? You know that this circumstance occurred in France a few months since. If we have travelled in France this autumn we may have met the ingenious gentleman who perpetrated this daring and successful coup. We may have found him a well-informed and agreeable man. I have been acquainted with two or three gentlemen who have been discovered after—after the performance of illegal actions. What? That agreeable rattling fellow we met was the celebrated Mr John Sheppard? Was that aimiable quiet gentleman in spectacles the well-known Mr Fauntleroy? In Hazlitt's admirable paper 'Going to a Fight', he describes a dashing sporting fellow who was in the coach and who was no less a man than the eminent destroyer of Mr William Weare. Don't tell me that you would not like to have met (out of business) Captain Sheppard, the Reverend Doctor Dodd, or others rendered famous by their actions and misfortunes, by their lives and their deaths.

Gilbert's operatic burlesques do not show much promise of future developments because they were all written before 1870, the *annus mirabilis* in which the *Princess* plot, the *Palace of Truth* technique, and topsyturvydom were added unto him. The second of them is *La Vivandière* (1868) which gives us the boorish behaviour of the Earl of Margate and his friends in France—the Earl's wife casts the first pale shadow of the formidable Gilbertian female who was to come. The behaviour of these loutish noble tourists is derived from Thackeray's chapters on Continental Snobbery in *The Book of Snobs*. In the following extract Colonel Cutler and Major Slasher discuss the Peninsular War. They are joined by Captain Boarder:[28]

> 'Hang the fellows,' says Boarder, 'their practice was very good. I was beat off three times before I took her' [referring to a ship]. 'Cuss those carabineers of Milhaud's,' says Slasher, 'what work they made of our light cavalry!' implying a sort of surprise that the Frenchman should stand up against Britons at all: a good natured wonder that the blind, mad, vain-glorious, brave poor devils should actually have the courage to resist an Englishman.

Gilbert's version of these sentiments in *La Vivandière* runs as follows:[29]

> LORD MARGATE: I've half a dozen Frenchmen tried to teach
> That I'm twelve times as brave and strong as each,
> And showed that this corollary must follow,
> One Englishman can thrash twelve Frenchmen hollow.
> In fact, my friends, wherever we have placed ourselves,
> I may say we have thoroughly disgraced ourselves.

Having thus reconnoitred the territory, Gilbert was able to make the same point more subtly in *H.M.S. Pinafore*:[30]

> He is an Englishman!
> For he himself has said it,
> And it's greatly to his credit,
> That he is an Englishman!

In *Ruddigore* the Thackerayan attack is renewed with even weightier irony. Richard Dauntless of the Revenue Sloop *Tom Tit* is the ultimate naval snob. He describes an incident in which his ship (broadside about 56 pounds) meets a French frigate (broadside about 376 pounds) off Cape Finisterre; one wonders what a Revenue ship was doing off the cape, which is in Spain. It would in fact have been folly for any sloop to fight a frigate, even a French frigate, but Richard's jingoism is fully equal to the interpretation of the encounter in terms favourable to the British:[31]

> Then our Captain he up and he says, says he,
>   'That chap we need not fear—
>   We can take her, if we like,
>   She is sartin for to strike,
>   For she's only a darned Mounseer,
>   D'ye see?
>   She's only a darned Mounseer!
> But to fight a French fal-lal—it's like hittin' of a gal—
>   It's a lubbery thing for to do;
>   For we, with all our faults,
>   Why, we're sturdy British salts,
>   While she's only a Parley-voo,
>   D'ye see?
>   While she's only a Parley-voo!

The *Tom Tit* very wisely runs away, and the British tars congratulate themselves on a moral victory while the French rejoice at their narrow escape from death. It is an amusing song which shows Gilbert still able to make imaginative use of an old idea. The idea emerges again in *Utopia Limited*, but this time without fresh impetus; indeed it is only Gilbert's reputation as a satirist which alerts one to the irony of the words. Captain Corcoran, imported from *H.M.S.*

Pinafore as one of the Flowers of Progress, describes the power of the British navy:[32]

> I'm Captain Corcoran K.C.B.,
> I'll teach you how we rule the sea,
>   And terrify the simple Gauls;
> And how the Saxon and the Celt
> Their Europe-shaking blows have dealt
> With Maxim gun and Nordenfeldt
>   (Or will when the occasion calls.)

In the treatment of patriotic snobbery we see a complete sequence of Gilbert's development from straightforward borrowing from a source through characteristic and original reworking into the flaccidity of decline. It is a neat curve which is not observable when Gilbert borrowed ideas on a one-off basis. Several small details of the libretti appear to be taken from Thackeray, notably the name Diddlesex used in the 'Railway' song in *Thespis*. Diddlesex is the main scene of operations of Thackeray's absurd footman-cum-railway-king Jeames de la Pluche.[33] However it is in the field of social snobbery at large that the debt is deepest.

Gilbert's literary dislike of the aristocracy—there is no trace of it in his private life—was not confined to himself. It was a shared prejudice of the staff of *Punch* in its early days, coming to a gloriously comic and biting climax in Thackeray. The lyrics in which Gilbert dealt with the House of Lords in *Iolanthe* are well known. However, as we have suggested, it was in his excised work that he came closest to satire. The following lyric was intended to be sung by the Duke of Dunstable in *Patience*, but was cut before the first performance; of Sullivan's setting only the accompaniment survives:[34]

> Though men of rank may useless seem,
>   They do good in their generation,
> They make the wealthy upstart teem
>   With Christian love and self-negation;
> The bitterest tongue that ever lashed
>   Man's folly drops with milk and honey,
> While Scandal hides her head, abashed,
>   Brought face to face with Rank and Money!

The style and subject matter of these words are so entirely Thackerayan that it would be hard to find a single source for them. Perhaps this passage from *The Book of Snobs* will serve as an example:[35]

> How can we help snobbishness with such a prodigious national institution erected for its worship? How can we help cringing to Lords? Flesh and blood can't do otherwise. What man can withstand this prodigious temptation? Inspired by what is called a noble emulation, some people grasp at honours and win them; others, too weak or mean, blindly admire and grovel before those who have gained them; others, not being able to acquire them,

furiously hate, abuse and envy. There are only a few bland and not-the-least conceited philosophers who can behold the state of society, viz, Toadyism, organized:—base Man-and Mammon worship, instituted by command of law: Snobbishness, in a word, perpetuated,—and mark the phenomenon calmly. And of these calm moralists, is there one, I wonder, whose heart would not throb with pleasure if he could be seen walking arm-in-arm with a couple of dukes down Pall Mall? No: it is impossible, in our condition of society, not sometimes to be a snob.

The second verse of Gilbert's excised lyric deals with the power of noble birth to nullify the consequences of immorality. Again this is the type of thought one finds in Thackeray *passim*. The following passage, close to the beginning of *The Book of Snobs*, sets the tone:[36]

> Suppose he is a nobleman of a jovial turn, and has a fancy for wrenching off knockers, frequenting gin-shops, and half murdering policemen: the public will sympathise good-naturedly with his amusements, and say he is a hearty, honest fellow. Suppose he is fond of play and the turf, and he has a fancy to be a blackleg, and occasionally condescends to pluck a pigeon at cards; the public will pardon him, and many honest people will court him, as they would court a house-breaker if he happened to be a Lord.

It will be remembered that the house-breaking pirates of Penzance are pardoned because they are 'all noblemen who have gone wrong.' The next sentence in the passage from Thackeray just quoted reads as follows, 'Suppose he is an idiot; yet by the glorious constitution he is good enough to govern *us*.' A little earlier, Thackeray has had this to say about the sons of Lords:[37]

> 'Your merits are so great,' says the the nation, 'that your children shall be allowed to reign over us, in a manner. It does not in the least matter that your eldest son is a fool: we think your services are so remarkable that he shall have the reversion of your honours when death vacates your noble shoes.'

In these passages we come very close to the familiar Gilbertian idea that the House of Lords is composed entirely of stupid people. The difference is that Thackeray's prose has a cutting edge while Gilbert, at least in those sentences he allowed his audience to hear, sounds positively friendly by comparison.

Below the ranks of the peerage lie the middle classes who ape them. This too was Thackeray's territory long before it became Gilbert's. The best known Gilbertian attack on middle class snobbery is in the duet 'Small titles and orders' (*The Gondoliers*), but once again the sharper material is to be found in an excised lyric, this time from *Ruddigore*; it is sung by Robin Oakapple in the second act after the ghosts have convinced him that he must after all commit his crime a day. Sullivan's setting is extant, but is deliberately self-effacing and mediocre:[38]

Ye well-to-do squires, who live in the shires,
    Where pretty distinctions are vital,
Who found Athenaeums and local museums,

With views to a baronet's title—
Ye butchers and bakers and candlestick makers
Who sneer at all things that are tradey—
Whose middle-class lives are embarrassed by wives
Who long to parade as 'My Lady',
Oh! allow me to offer a word of advice,
The title's uncommonly dear at the price!

Once again the ambience of these lines is so thoroughly Thackerayan that it does not require to be tracked to a specific source in Thackeray's work. These words from *The Book of Snobs* are enough to make the point:[39]

Read the fashionable intelligence; read the Court Circular; read the genteel novels; survey mankind from Pimlico to Red Lion Square, and see how the Poor Snob is aping the Rich Snob; how the Mean Snob is grovelling at the feet of the Proud Snob; and the Great Snob is lording it over his humble brother. Does the idea of equality ever enter Dives' head? Will it ever?. Will the Duchess of Fitzbattleaxe (I like a good name) ever believe that Lady Croesus, her next-door neighbour in Belgrave Square, is as good a lady as her Grace?

As his biographers make clear, Gilbert had no kind of sympathy for, or understanding of, the working class.[40] However, he was prepared to use them as a stick with which to beat the aristocracy, as an excised song from *Iolanthe* shows. The song, which was actually heard at the Savoy, was sung by Strephon in the second act:[41]

Take a wretched thief, through the city sneaking,
Pocket handkerchief ever, ever seeking:
What is he but I, robbed of all my chances,
Picking pockets by force of circumstances?
I might be as bad, as unlucky, rather,
If I'd only had Fagin for a Father!

What these words express is not insight into the lot of the lower orders—except insofar as that may be obtained from Dickens or Thackeray—but contempt for the snobbish idea that aristocrats are naturally virtuous. Gilbert seems to have been annoyed by the phrenological notion that character is determined by bumps on the head. He wrote a *Bab Ballad*, 'Phrenology' (1870), in which a criminal proves to have bumps of Faith, Hope, and Charity, while a nobleman is covered in bumps of viciousness.[42] The moral is that the nobleman has been kept from a life of crime only by his social position, whereas on the other hand an intrinsically virtuous man has been demoralised by his circumstances. The leading idea behind Strephon's song is not therefore a modern social conscience but a thoroughly Victorian concern with phrenology combined with a thoroughly Thackerayan dislike of aristocrat worship. Considering his father's concern with social questions, and the similar concern of Dickens, whom he admired, it is surprising that Gilbert avoided them so completely. Only in Josephine's first act aria in *H.M.S. Pinafore* and in a single line in the second act of *Utopia Limited* did he allow what one might call true realism to break into his elaborate fantasy.[43]

The second verse of the excised song from *Ruddigore*, quoted above, refers to another favourite Gilbertian theme—the stupidity of Members of Parliament. The classic statement of this case is the sentry's song in the second act of *Iolanthe*:[44]

> When in that House M.P.s divide,
>   If they've a brain and cerebellum, too,
> They've got to leave that brain outside,
>   And vote just as their leaders tell 'em to.
> But then the prospect of a lot
>   Of dull M.P.s in close proximity,
> All thinking for themselves is what
>   No man can face with equanimity.

These lines reflect Walter Bagehot's well known judgement that the success of the British Parliamentary system is due to the stupidity of the politicians, who do not share the intellectualism which makes politics so volatile in other countries. Bagehot was editor of *The Economist* from 1860 onwards, where many of his influential articles appeared. So paradoxical an idea as that the success of a system is due to the unintelligence of its practitioners was not likely to escape the notice of Gilbert.

To accompany its general lack of focus and its debt to Thackeray, Gilbert's satire also tends to be somewhat out of date. For sound artistic reasons he eschewed the introduction of topical jokes, but on more than one occasion the basic subject of his jibes had long since ceased to be of current interest. Perhaps the most notable instance of this tendency is to be found in the second act of *The Pirates of Penzance*.

The second act of the *Pirates* is set in a ruined Gothic chapel by moonlight. To the chapel comes Major General Stanley to abase himself in front of the tombs of his ancestors on account of the lie he has told the pirates:[45]

> FREDERIC: But you forget, sir, you only bought the property a year ago, and the stucco on your baronial hall is scarcely dry.
> GENERAL: Frederic, in this chapel are ancestors: you cannot deny that. With the estate, I bought the chapel and its contents. I don't know whose ancestors they *were*, but I know whose ancestors they *are*, and I shudder to think that their descendant by purchase (if I may so describe myself) should have brought disgrace upon what, I have no doubt, was an unstained escutcheon.

By the time *The Pirates of Penzance* came to be written the cult of the Gothic ruin had been in existence for well over a century, owing its origin ultimately to Horace Walpole's house at Strawberry Hill (1747). The heyday of romantic Gothicism was probably the first half of the nineteenth century; by Gilbert's day, certainly, it was long-established and not remotely a topic for current satire.

Similarly the fashion for acquiring ancestors belongs to the first part of the century. The great passion for recovering one's lost medieval barony achieved its masterpiece in the antics of Sir Egerton Brydges (1796-1837) who spent well over £100,000 in vain pursuit of his claim to the barony of Chandos. Ancestor hunting in general was possibly at its height in 1845, when Disraeli mocked it in *Sybil*.

Much the same comments apply to *Ruddigore*, which Gilbert called a burlesque of the kind of melodrama seen at the Surrey Theatre. The Surrey had been the home of melodrama since 1806; at the time of *Ruddigore* it was under the management of George Conquest, who produced sensational dramas and fine pantomimes whose scenic effects Sullivan compared favourably with those at Bayreuth. As a *Gothic* melodrama, however, *Ruddigore* tilts at a distinctly ageing windmill, one whose sails had long since ceased to turn with any show of vigour.

In *Patience* Gilbert found a subject which was not entirely moribund, though it was by no means new. If we date the emergence of aestheticism from the founding of the Pre-Raphaelite Brotherhood in 1848, then the subject matter of Gilbert's opera was over thirty years old when it was produced. The aesthetic movement was attacked as early as 1866 by Robert Buchanan in an article entitled *The Fleshly School of Poetry*. The first stage burlesque seems to have been *The Grasshopper* by John Hollingshead (Gaiety 1877), followed by *Victims* (1878) and James Albery's *Where's The Cat?* (1880) in which Beerbohn Tree played a poet who admired sunflowers and blue and white china.[46] The most sucessful of the predecessors of *Patience* however was F.C. Burnand's *The Colonel* (21 February 1881), which survived for years in provincial tours and revivals. Besides this the aesthetes featured as characters in many pantomimes dances and burlesques. One begins to wonder whether the craze for satirising aestheticism was not greater than the craze for aestheticism itself. In joining in the attacks on it in 1881 Gilbert showed sound commercial judgement and superior artistic ability, but enterprise and courage not at all.

It is perhaps superfluous to point to the remote and dated nature of some of the satire in *The Grand Duke* when the libretto as a whole misfires. Nevertheless by way of partial explanation of the misfire we may notice the abstruseness of the duel as a topic in Gilbert's day. The lyric in which duelling is attacked has an odd ring of sincerity, as though proceeding from personal conviction:[47]

> Strange the views some people hold!
> Two young fellows quarrel -
> Then they fight, for both are bold -
> Rage of both is uncontrolled -
> Both are stretched out, stark and cold!
> Prithee, where's the moral?
> Ding dong! Ding dong!
> There's an end to further action,
> And this barbarous transaction
> Is described as 'satisfaction'!
> Ha! ha! ha! ha! satisfaction!
> Ding dong! Ding dong!

Each is laid in churchyard mould—
Strange the views some people hold!

In 1896 duelling had no significance for the British public. Duelling had been banned in the British Army since 1844 on the instigation of Queen Victoria; the last fatal duel took place in 1852—forty four years before *The Grand Duke*. The practice lingered on the continent, but it was not an issue in England from the time of the Queen's ban.[48] Yet Gilbert saw fit to introduce it as an important part of his play.

Similar strictures apply to the satire on acting in *The Grand Duke* and the treatment of the Joint Stock Companies Act in *Utopia Limited*. In the first case scorn for the jealousies and bad taste of actors was a personal fetish of Gilbert's not shared by the public, who enjoy such things if anything. In the second case the Joint Stock Companies Act (1862) was thirty years old at the time of *Utopia Limited*. Even if we drag in the Directors' Liability Act of 1890 and the Companies (Winding Up) Act of 1893 the degree of topicality attained is hardly such as to stimulate the phagocytes. As we have seen, some of Gilbert's successful works contain untopical material; what is different in the last two libretti is not so much that the material was untopical as that it was of more interest to Gilbert than to the world in general. This was the result of increasing self-absorption accompanied by a correspondingly diminished power of self-criticism.

No sooner had the good ship *Pinafore* set sail than it was taken for granted by contemporaries that Sir Joseph Porter, First Lord of the Admiralty, was a caricature of W.H. Smith (1825-91). Smith, son of the founder of the still-flourishing chain of bookshops, had been made First Lord in 1877 with no experience of the sea; the parallel was too obvious to be missed. Gilbert had the foresight to realise that his intentions might be misunderstood and took the trouble to clarify them in a letter to Sullivan written before the production, 'Of course there will be no personality in this - the fact that the *First Lord* in the opera is a *Radical* of the most pronounced type will do away with any suspicion that W.H. Smith is intended.'[49] This denial has been regarded as the joke of the century, and thought of as a *locus classicus* in the ultimate obtuseness of wit. Yet Gilbert undoubtedly meant to be taken at his word, as the derivation of Sir Joseph's *Palace-of-Truth*-style entrance song shows.

It will be remembered that Sir Joseph traces his career from his early days as an office boy in an attorney's firm, through a junior clerkship and a junior partnership to a Parliamentary seat and the Admiralty, culminating in the immortal advice:[50]

Stick close to your desks, and never go to sea,
And you all may be rulers of the Queen's Navee!

So far from deriving from the career of W.H. Smith, Sir Joseph's rise is in fact another instance of Gilbert's borrowing from *The Book of Snobs*. In the chapter on 'The Great City Snobs' we read this:[51]

OLD PUMP sweeps a shop, runs messages, becomes a confidential clerk and partner. PUMP THE SECOND becomes chief of the house, spins more and more money, marries his son to an earl's daughter. PUMP TERTIUS goes on with the bank; but his chief business in life is to become the father of PUMP QUARTIUS, who comes out a full-blown aristocrat, and takes his seat as BARON PUMPINGTON, and his race rules hereditarily over this nation of snobs.

Gilbert has compressed the activities of several generations of Pumps into the single lifetime of Sir Joseph, but his Thackerayan source is hardly open to doubt. Further confirmation of the non-specific nature of the satire in Sir Joseph's song is forthcoming from *The Happy Land* (1873), the burlesque of *The Wicked World* which Gilbert wrote in collaboration with Gilbert à Beckett. *The Happy Land* is one of the seminal works of Gilbert's career even though, as he more than once insisted, he was responsible for the scenario but not the written text.[52] The work directly ridiculed Gladstone and two members of the Cabinet, and was therefore the only directly political satire with which he was associated. In the first act Mr A (A.S. Ayrton, that is, Commissioner of Public Works in the Gladstone Government) examines the fairy Darine with a view to ascertaining her degree of unfitness for high office. He asks her 'the average cost of a first-class ironclad ship':

DARINE: Please, sir, a first-class ironclad *what?*
Mr A: Ship, my dear - ship, *ship*.
DARINE: (*Innocently*) - Please sir, what *is* a ship?
Mr A: Here's a First Lord ready made! Take 'em all down.
        Gives her a portfolio labelled 'First Lord of The Admiralty'.
        Darine goes to top of class.
DARINE: But, please sir, I don't know anything about ships!
Mr A: My dear, it's one of the most beautiful principles of our system of government never to appoint anybody to a post to which he is at all fitted.

In the second act we learn that 'the entire fleet has run aground, even though a retired solicitor was in command.' *The Happy Land* was written four years *before* W.H. Smith went to the Admiralty. It is impossible to determine how many of its ideas were included in the scenario handed to Gilbert à Becket, but it is sufficiently apparent that the character of Sir Joseph Porter has nothing to do with W.H. Smith—he derives from Old Pump and the fairy Darine, not from a real politician.

Walter Bagehot once remarked that few good books are written because authors live in rooms rather than the world and read other authors rather than employing their own eyes and ears. Gilbert was, of course, a good author, but he lived very much out of the world by virtue of his cynicism and egocentricity. He compensated for the unreality of his words by minute attention to realism in matters of costume, but he remained detached. As a result his satire is derived from books, notably those of Thackeray, rather than from anything a novelist would recognise as first hand observation; it touches the real world only when, as in the cases of Oscar Wilde and W.H. Smith, life begins to imitate art. On the other hand the remoteness and unreality of his satire has probably helped to give it permanence by detaching it from the arena of current events and mores. *Patience*, which looks like a topical satire, endures because it is not a palpable hit at anything one can positively identify.

As his blank verse plays show, Gilbert's satire had a root in sincerity; but sincerity is very bad for art. Gilbert became an artist in the proper sense only when he abandoned his 'true' self in favour of his inversions and improbabilities, his ironies and his mechanical whimsies. These qualities are seen at their best in the superb lyric from *Patience* in which Bunthorne gives his recipe for aesthetic success: [53]

> If you're anxious for to shine in the high aesthetic line as a man of culture
>> rare,
> You must get up all the germs of the transcendental terms, and plant them
>> everywhere.
> You must lie upon the daisies and discourse in novel phrases of your
>> complicated state of mind,
> The meaning doesn't matter if it's only idle chatter of a transcendental kind.
>> And every one will say,
>> As you walk your mystic way,
> 'If this young man expresses himself in terms too deep for *me*,
> Why what a very singularly deep young man this deep young man must be!'

In these lines any possible satirical intention has been absorbed into a fantasy which makes of aestheticism a thing more wonderful than anything it can have been in the drawing rooms of life. The same transformation is wrought with Sir Joseph Porter and the Lord Chancellor and the policemen of *The Pirates of Penzance*. Retaining only a formal and external connection with the sublunary world, they dwell in the palace of their own particular truth for ever. After all, *Bab*, the eternal baby, did know how to play.

7: *The Composer*

It is customary for all writers on Gilbert and Sullivan to pay tribute to the bicephalic nature of the partnership. Comments on the artistic interdependence of the two men are a standard part of any account of their achievement. In practice, however, much more space is devoted to the author than to the composer, no doubt because it is easy for words to beget words, whereas music is intangible outside its technicalities. By way of compensation Sullivan has been made the subject of a number of independent studies, of which that by Arthur Jacobs is the most recent. The composer is, so to speak, a much more substantial figure in his own right than is Gilbert. The difference may be expressed by saying that whereas no one has suggested that Gilbert was capable of better things than his libretti, Sullivan was almost universally regarded by his contemporaries as wasting his time in comic opera. Whether, and to what extent, this may be true will form a main theme of the second part of the present book.

As a personality Sullivan does not appear to have been so complicated as Gilbert. The universal testimony of those who knew him is that he was equable and gracious, kind and patient. Since we have quoted Seymour Hicks on Gilbert, it may be fitting to let a quotation from the same source stand for many:[1]

> Arthur Sullivan was surely one of the most lovable men who ever lived. Unlike his giant partner, he was quite short. He had a gentle, kindly face and two merry eyes which looked out upon the world, one of them through an eyeglass, always searching for the sunshine....
>
> Towards the end of his life he leaned somewhat heavily on a stout strong malacca cane and limped slightly. His health was extremely poor, and his nephew, Herbert Sullivan, told me that many of his happiest melodies were written when, in great pain, he lay stretched on a sofa in his London library.
>
> He was the most modest of 'masters', and time and again had been

known to sit down after dinner at a friend's house and accompany some young lady or amateur tenor in their songs at the piano.

Often I have been told that these delightful assassins were quite unaware of the identity of the charming little man who played for them, and though they many a time murdered one of his own compositions, he remained only an ever gracious and never critical accompanist.

Naturally of an even temper, in his later days the agony of the internal complaint from which he suffered made him at times very irritable. Often he would attend a rehearsal in the morning and, unlike his real self, become very difficult. It was then that, realizing his ailment to be the cause of his intolerance, he would go to his room in the Savoy Theatre and seek relief from hypodermic injections. Returning to the stage temporarily free from suffering, he was once more the dear Arthur Sullivan who was without an enemy in the world.

These words are echoed without exception by every writer who recorded impressions of Sullivan. We may take it therefore that they represent something fundamentally true about him. However he was not merely good natured, for the energy which must of necessity burn within any man of genius was active in him also. This energy found its outlet in a personal and professional life so strenuous that already by 1867 it was being said of him that he would make himself an old and broken down man at forty. [2] Because his fame owes nothing to them, it is easy to forget Sullivan's labours as a conductor, educator and administrator—the labours which brought him his knighthood. His methods of composition are well known; he would delay work until the last possible moment, and then proceed at intense pressure. Part of his reason for acting in this way was the desire to avoid unnecessary work, but it is hard to resist the suspicion that he also enjoyed the exhilaration of functioning at the limits.

Desire for excitement certainly seems to have lain behind his love of gambling and the turf. Several writers have remarked on the feverish way he played, seemingly oblivious to the amounts of money won and lost. [3] To this must be added his all-night parties and an active sexual life, conducted mostly with anonymous partners, often on the continent to avoid possible scandal at home. Not the least of the attractions of Paris for him lay in the prospect it afforded of pre-arranged sexual encounters. [4]

No man is a hypocrite in his pleasures. Sullivan's pleasures show that in some respects at least he was not more sophisticated than the average *homme moyen sensuel*. Johann Strauss was another such, and so too was Offenbach. Sullivan, however, like the other two, was also a gifted artist, with an artist's refinement and sensibilities. Outside music he expressed his refinement by his association with cultivated aristocrats and Top People generally. This aspect of his social life has been misunderstood, especially by Hesketh Pearson, as reprehensible tuft-hunting. We need not doubt that a man born in a cheap terrace in Lambeth felt gratified to walk with princes, but, as the enlightening researches of Marc Girouard have shown, the aristocracy of Sullivan's day were also the last heirs of the high eighteenth-century civilisation as it was embodied in the country parks of Capability Brown and the interiors of Robert Adam. [5] In visiting the aristocracy in their houses Sullivan was not climbing the social ladder in any crude sense—he belonged by virtue of ability to the top drawer—but simply living the most civilised life his society had to offer. A glance at the houses he visited or rented for himself, such as Pencarrow or Stagenhoe Park, is sufficient to indicate what he was doing. Pencarrow, for instance, has an elaborate music room. So far from being snobbish, his association with the aristocracy was a mark of his own civilised qualities.

Besides aimiability, intensity, and civilisation, the fourth important element in Sullivan's personal life was undoubtedly his kidney disease. Kidney pain is one of the most acute of all pains. Sir Walter Scott, who suffered from it, used to lie shouting in bed during an attack, and Samuel Pepys reserved as a day of special thanksgiving the anniversary of his sucessful operation for the stone. The Stoic philosophers used to hold that a wise man may be happy on the rack; if that is so, Sullivan must have been a wise man indeed, for some of his best known works were composed through attacks of kidney pain. According to contemporary medical opinion, prolonged suffering from kidney disease led to loss of vitality and weakening of judgement. Sullivan barely survived the severe attack of 1892, which left him permanently changed. Although he died early by modern standards, it is surprising that he lived as long as he did.

Any consideration of Sullivan's music must begin with his great natural gifts. From childhood onwards he stood out as a person of whom something exceptional might be anticipated. This was undoubtedly why educational doors were flung open for him, and rules were waived in his favour. As we have seen, his teachers in Leipzig regarded his native powers greater than those of Brahms, who is himself considered one of the greatest of all composers. J.A. Fuller Maitland, one of the unkindest of his many unkind critics, thought his ability 'greater, perhaps, than fell to the lot of any English musician since the time of Purcell.'[6] Comments to similar effect may be found in numerous other writers, generally made in connection with his orchestral and choral works, and generally also regretting his involvement with comic opera. What such comments mean in round terms is that Sullivan stood out as conspicuously in his own day as Britten did in ours. Indeed it would be hard to deny that he created a larger body of living music than any native composer between Purcell and Elgar. Even his unwritten works have been considered significant. Percy M. Young looks on his projected Symphony in D (1868) as 'one of the most important non-works in British music'.[7]

Ability is one thing, achievement another. The fundamental reason why Sullivan's reputation declined so catastrophically after his death, and has remained ambiguous ever since, lies in the word *greatness*, which in music criticism has specific and somewhat rigid connotations. Before the time of Beethoven composers were for the most part the paid employees of individual or institutional patrons. Thus Bach served the Leipzig town council, and Haydn lived as something very like a liveried flunkey in the household of Prince Esterházy. Mozart stood out against this system, attempting to earn his living independently by composition. By the beginning of the nineteenth century independence had become entangled with romanticism, so that Beethoven regarded himself not simply as a free tradesman but as a hero defying the world and fate. A new value, which Wordsworth aptly called the Egotistical Sublime, had come into being, achieving its masterpiece in the career of Wagner. All subsequent music and music criticism have been dominated by the enormous egos and achievements of Beethoven and Wagner. No composer can be called 'great' in this scheme of things if he does not in some sense follow them up the winding stair of egotism.

In the particular case of Sullivan the difficulty for critics has always been to reconcile his obvious gifts with his equally obvious failure to use them according to the prescribed romantic formula. With a talent greater than Brahms' he *should* have been a thundering egotist; in fact he sat down to accompany young ladies at the piano or to write trifling entertainments for the Savoy. Music cristicism then, as now, had no way of dealing with such a man except to dismiss him. For Sullivan the classic notice of dismissal was written by Ernest Walker in his *History Of Music In England* (1907). [8] It has been repeated at intervals throughout this century as the histories of English music have appeared. In recent years the durability of his comic operas has enforced revision, but the condemnatory attitude has found fresh vigour in the very emphasis laid on Gilbert and the Savoy. Sullivan, we now learn, was essentially a damp squib who became a shining light only as an appendage to his librettist. The defence of his neglected music has become a matter of some difficulty; to think well of him is by no means a passport to respect among musical people.

The most direct way to the understanding of Sullivan's position is to think of him as belonging in spirit to the age of Haydn, that is to the period before the Egotistical Sublime became a necessary part of the equipment of a man of genius. Sullivan began not with his own subjectivity but with Victorian musical life as he knew it; in that context he was as ready to make pots as dishes. Having no personal message to impart, he felt no need to compose works which nobody wanted but himself. To him 'devotion to art' meant not the service of a private ideal but the maintenance of the finest possible standards of craftsmanship in whatever he undertook. Thus it came about that without loss of integrity he could write those ballads for the drawing room and hymns for the church whose existence has done his reputation so much harm: [9]

> I was ready to undertake anything that came my way. Symphonies, over-tures, ballets, anthems, hymn tunes, songs, part-songs, a concerto for the violoncello, and eventually comic and light operas—nothing came amiss to me, and I gladly accepted what the publishers offered me, so long I could get the things accepted.

The nature of the conditions in which Sullivan worked may be estimated from a remark made by one of Elgar's publishers in 1914. Elgar was then at the height of his fame, an acknowledged master, but the publisher's financial judgement was this, 'I don't want any more Elgar symphonies or concertos, but am ready to take as many part-songs as he can produce, even at exorbitant rates'.[10] Sullivan's symphony was not published till 1915. Not all of his *gebrauchsmusik* is as bad as its unsavoury reputation suggests, but a composer who supplies the market is vulnerable to the current level of public taste. Sullivan undoubtedly abused his gifts on more than one occasion.

Sullivan's objective approach to the opportunities before him was supported by two qualities, both highly personal to himself, and both the very negation of egotism. The first of these was an acutely sensitive musical response to external stimuli, the second a vast and precise store of memory and knowledge which enabled him to be equal to almost any demand made on him.

Among his early appointments Sullivan spent some time as organist at Covent Garden, where he made himself familiar with the standard operatic repertory of the day (much of it still familiar). In 1864 he wrote a ballet for Covent Garden under the title *L'Île Enchantée*. He described the rehearsals himself in these terms:[11]

> "On one occasion ... I was admiring the 'borders' that had been painted for a woodland scene. 'Yes', said the painter, 'they are very delicate, and if you could support them by something suggestive in the orchestra, we could get a very pretty effect.' I at once put in some very delicate arpeggio work for the flutes, and Beverley [the artist] was quite happy. The next day probably some such scene as this would occur. Mr Sloman [the stage machinist], 'That iron doesn't run in the slot so easily as I should like, Mr Sullivan. We must have a little more music to carry her [Salvoni] across. I should like something for the 'cellos. Could you do it?'
>
> 'Certainly, Mr Sloman, you have opened a new path in the beauty of orchestration,' I replied gravely, and I at once added sixteen bars for the 'cello alone. No sooner was this done than a *variation* (solo dance) was required, at the last moment, for the second *danseuse*, who had just arrived.
>
> 'What on earth am I to do?' I said to the manager; 'I haven't seen her dance yet, and know nothing about her style.' 'I'll see,' he replied, and took the young lady aside. In less than five minutes he returned. 'I've arranged it all,' he said. 'This is exactly what she wants'—giving it to me rhythmically— *'Tiddle-iddle-um, tiddle-iddle-um, rum-tirum-tirum*, sixteen bars of that; then *rum-tum, rum-tum, rum-tum*, heavy, you know, sixteen bars; and then finish up with the overture to *William Tell* last movement, sixteen bars and *coda*.' "
>
> With a celerity which he has equalled on many occasions at a much later date, the composer wrote the necessary quantity of "that", and it was in process of rehearsal in less than a quarter of an hour.

These extraordinary proceedings—unthinkable in the case of Wagner—show Sullivan writing music in response to scenery, to a stage machinist's suggestion, and wishing to write for a dancer only after he had grasped her personal qualities; in the end he wrote to a rhythm selected by her. At this stage in his career Sullivan in fact objected to being asked to write music to order; what concerns us is to note the sensitivity of a composer who felt he could not write music for a dancer until he has seen her perform. In 1888 much the same thing happened when Sullivan provided music for Irving's production of *Macbeth*:[12]

It was a lesson in collaboration to see the way in which these two men, each great in his own craft, worked together. Arthur Sullivan knew that with Irving lay the responsibility of the *ensemble*, and was quite willing to subordinate himself to the end which the other had in mind.

The ends Irving had in mind are described thus in a letter he wrote to Sullivan on the subject of the production:[13]

> Trumpets and drums are the things *behind scenes*.
> Entrance of Macbeth, only drum.
> Distant march would be good for Macbeth's exit in 3rd scene—
> or drum and trumpets as you suggest.
> In the last act there will be several flourishes of trumpets.
> Make all our trumpets speak, etc.
> Really anything you can give of a stirring sort can be brought
> in. As you say, you can dot these down at rehearsals—but one
> player would be good to tootle tootle so that we could get the
> exact tune.

Sullivan was able to employ these primitive hints to make a substantial contribution to the success of the production. The same process may be seen in the comic operas, each of which has an 'atmosphere' of its own, derived from the stage setting, the costumes, and the general tenor of the story. Thus the music of *Patience* largely reflects the pastel shades of the aesthetic draperies and the langour of the maidens; the grim atmosphere of the Tower of London is captured in *The Yeomen of the Guard*, and in *Utopia Limited*–'Utopia' means 'Nowhere'–the music is mostly null and void.

The sensitivity to externals was carried over into an equivalent or greater sensitivity towards the written word. By a microfine but well-nigh infallible process Sullivan was able to set words to music which not only captured their diction and meaning, but reflected their quality as well. Among his songs the best are those which, like the passionate *Arabian Love Song* (Shelley), are set to the best words; a shoddy ballad text like *The Distant Shore* drew from him a shoddy ballad, with many shades of distinction between. The famous word setting of the comic operas is not confined to them, but is a particular instance of an ability which is manifest in everything he wrote.

Sullivan's methods of dealing with words are well known. He began by marking out the text in various alternative rhythms with a view to discovering which would be most interesting. Having settled on a rhythm the melodic outline then apparently formed itself in his mind without further effort as a natural outcome of the rhythm chosen. Sometimes, as in the case of *The Lost Chord* and 'I hear the soft note' (*Patience*), the rhythm itself is allowed to form the melody—though beginning with repetitions of a single note these two pieces appear to have completely different tunes. Sometimes, notably in *The Light of the World*, Sullivan employed his rhythm-tunes as a substitute for something more enterprising, but in general the ear hardly detects the device in use.

Turning now to the variety and depth of Sullivan's resource it is hard to single out individual examples as more characteristic than others. At the simplest level Sullivan knew exactly how to conjure up nautical music for sailors, military music for soldiers, graceful music for young girls and weird music for ghosts. When Gilbert offered him the chance in *Utopia Limited* he showed that he knew precisely how to make an orchestra sound like a collection of buzzing banjos, [14] and when Sydney Grundy offered him the bagpipes in *Haddon Hall* he showed himself capable of producing their sound as well. This sort of thing may seem facile, but it is not done by jostling in the street. It can be achieved only by a man with a perfect ear for sound who is also equipped with an accurate aural memory, plus the technical understanding of the orchestral instruments necessary to translate the remembered sound from one medium to another.

Wherever one turns in Sullivan's music this same ability is apparent. Sometimes it manifests itself as burlesque, like the mock Handel that introduces the judge in *Trial by Jury*, and sometimes, where it is not properly digested, as a rather embarrassing crib, like the borrowing from *Carmen* in 'Here is a case unprecedented' (*The Gondoliers*). At a rather less obvious level come the moments when the music sets the atmosphere, as in the dewy nocturnal introduction to the second act of *The Pirates of Penzance*, or the feverish accompaniment to the Lord Chancellor's Nightmare song in *Iolanthe*. Outside the operas one thinks of the splendid evocation of Venice at carnival time in the *Merchant of Venice* music (1871) and the glorious Elgarian sunset that opens the second scene of *The Golden Legend* (1886). Such things were not written by accident; they are part of a comprehensiveness of consciousness that made Sullivan a microcosm of the musical world as he knew it.

In spite of the fame of his melodies Sullivan's imagination was probably most truly itself in the creation of sound as such. The sensitivity and brilliance of his orchestration in the comic operas has always been recognised, even though in these works display is deliberately held in check lest the words be obscured. Outside the works with Gilbert the orchestra and its sonorities become the single most important feature. Sullivan's symphony for instance is no masterpiece of tonal drama, but it *is* a masterpiece of living and subtle tone colour. Bernard Shaw, who advised Sir Hubert Parry to burn *Job*, was prepared to exempt *The Golden Legend* from the strictures he passed on Victorian music generally because of the way it expressed the composer's sheer love of sound. Modern performances confirm Shaw's judgement; whatever the intellectual shortcomings of *The Golden Legend*, it is a feast of beautiful noises, for which the story is only a pretext. In the late operas, *The Beauty Stone* (1898) and *The Rose of Persia* (1899), Sullivan has begun to abandon the formula of tune plus accompaniment in order to absorb the vocal parts into the tissue of orchestral sound. Gervase Hughes points out that even in the familiar operas some of the best songs are more orchestral than vocal in character. [15] Towards the end this became true to such an extent that some of the late music, including *The Grand Duke* (1896), actually benefits from being heard in purely orchestral form.

One of the major obstructions to appreciating Sullivan as an artist in sound lies in the piano scores of his works. Sullivan himself made no use of the piano when composing because, as he said, that would limit his ear for the effect he desired. In the theatre the singers were handed simple melodic lines, while the répétiteur either vamped an accompaniment or played from a figured bass. Sullivan in the meantime carried in his head the true sonority of the accompaniment, only transferring it to paper when the time came to prepare the full orchestral score. The piano vocal scores which were sold in the shops were, and are, misleading reductions by another hand of Sullivan's full scores. Often greatly simplified, they give a very inadequate idea of what is heard in performance. In the case of a familiar work like *Iolanthe* no great harm may be done, because the nature of the orchestral accompaniment is known. Where the work is unfamiliar the piano score generally offers a very unreliable guide to its quality. A case in point is the magnificent orchestral opening of *The Martyr of Antioch*, which appears from the piano score to be thoroughly banal. This being so, it is safe to say that no work of Sullivan should be judged from the piano score. Having been conceived as sound it must be heard as sound; nothing else will do.

As a corollary to his objectivity, his sensitivity to stimuli and his love of sound as such, Sullivan showed little capacity to grasp what one might call the literary side of music, that is, in broad terms, the intellectual climate created by romanticism. The poet William Allingham, who met him in 1863, remarked that he thought Faust the best of all operatic subjects, but had 'no ideas outside music'.[16] This remark is wholly true. Sullivan met most of the distinguished people of his time, but nowhere is it recorded of him that the relationship extended to an exchange of ideas. Rachel Scott Russell, his early fiancée, laboured in vain to turn him into an intellectual, marking the difference between them by herself preparing the first English translation of the Memoirs of Berlioz.

Whether a bluestocking wife would have turned Sullivan into a literary musician after the pattern of Berlioz may be doubted. Intellectual culture is by no means necessary to a musician, but in the particular case of Sullivan a purely musical sensibility did have one literary drawback. The musical relationships between the various movements of his works are all beautifully calculated for pace and contrast, but he seems neither to have known nor cared whether the corresponding texts made up a coherent whole in the literary sense. The characteristic form of his works is a series of tableaux (Berlioz!) illustrating a story rather than a developing drama whose end is drawn out of the beginning by conflict between the characters. In this connection an anecdote related by Joseph Bennett, the librettist of *The Golden Legend*, is illuminating:[17]

> I now come to a work in which Sullivan and myself were associated. I mean of course the *Golden Legend*. The first letter received from him relating to this subject has unhappily disappeared from my collection and gone I know not whither. But I recollect that a copy of Longfellow's poems came with it.... There was ample proof of much searching in the volume itself, which opened as though instinctively at the poem and was adorned with many pencil marks on many pages. Sullivan begged me to come to his relief in the making of a 'book', saying he felt the task, so far as he was concerned, was hopeless. It appeared to me, on going carefully through the marked passages, that Sullivan had selected incidents and scenes admirably adapted for musical effect, but having, in many cases, no relationship to one another. Of course a

libretto could not be constructed in that way, and I determined, without hesitation, to take the story of Prince Henry and Elsie out of the mass of matter in the poem and deal with it alone.

It is apparent from Bennett's remarks that Sullivan could perceive the musical potential of a text but could not, evidently, organise disparate scenes into a consistent whole. This can hardly be considered a musical weakness as such, but it is apparent that a composer who lacks the power of literary organisation must either write symphonies or be dependent on a librettist for a dramatically sound job. Moreover, such a composer will not be able to mend matters if he is given a broken-backed libretto. In Gilbert, Sullivan was fortunate enough to find a librettist with a natural sense of form, but elsewhere, and even with Gilbert, he acquiesced in seemingly obvious structural deficiencies. *Ivanhoe* is conceived from the outset without internal form, and so is *The Light of the World*, except that it begins with the Nativity and ends with the Resurrection. Among the Savoy operas *The Chieftain*, *Haddon Hall*, *Ruddigore* and *Utopia Limited* all suffer from structural weaknesses which the composer presumably could not correct. Part of his problem lay in his habit of leaving the libretto to the librettist; sometimes, as with *The Yeomen of the Guard*, he discovered difficulties only after rehearsals had begun.

Egotistical men—Gilbert will do as an example—are not normally blessed with a sense of humour. The reason is simple enough: humour first pricks then deflates the exaggerated pretensions and emotions with which the self-centred mind sustains its *folie de grandeur*. Once one has seen the funny side of romanticism there is no going back. Sullivan's sense of humour effectively disqualified him from sharing in the intellectualised high seriousness of romanticism even if his other-directedness did not. His contemporaries speak of him—and his brother—as 'brimful of humour'; this quality is a marked characteristic of his letters, and is fully expressed in his music. It is humour from which sardonic or unkind elements are completely missing; in their place is something Edmund Burke summed up in his phrase 'the unbought grace of life'. If the world is a vale of soul-making, then we may properly ask what is the spiritual end product at which the process aims. The goal of the romantic agony cannot be agony; it must, in some sense, be reconciliation and peace. Sullivan had no understanding of such things, but he did, by nature, possess the qualities of lightness of heart and emancipation of spirit which we may suppose to lie at the journey's end of more sophisticated travellers. These are the characteristics for which he was loved by his contemporaries as a man, and by his public as an artist. As Colin Wilson has pointed out, [18] the music of Sullivan seems to say that the world is a good place after all, in which lightness of heart—the aristocratic virtue—is the one to count. In the same context we may note that the energy of Sullivan had nothing of the frenetic in it, no sense of dark forces lurking beneath the surface; it is pure and natural, like a spring at source. Here too lies a major reason for the affection in which he is held, and for the ability of his work to give constantly renewed pleasure through the countless thousands of performances it has received. We may tire rapidly of the Gilbertian mechanisms, but energy—Sullivan's energy—is eternal delight.

As we have seen, Sullivan's association with the aristocracy enabled him to participate in the latter stages of the great eighteenth-century civilisation of the country house. The virtues of eighteenth-century art—restraint, grace, harmony, proportion, dignity, delicacy—are notably to the fore in his work, just as he adopted an eighteenth-century attitude to the artist's social role. Even in the most unbuttoned moments of the comic operas an aesthetic decorum is preserved; outside them decorum was sometimes carried beyond the call of duty, but sometimes, equally, it blossomed into something one can only call nobility. A good example is the stately aria 'When thou tookest upon thee to deliver man' in the *Festival Te Deum* (1872); another is 'The night is calm' in *The Golden Legend* (1886). More familiarly one might cite the overture to *The Yeomen of the Guard* as an example of power harnessed by deliberate restraints. Even such an apparently insouciant tune as 'Prithee pretty maiden' (*Patience*) was described by Chaliapin as 'noble', thus implicitly giving recognition to the values within which Sullivan worked.

French music preserved the aesthetic of the eighteenth century much longer than did that of Germany. It is not surprising therefore to find that Sullivan's main stylistic affinities lay with the French school as represented by Gounod, Massenet, Bizet, Delibes, Thomas, and Offenbach. Sullivan's music can sound very like that of Bizet, another composer who—consciously this time—abandoned inner-direction in favour of response to outside stimulus. The early influence of Mendelssohn tended by its very nature to turn Sullivan away from *Sturm und Drang* towards Sweetness and Light. The upshot is that Sullivan's music in all its aspects represents civilisation as against the disruptive forces of the power-seeking ego of romanticism. Bernard Shaw quite rightly pointed out that the supposedly antagonistic Saxons and Normans of *Ivanhoe* are 'eminently gentle-manly'. In his eyes, and perhaps in those of many other people, that would be sufficient to damn them. Sullivan, however, thought differently.

We have seen that Sullivan had no trace of the intellectual about him. His literary tastes, so far as we have them, were straightforward and unremarkable, running to such authors as Anthony Trollope (a personal friend) and Anthony Hope. In one respect, however, he had a definite predilection—he shared to the full the Victorian view of history. In our own day history has become little more than a branch of sociology, the deeds of kings having yielded pride of place to the revolts of peasants. To the Victorians, by contrast, it was a branch of literature; the historian's first task was to tell the exciting tale of the heroes and heroines whose battles had led up to the constitutional glories and domestic felicities of the nineteenth century.[19] The inspiration of the movement was Sir Walter Scott, whose romantic historical novels combined exciting storytelling with seeming accuracy of historical detail. The result was the creation of a colourful pageant-world known generically as 'Merrie England'—a source of ideas to writers, artists, and musicians alike. To celebrate this world was also an act of patriotism, a declaration of belief in England and all that went to make it.[20]

Victoria and Merrie England, 1897
Scene 3 - The May Pole Dance

Sullivan was an enthusiastic subscriber to history and patriotism as thus described. Insofar as his work has a detectable leading theme, that theme was historical romance. He first essayed it in 1864 with his cantata *Kenilworth*, an imaginary version of the masque presented by the Earl of Leicester to Queen Elizabeth at Kenilworth Castle in 1575. The same spirit, which was by no means foreign to Shakespeare himself, animated much of the Victorian production of Shakespeare; Sullivan kept in touch with it by writing his various suites of incidental music to Shakespeare's plays: *The Merchant of Venice* (1871); *The Merry Wives of Windsor* (1874); *Henry VIII* (1877); *Macbeth* (1888). As his reputation and ambition grew he conceived the idea that he should write a work which would become a classic of patriotism, an embodiment of the essence of Englishness. It seemed to him, as to most Victorians, quite natural that such a work should be cast in historical/romantic mould, and he spent much energy in the last years of his life attempting to write it.

The first step was taken when Gilbert offered him *The Yeomen of the Guard* (1888), but D'Oyly Carte's Royal English Opera House seemed to hold out the best chance of writing the national masterpiece. The choice of *Ivanhoe* was therefore no whim; Walter Scott was the fountainhead of historical romance, and the Norman dominance of Saxon England was one of the foundations of the national story. Following the disappearance of Carte's grand opera house Sullivan continued to work in the same vein with *Haddon Hall* (1892), a romantic tale of elopement set in the days of Charles II. In 1895 he associated himself with the great national hero King Arthur by writing incidental music for Comyns Carr's play of that name, and in 1897 he supplied the music for a 'Grand National' ballet, *Victoria and Merrie England*, which implicitly equates Queen Victoria with Good Queen Bess, so drawing the Elizabethan and Victorian ages together. Finally, he commissioned Comyns Carr to turn his *King Arthur* play into an operatic libretto which he did not live to set. Another Arthurian subject, *Guinevere*, came to nothing twice: once in 1868, and again in 1870 when Lord Tennyson failed to respond to Sullivan's request for a libretto.

It is most unfortunate for Sullivan's continuing reputation that the historical romance which must have seemed to him a part of the natural order of things has been so completely repudiated in the twentieth century. The change could not possibly have been predicted, but it has deprived a considerable part of Sullivan's output of the fundamental audience sympathy without which no music can be appreciated. If one includes also *The Golden Legend* and *The Beauty Stone*, both of which have a medieval setting, the loss becomes even more substantial. Already, less than a century after his death, some of his works require the same kind of historical understanding that one brings to, say, Purcell's *King Arthur* or the operas of Handel.

If we now list, as for Gilbert, the separate components of Sullivan's musical personality we obtain something along the following lines:

1) Outstanding natural ability.
2) Unromantic objectivity of approach.
3) Sensitivity of response to external stimuli, especially words.

4) Depth and variety of resource.
5) Power of rhythmic and melodic invention.
6) Fertile aural imagination.
7) Non-intellectualism.
8) Small power of literary construction.
9) Sense of humour; lightness of touch.
10) Energy.
11) Adherence to civilised values and restraints.
12) Adherence to historical romanticism.

Taken together, these qualities manifestly render Sullivan unfit for the role of composer-hero, either as a symphonic thinker or as a musical dramatist in the sense one applies the term to Verdi in *Otello*. One might with as much sagacity expect Herrick to be Milton or Fragonard to be Rembrandt. And yet this really stupid error has been, and is, constantly made in the judgement of Sullivan. He is known to have harboured ambitions beyond the Savoy, as was his privilege. The works he produced as a result of those ambitions have invariably been judged—and necessarily found wanting—by the very highest standards known from the Germanic composers. These standards are real; but they are not the only standards, or we should all end like the conductor Klemperer, who seasoned his reading of Goethe only with a little Shakespeare. Very little of the music performed or broadcast in the course of a week conforms to the highest standards. For the most part it is good or very good, and is accepted as such on its own terms. Whether one likes or dislikes a merely good work depends on the extent to which one's own temperament or values find an echo in those of the composer. The point was put by Bernard Shaw in his review of Stanford's *Irish* Symphony:[21]

> If you try to form a critical scheme of the development of English poetry from Pope to Walt Whitman, you cannot by any stretch of ingenuity make a place in it for Thomas Moore, who is accordingly either ignored in such schemes or else contemptuously dismissed as a flowery trifler. In the same way you cannot get Meyerbeer into the Wagnerian scheme except as the Autolycus of the piece. But this proves nothing except that criticism cannot give an absolutely true and just account of any artist: it can at best explain its point of view and then describe the artist from that point of view. You have only to shift yourself an inch to the right or left of my own point of view to find this column full of grotesque exaggerations and distortions; and if you read the musical papers you will sometimes find some *naif* doing this, and verdantly assuming that *his* point of view commands the absolute truth and that I am the father of lies.

Autolycus was not a Mastersinger but a snapper-up of unconsidered trifles. Sullivan, by the same token, was not Beethoven, but that need not mean that his music was not as beautiful as the songs of Autolycus. If we stand an inch to the right or left of Beethoven or Wagner it is possible that we may find among the 'unconsidered trifles' of Sullivan's art something pleasurable, albeit not 'great' in the full romantic sense. English music critics, including those who have made a study of Sullivan, have almost to a man failed to perceive that his music may have merits as well as defects, that the twelve gifts which illuminate the comic operas may have found expression even in those works which have been described as 'the worst music ever written'. Among recent writers only Henry Raynor has appraised Sullivan's qualities for what they were rather than for what they were not:[22]

> What Sullivan wrote is never portentous and never inflated; it is beautifully scored, with instruments used neatly and idiomatically, closer to the style of Sterndale Bennett than to the unrelieved seriousness of Sullivan's immediate contemporaries. Generally speaking, it is conservative in harmony and in the symmetry of its construction. Whether or not it was a major contribution to the repertoire (in the sense that a composer after Beethoven had, to prove his worth, to wrestle with his fate, defying a hostile destiny) it is hard to say. What Sullivan wrote is skilful, inventive, stylish and natural; he was a craftsman who knew how to do what he found necessary. If his society imposed upon him tasks not necessary or natural to his gifts, the fault cannot be laid at his door.

Sullivan regarded himself, and was regarded by his contemporaries, not simply as the author of comic operas but as an all-round composer, capable of doing anything he wished. Is it possible, therefore, that he may after all have merit outside his collaboration with Gilbert?

To some extent this question has been answered by events. Certain works by Sullivan have never disappeared from view. These include the overtures *Di Ballo* and *In Memoriam*, *Onward Christian Soldiers*, *The Lost Chord* and *Orpheus With His Lute*. A recorded performance of the *Irish* Symphony, conducted by Sir Charles Groves, has brought this work out of obscurity and established it as a regular part of the broadcast repertory of the BBC. Much the same has happened with the suites to *The Tempest* and *The Merchant of Venice*, and will happen with that to *The Merry Wives of Windsor* when it is recorded. *The Zoo* (1875), a one-act operetta, has recently come to life and is now in regular amateur performance all over the world.

The large-scale choral works are a more difficult matter. To perform any of them properly is an expensive and elaborate undertaking. Moreover there is no natural audience for such works as there was in Sullivan's time. Individual oratorios like *The Dream of Gerontius* compel performance by their majesty, but there is no longer an oratorio tradition *per se*. This being so the most suitable modern home for works like *The Golden Legend* or *The Martyr of Antioch* is the gramophone record.

As an embodiment of the Sullivanesque *The Martyr of Antioch* has much to recommend it. This work should be regarded as the musical equivalent of one of Lord Leighton's or Edward Poynter's neoclassical paintings. Poynter (1836-1919) gave expression to a humanly credible—though Victorian—vision of the classical golden age.[23] The pagan maidens of Sullivan's work share this vision in music of infinite grace and charm, whose nearest equivalent in the Savoy operas is 'Comes a train of little ladies' (*The Mikado*). The opening chorus, a Hymn to Apollo, is surely one of the fine things in English music. Taking twenty minutes to perform, it moves with effortless ease and resource through a range of bright sonorities until it culminates in a tremendous appeal to the god to manifest himself. A later pagan chorus, 'Io Paean', is boisterous beyond anything Sullivan thought suitable for the prim stage of the Savoy. Only the Christians do not come off so well, showing by their music that Sullivan, like Milton, was of the Devil's party without knowing it. However the Christian heroine, St Margaret, dies in a truly ecstatic aria which sweeps her up to heaven in a state of vision far beyond the pains of the fire in which she is supposed to be burning.

As an accompaniment to his neoclassical style Sullivan had an exotic or oriental style which is also the musical counterpart of a contemprary movement in the visual arts. This style first found expression in a stirring Bacchanal in *The Prodigal Son* (1869), 'Let us eat and drink.' It is continued in a Moresque and a 'Chorus of Muslim Triumph,' 'Alla'hu akbar', in the cantata *On Shore And Sea* (1871), which tells a tale of conflict between Moors and Christians. Though the reader may not believe it, the Savoy operas are tame stuff by comparison with some of the music Sullivan put into his supposedly inanimate choral works. His final fling in orientalism came with *The Rose of Persia* (1899).

The Golden Legend is perhaps less likely to appeal to modern taste than is *The Martyr of Antioch*. It is more sophisticated as sheer sound, but the text does not entirely permit Sullivan's emancipation from Victorian values. The noisy Prologue is the least convincing part of the work, mainly because the bells of Strasbourg Cathedral do not struggle musically with the agents of Lucifer who are trying to tear them down from the spire. However, when it is a question of depicting the effects of alcohol Sullivan responds with a superb evocation of the swimming head and faltering senses of the hero, Prince Henry. Comic opera is not neglected in the third scene, wherein Lucifer mocks a band of pious pilgrims. The general effect—with the addition of a riot of brass sound—is not unlike that of 'When the foeman bares his steel' in *The Pirates of Penzance*. The sixth scene commences with an evocative tone-picture of wedding bells ringing out over the valleys of the Rhine; the love duet which follows is Sullivan's most beautiful achievement in this kind. At length all ends with a vast fugue, beginning with a 'big tune' of the kind that ends the finales of the comic operas, but more dignified and grandiose. *The Golden Legend* was regarded as a masterpiece by every contemporary judge. The best way to approach it in our own time is that of George Grove:[24]

> As to Sullivan I don't care for *Ivanhoe*—but I do like the *Golden Legend*. I have heard it 6 or 7 times and every time I like it better. Take it as it is meant to be and don't compare it with Bach or Beethoven or Schubert and it is *lovely*—the duet always makes me weep, and so does the point of imitation where the chorus comes in 'the night is calm'.

Of the choral works with religious texts the most immediately viable is the *Festival Te Deum* of 1872. Written to celebrate the recovery of the Prince of Wales from typhoid, this work serves exactly the same sort of purpose as Purcell's Odes and Welcome Songs. Extremely buoyant, it would make a popular item for the last night of the Proms. Apart from the Bacchanal, *The Prodigal Son* is notable for a stark canon, 'They went astray in the Wilderness,' a joyful bass aria, 'For this my son', and a finely scored tenor aria, 'How many hired servants', which survived for many years as a concert item.

The Light of the World (1873) is a sprawling work of forty-two numbers, which can rarely have been performed at full length. Sullivan's Christianity was of the most summary Anglican kind; his natural sympathies lay with sun worshippers and those who eat and drink. Theology meant nothing to him, and for this reason the theological parts of *The Light of the World* are musically dead. However, where human emotion is involved the music often becomes effective. In particular Sullivan expressed the loneliness which sometimes appears in his diaries in two moving passages - 'In Rama was there a voice heard' (as bleak and comfortless as Purcell's Funeral Sentences), and 'Lord, why hidest thou thy face?', a soprano aria preceded by an exquisite tone picture of the Garden of Gethsemane in the cold dawn light. There is an entertaining children's chorus, 'Hosanna to the Son of David', and a charming *Andante Pastorale* for the shepherds keeping watch over their flocks by night.

It would be foolish to claim that Sullivan's choral works do not have weaknesses or moments of failed inspiration. On the other hand these weaknesses do not amount to some unique private crime but are common to all Victorian artists. If he had been a member of a group of young musicians, comparable to the Pre-Raphaelite Brotherhood, his art might be better understood today. As it is it makes sense to see him as the equivalent in music of one of the successful Victorian painters. His music has been rubbished as Victorian painting has been rubbished - but we have seen Leighton's *Flaming June* (1895) rescued from a Battersea junk shop to become one of the most prized of British pictures. Sullivan loved beauty of sound as much as any aesthete loved beauty of colour. Inasmuch as he tended to work in the brighter shades, and to evade dramatic issues, he may fittingly be compared to one of the Pre-Raphaelites, who today are so much appreciated.

We may now turn once again to the subject with which we began, that of greatness and the ego. Sullivan was unqualified to achieve greatness as we have learned to accept it from romantic sources. There is however another greatness, familiar in religious language in the phrase 'He that humbleth himself shall be exalted' (Luke 14:11), or again 'He that findeth his life shall lose it' (Matthew 10:39). What this means in the artistic sense is that fullness of being is achieved only when the boundaries of the ego—apparently protective but actually damaging—are broken down in order to admit all that the world contains as part of experience:[25]

> To *experience* - and only thus to *understand* - both Nature and Human Nature: it is possible only by unique *empathy*; by somehow *joining, identifying with them* in all their forms. For *only this course* will effectually turn on the full power of creative imagination, produce something of what we find supremely in Shakespeare.
> But in the process to import or impose *one's self*—whether in opinion,

preference, or judgement, as almost everyone cannot help doing—is at once to pull the switch, cut the mysterious current off. The *genius* vanishes; the man remains. *Self* or *identity* makes him no more than poetical.

With these words of Dr Leslie Hotson the characteristics of Sullivan come into a new focus. One realises that his artistic nature, so far from indicating weakness, was the expression of a marvellous strength. His self-effacement, his sensitivity to stimuli, his open-mindedness, his many-sidedness, indicate that he belonged psychologically to the finest of all artistic types - that of Shakespeare:[26]

> He [Shakespeare] was just like any other man, but that he was like all other men. He was the least of an egotist that it was possible to be. He was nothing in himself; but he was all that others were, or that they could become. He not only had in himself the germs of every faculty and feeling, but he could follow them by anticipation, intuitively, into all their conceivable ramifications, through every change of fortune, or conflict of passion, or turn of thought.

This description of Shakespeare's mind by Hazlitt was taken up by Keats, who condensed it into his concept of 'negative capability'. Negative capability. The phrase sums up Sullivan's apparent passivity and dependence, while revealing them as the key to his multiple powers. 'A poet is the most unpoetical of any thing in existence,' wrote Keats, 'because he has no Identity.' So too was Sullivan the non-intellctual musician all the more musical for his lack of a powerful self; and yet, paradoxically, he remained himself through all his many changes. When, in *Ivanhoe*, he finally bowed to convention and made a grand gesture of self-assertion the result was not fully successful because the gesture itself represented a departure from his true nature.

The full Shakespearean myriad-mindedness was of course denied to Sullivan as it is denied to us all. Sullivan had no Iago in him, no King Lear. In addition his entry into the Chapel Royal may be regarded as the most grievous blow ever suffered by English music, for it tainted him with the spiritual bankruptcy of Victorian Anglicanism. He would have done better to enter a circus. On the other hand he possessed, as no other native artist—except perhaps Benjamin Britten—has possessed, the ingrained humility which has been described as Shakespeare's greatest endowment.[27] Contemporary testimony to this quality in him is universal, coming even from its greatest beneficiary, W.S. Gilbert:[28]

> . . .a composer of the rarest genius, and who, because he was a composer of the rarest genius, was as modest and unassuming as a neophyte should be, but seldom is.

Through humility, genius. Sullivan had no knowledge of himself. He lived for the moment, and died perhaps in despair of immortality. By all conventional standards he was an insubstantial figure, but is it absolutely certain that the admired egotists of the nineteenth century were wiser or more profound than this man who had nothing whatever to say? If Mr David Holbrook is to be believed, the neurosis of Mahler holds the key to the salvation of the European soul.[29] Let us hope so. But it may also be that the humility of Sullivan might make an even more fruitful starting point for the diagnosis—and cure—of the sickness of contemporary civilisation and art.

8: *The Creative Conflict*

It is commonplace to describe the Gilbert and Sullivan operas as unique, meaning that in them the sphere-born harmonious sisters, voice and verse, meet on something like equal terms. Too often, however, the partnership is treated in isolation, as though it had nothing in common with other collaborations between composer and librettist. In fact the achievements—and disagreements—of the two men form part of the wider history of opera, in which the balance of power between words and music has not always remained the same. The subject is too large to be treated fully here, but it may be worth glancing at operatic history in order to see Gilbert and Sullivan in perspective.

The origins of opera lie in Florence during the years in which the sixteenth century turned into the seventeenth. As part of their admiration for ancient Greece the *virtuosi* of the Florentine Camerata attempted to revive the Greek method of performing plays. It was known that Greek plays were sung or declaimed, and the Florentines attempted to give a truly antique flavour to their own pastoral plays by having them set to declamatory music.[1] From the first these plays were regarded as poetic texts with additional music; Monteverdi introduced a degree of dramatic characterisation, but opera soon settled down to what it was to be throughout the seventeenth century—a highly elaborate concoction of stage spectacle, machinery, costume and elevated language, with music serving to integrate the whole. The dominant force was the poet, who arranged the effects, and had the satisfaction of seeing his work in print; the music remained in manuscript, and the composer—if he was mentioned in the libretto at all—yielded precedence to the stage machinist.

The pattern thus laid down maintained itself for most of the eighteenth century, changing slowly as the composer began to come to the fore. This process might have taken place more rapidly but for the extraordinary success of the poet

Metatasio (1698-1782) whose libretti dominated *opera seria* almost to the extinc-
tion of the composers. Some of his works were set by over twenty different
composers, and sometimes the same composer would set a libretto several times
over. Metatasio was enough of a musician to be able to set his own words, and he
was quite capable of sending instructions to his composer on how to carry out his
intended characterisations through the orchestra.[2] In England the continental
concept of opera was mocked by John Gay in *The Beggars Opera* (1728). This
ballad opera, in which the lyrics are written to existing tunes, established the
only operatic form which has ever been throroughly at home in *Das Land ohne
Musik*.

The reform of opera commenced by Gluck (in collaboration with his
librettist Calzabigi) involved replacing the artificialities of *opera seria* with
something more human, and more direct. Gluck did not, however, abandon the
traditional relationship between words and music, 'I have striven to restrict
music to its true office of serving poetry by means of expression and by following
the situations of the story....'[3]

It was in fact only with the advent of Mozart that the literary dominance of
the libretto was broken. In 1781 Mozart wrote that 'in an opera the poetry must
be altogether the obedient daughter of the music.'[4] He spent his adult life
searching for a librettist able to meet his demands, and at length found one in
Lorenzo da Ponte, who was not so much a poet as an adaptor.[5] From this time
forward the operatic libretto came to be seen increasingly as an adaptation for
musical purposes of some already-existing work or plot.

In part the new-found dominance of music was due to the increased power of
the orchestra, which during the course of the nineteenth century became more
and more capable of noisy and violent effects. Singers expanded their voices to
match, thus ending any possibility that music might serve poetry in opera. The
effect may be seen in the career of the librettist Eugene Scribe (1791-1861), who
functioned as a planner and organiser of theatrical effects rather than as a writer.
Scribe readily collaborated with other men, and regularly, in his work with
Auber, wrote words to existing music. In general terms, this is the relationship
between librettist and composer that the modern operagoer takes for granted.

The final apotheosis of the composer as dramatist arrived with Wagner, who
became his own librettist, thereby eliminating any possibility of rival claims
between words and music. Almost as dominant was Verdi, who supervised his
libretti in detail, insisting that the librettist should provide him with strong
words and red-hot situations, together with a degree of credible characterisation.
Verdi sometimes even suggested the words he wanted to set; so did Puccini. Yet
even the most dominant composer cannot write an opera without a libretto. And,
except with Wagner, this libretto must be supplied by a librettist, who must in
turn be capable of doing his job:[6]

> The fatal temptation is to assume that the omnipotent composer is therefore
> omniscient, the librettist but a utilitarian appendage employed to crank the
> composer's ideas into some sort of serviceable verse. We accept this as the
> lesson of the Verdi-Ghislanozi *Aida*: we tend to infer beyond. As we shall

see, even Verdi had distinct limitations as a dramatic librettist.

This belief in the omniscience of the composer, which may be termed the Pathetic Fallacy of Opera, is perhaps the most consistent mistake of those who write about opera. It consists in ascribing to the music qualities that can be found only in the libretto or qualities that cannot empirically be traced to the composer. It is rife for two reasons: because it is easier to write 'Verdi' than to check which one of his librettists the comment applies to, and because we have known very little about librettists and a good deal about composers.

The librettist therefore cannot be considered merely a word-smith stringing out lines of mellifluous verse: he is at once a dramatist, a creator of word, verse, situation, scene, and character, and—this is of vital importance— an artist who, by dint of his professional training as a poet and/or dramatist, can often visualise the work *as a totality* more accurately than the composer. This totality includes not only the 'story' but also the means by which that story will be most effectively presented on stage both organizationally and scenically.

Thus Patrick Smith, the historian of the libretto. If the librettist is important in grand opera, a form in which the music claims dominance, it is hardly surprising if he is also important in comic opera, a form in which it would be artistically impermissable for the composer to sweep the board. Gilbert is certainly one of the finest of all librettists, but his position *vis à vis* Sullivan is no more than a special instance of a general trend. Most surviving operas are written to good or at least serviceable libretti. If Sullivan hit upon a librettist of genius this does not mean that Gilbert was functionally unique. All opera is struck out of the tensions of words, stage situation, and music. In operetta also one tends to write 'Offenbach' for 'Meilhac and Halévy', 'Bizet' (*Carmen*) for 'Meilhac and Halévy', or 'Strauss' (*Die Fledermaus*) for 'Genée and Haffner—after Meilhac and Halévy'. If enthusiasts have sometimes written 'Gilbert' for 'Sullivan', that is perhaps no more than a *quid pro quo*.

As we have seen, Gilbert was exposed to opera from an early age, probably earlier than Sullivan. Throughout his life he took the conventional musical view that in grand opera the position of the librettist is humble or subordinate. By the same token he had rather fixed ideas about the proper function of music in a comedy. These ideas were derived from his work in burlesque and pantomime, wherein the music consisted of detached songs interpolated from time to time in a spoken text. The function of these songs was to entertain, naturally, but the music was not required to do more than add to the prevailing levity. The mere fact that the music in burlesque was not original but culled from any popular source gave the writer a free hand to do with it as he liked.

When he came to collaborate with composers in the theatre, Gilbert adhered to the simple comedy-with-songs formula. Even *Ages Ago* (music by Frederic Clay), which is the most sophisticated of his works of this type, is undeveloped by later standards. Nor can there be any doubt that left to himself Gilbert would have persisted in the same vein throughout his career. It follows that the development he underwent was due to the challenge of writing for Sullivan. In 1871, when the collaboration began, Sullivan was well established as a young genius, albeit one unfit to marry into a middle class family. He was therefore in a position of independent power with regard to Gilbert, able to treat his own substantial contribution to any work as a matter of course. Neither man looked on *Thespis* as the summit of his ambitions, but the effect of Sullivan's presence can already be detected in a first act finale which provides a short scene of continuous music. This finale also exhibits a Gilbertian weakness which was to recur; it consists not of a development of the story but of a succession of characters who simply step up and sing about themselves. Even so the little work may be regarded as Gilbert's first move on the way to the Savoy libretti.

If there was artistic tension between Gilbert and Sullivan in the early years of their collaboration the evidence for it has not survived. The text of *Trial by Jury* was not written for Sullivan but for Carl Rosa, whose only venture into composition this would have been; no doubt the existence of Rosa's opera company determined the thorough-composed form. It may be worth remarking, by the way, how little experience in comic opera Sullivan brought to this masterpiece. *Cox and Box* (1866) was written in great haste, which probably means ten days or a fortnight; *The Contrabandista* (1867) was written, composed and rehearsed in the space of sixteen days.[7] *Thespis*, described by Gilbert as 'a hasty bit of work', cannot have taken much longer. The conclusion must be that Sullivan wrote *Trial by Jury* with something like six weeks' work in comic opera behind him. It has remained ever since a model of his precision, variety, and economy of touch.

With the success of *Trial by Jury* Sullivan and Gilbert no doubt began to sense the possibilities of the future. As Gilbert's speech quoted on page 23 shows, they must have sat down together to reach mutual agreement on what form their next work should take. It is at this point that Sullivan's unrecorded contribution to the finished result becomes apparent, for *The Sorcerer* is by no means another of Gilbert's comic plays with divertive songs.

On his side Gilbert began to gather together a company of talented but inexperienced performers to whom it would be possible for him to dictate the reforms in acting and production methods he wished to introduce. Sullivan acquiesced in this, but obtained in return a *libretto*, that is a dramatic work intended for musical setting. The librettistic nature of the *Sorcerer* text is to be seen in the lengthy and eventful finale to the first act, the use of recitative, and the presence of self-contained musical scenes, like that in the first act which culminates in the signing of the marriage contract. It was the practice in British operas of the nineteenth century to write songs which could translate easily to the home and concert hall; true to this tradition, the tenor songs in *The Sorcerer* are aimed sweet and low at the ballad market. Sullivan looked on the success of *The Sorcerer* as a blow struck at French operetta; this being so, the decision to make an opera out of Gilbert's story *An Elixir of Love* may well have been clinched by the possibility of an English setting. Gilbert will have been pleased by the transformations and magic, Sullivan by the English country mansion in the background.

In *H.M.S. Pinafore* the balance between words and music is much what it is in *The Sorcerer*, except that Gilbert now boasts a fuller command of his own style—the style in which everything he had previously written is consummated and consumed. However it is in connection with this work that we first find evidence of the antagonisms between Gilbert and Sullivan that were to end disastrously in the carpet quarrel. It will be remembered that in October 1879 Gilbert and Sullivan sailed to America in order to produce the authentic version of *H.M.S. Pinafore* and introduce *The Pirates of Penzance* on Broadway. For the only time in their lives they found themselves regularly in each other's company. *Bab* did not like what he then discovered:[8]

> Their association in America had been highly successful but not always harmonious. Gilbert, more than a little nettled by the immense popularity of the *Pinafore* music, which he heard praised wherever he went while only the silliest of his own words were quoted, could not help displaying the superiority of wit to tunes in public; and when the partners were being entertained he was inclined to make a butt of Sullivan. No doubt he believed that his fun was good-natured, but the pointed way in which he expressed it pained the more sensitive nature of the composer, who confided in Fred Clay that Gilbert's jokes never failed to get a laugh at his expense.

By the time *H.M.S. Pinafore* was produced in America *The Pirates of Penzance* was already substantially written. In this work, therefore, Gilbert was not in a position to obtain artistic revenge on Sullivan. He must certainly have desired to do so, for he desired—and generally obtained—revenge on anyone who thwarted him in any way. His intention must have been reinforced by the full and vigorous nature of the *Pirates* music, which often threatens to break out into opera on a Verdian scale. Whether he recognised it or not, Gilbert had been hoist with his own petard, for he himself had supplied the mock-melodramatic situations and manly men (pirates and policemen) that Sullivan had characterised in such appropriate music.

Those who wish to attribute the nature of the next opera, *Patience*, to accident are of course free to do so. It *may* be coincidence that in this work the forward stride of the music—apparent in the progression from *The Sorcerer* to *The Pirates*—is halted: on the other hand we have seen *Bab* involved in such coincidences before. Whatever the truth of the matter the music of *Patience* is not as dominant as that of the previous opera. Apart from the extended first act finale the music is confined almost entirely to individual 'set piece' numbers, and is not given the chance to carry the action forward. Besides this, the 'pallid and thin' aesthetic background drew from the chamelion Sullivan the appropriate musical expression. Burlesque Verdi would have been quite unsuitable for a chorus of love-sick maidens.

As he was soon to show Sullivan was not unaware of the nature of the libretti he was setting. Since *Patience* is as it is he must at least have acquiesced in it, even if he did not approve. Why then did he permit such things to happen? Why is there a popular (albeit mistaken) impression to the effect that the Savoy libretti simply represent Gilbert's *fiat*?

The answer to this question lies in both the weaknesses and in the strengths of Sullivan's nature as man and artist. At the most superficial level he saw that his work with Gilbert enabled him to pay himself for those expensive tastes which in the case of Wagner were paid for by other people. Since his way of life depended on theatrical success he had strong reasons for keeping to any formula which proved profitable. Besides this, he was an easy going man with a great capacity for failing to take offence, even under provocation. On the artistic level he seems to have drawn the logical conclusion of his own shortcomings in dramatic literature: since he could not perform the task himself, it was better to leave libretto-writing to someone who knew what he was about. In the last resort he shared Gilbert's view of comic opera in one vital respect; he thought the words should be heard, and judged it artistically necessary to sacrifice musical ambition to this end. No one, not Gilbert nor Sullivan nor the Victorian critics, thought of comic opera as an elevated art form. If conscience pricked, therefore, the composer could console himself with the thought of higher things.

But behind such rationalisations lay Sullivan the man of Shakespearean humility. To have attempted to impose conditions on Gilbert would have been a violation of the very principles on which his genius operated. One might put it another way by calling him an unwitting Hindu, taking as his principle 'Thou art That'; to endeavour to define 'That' in advance is to pervert the whole basis of one's position. Sullivan cannot consciously have thought like this, but he must have been aware of his own powers, which were sufficient to enable him to do anything he chose. At the deepest artistic level it was a matter of indifference to him what Gilbert wrote, for he knew he would be equal to it. He could therefore afford to wait, remembering all the while his right to reject anything he found really unusable. If on the other hand—and here's the rub—Gilbert failed seriously in his task, there was little Sullivan, from his position, could do about it.

For his part Gilbert seems to have taken for granted Sullivan's ability to set anything, whether musically conceived or not—it is not entirely clear whether he knew the difference. On the other hand the freedom granted by Sullivan's waiting approach did, in practice, place a great strain on Gilbert, especially after a series of triumphs had raised public expectations. Gilbert took pride in describing his works as 'original', meaning not copied or adapted from an outside source. At the same time his creative scope was narrow, being circumscribed by the infantile and mechanical foundation of his personality. From this base he was required to supply a composer whose strength lay in variety, who could, as the proverb has it, give a musical realisation of a teaspoon standing in a cup—provided someone asked him to do it. The inherent tendency of the partnership was therefore to exhaust Gilbert while leaving Sullivan fresh. As Bernard Shaw put it, Gilbert 'got worked out very desperately,' while Sullivan 'was as good at the end as at the beginning.'[9]

For the time being there was no difficulty as *Iolanthe* followed *Patience* at the Savoy. *Iolanthe* is arguably the finest of the Savoy operas, for in it Gilbert reaches the most sophisticated development of his own essential character as *Bab*, while Sullivan, the inexhaustible, transforms the penny-plain puppets of Gilbert's imagination into the twopenny-coloured exotics we experience in the theatre. It is Sullivan, not Gilbert, who makes the fairies fairy-like, and the Peers noble; it is Sullivan who gives the pastoral quality to Phyllis and Strephon and the sturdiness to Private Willis. [10] This is as it should be; the ability to provide stimulus to a composer—painfully arrived at, and perhaps not deliberate—is what marks out Gilbert as a *librettist*, and not simply as a comic writer.

As we contemplate the skill of the *Iolanthe* libretto it is hard to see how Gilbert could possibly have matched it again in his next work; everything he had previously done is done here to perfection, leaving no room for further advance. Gilbert himself evidently found the problem insoluble, for he treated it by regressing to his own earlier play, *The Princess*. Nothing actually obliged Gilbert to spin his libretti out of his own bowels; he could, for instance, have offered Sullivan a libretto based on *The Three Musketeers*, or even *The Three Bears*; but ego forced him to be 'original', even at the cost of being repetitious and somewhat stale.

The original *Princess* play of 1870 conformed to Gilbert's regular prescription in having a few interpolated comic songs, one employing the tune of 'Largo al factotum'. Not having been conceived in operatic terms, it did not translate into an entirely satisfactory libretto. In particular the chorus has no dynamic function, either within the plot or as a means of creating dramatic tension between opposing groups of men and women. Prince Hilarion invades Castle Adamant with two companions, not with the chorus of retainers who would have set up an opposition to the girl graduates. When the men *do* arrive the action is almost over. As a result Sullivan was denied the chance to build up dramatic *scenas* and even, at the exiting moment when the Princess falls in the river, found himself writing an elementary *melodrame* to accompany speech when a full choral treatment was self-evidently called for. Gilbert, it seems, wished to preserve his graceless joke about Princess Ida's back hair.

The character of Princess Ida herself gives evidence of failure by Gilbert and Sullivan to agree on a common purpose. As depicted in her songs the Princess has humanity and dignity—even pathos. Her spoken lines, by contrast, are unregenerated burlesque, intended to demean her and her aspirations. Gilbert was unlikely to have given the Princess a dignified character of his own accord; probably therefore the nature of her sung words is due to pressure from Sullivan for the opportunity to write music of emotional substance; for the rest, Gilbert simply let the spoken text stand unaltered.

By an agreement of 8 February 1883 Gilbert and Sullivan had bound themselves for five years to supply Richard D'Oyly Carte with a new opera on receipt of six months' notice. This agreement had been signed in the first flush of the success of *Iolanthe*, and before Gilbert had seen fit to offer the composer resurrection pie in the shape of *Princess Ida*. Sullivan had expressed the wish to write a substantial opera even before *Iolanthe*. Now, on 29 January 1884, little more than three weeks after the production of *Princess Ida* (5 January) he began to set in motion the chain of arguments and events that ended in *Ivanhoe* and the Carpet Quarrel. What one might call the parameters of the argument were determined by the personalities of the men. Strauss and Hofmannsthal *discussed* their differences as intellectuals; Gilbert and Sullivan *argued* because neither was an intellectual and because Gilbert was not by nature an accommodating man.

Nevertheless the positions taken on both sides go to the heart of the collaboration between author and composer in opera, and reveal Gilbert and Sullivan at their most interesting.

Sullivan made his announcement of 29 January straight to Carte, telling him of a decision already made to write no further operas for the Savoy. [11] Carte responded on 22 March by formally invoking the agreement of 1883 by which the composer was committed to providing a new work, whereupon Sullivan flatly refused to do so. Carte communicated the news to Gilbert, who wrote on 30 March expressing his 'unbounded surprise'. In spite of his surprise Gilbert must have known well what lay in the wind, for he immediately began to defend himself against a charge Sullivan had not openly made, [12] 'In all the pieces we have written together I have invariably subordinated my views to your own. You have often expiated to me, and to others, on the thorough good feeling with which we have worked together for so many years'.

Sullivan's reply cannot have been born of a moment's irritation for it expresses his artistic credo, while revealing just how accurately Gilbert had diagnosed his complaint: [13]

> I will be quite frank. With *Princess Ida* I have come to the end of my tether—the end of my capability in that class of piece. My tunes are in danger of becoming mere repetitions of my former pieces, my concerted movements are getting to possess a strong family likeness and I have rung all the changes possible in the way of variety of rhythm. It has hitherto been word-setting, I might almost say syllable-setting, for I have looked upon the words as being of such importance that I have been continually keeping down the music in order that not one should be lost.
>
> And this very suppression is most difficult, most fatiguing, and I may say most disheartening, for the music is never allowed to rise and speak for itself. I want a chance for the music to act in its own proper sphere—to intensify the emotional element not only of the words but of the situation.
>
> I should like to set a story of human interest and probability, where the humorous words would come in a humorous (not serious) situation, and where, if the situation were a serious or tender or dramatic one, the words would be of a similar character. There would then be a feeling of reality about it which would give a fresh interest in writing, and fresh vitality to our joint work.

As used by Sullivan the term *word-setting* meant, in effect, the principle of setting one syllable to one note in order to preserve the clarity of the diction; it was a special technique with him, to be distinguished from his practice outside comic opera where the vocal line paid less attention to the need for audibility. What Sullivan meant by 'keeping down the music' may be gauged by comparing, say, the sonorous Moorish exoticism of the cantata *On Shore And Sea* (1871) with the deft but subordinate accompaniment to Ko-Ko's 'Little list' song in *The Mikado*. Sullivan makes it clear that subordination was a matter of deliberate artistic choice arising, as we have seen, from the very centre of his nature as an artist in sympathetic imagination. For too long this gift of the spirit has been interpreted in a negative sense as dependence or inferiority. Sullivan himself evidently failed to understand his most priceless possession, presumably because he had been schooled from his youth up in the romantic idea of ego-greatness. The desire to set a story of human interest speaks for itself. Sullivan regarded Wagner's *Mastersingers* as the greatest comic opera ever written, partly no doubt because of the humanity of the characters. He cannot have expected or desired such a libretto from Gilbert, but nevertheless *The Mastersingers* shows the direction in which his mind was turned. Given the range of his creative powers it cannot be called an illegitimate one.

The same applies to his wish for the music 'to act in its own proper sphere.' The request is not for musical dominance but for the opportunity to do more of the things music can do outside the range of the comic song. Once again there is nothing unwarrantable here; one might cite the incident in which Princess Ida falls from the bridge as an example of the way in which Gilbert was beginning to fail in his elementary responsibilities towards the musical dramaturgy.

Gilbert's response to so much musical reason is a characteristic piece of bluster encapsulating the whole man:[14]

> Your reflections on the character of the libretti with which I have supplied you have caused me considerable pain. However, I cannot suppose that you have intended to gall and wound me, when you wrote as you did. I must assume that your letter was written hurriedly.
>
> When you tell me that your desire is that I shall write a libretto in which the humorous words will come in a humorous situation, and in which a tender or dramatic situation will be treated tenderly and dramatically, you teach me the ABC of my profession. It is inconceivable that any sane author should ever write otherwise than as you propose I should write in future.

Sullivan was perhaps the only person whose independent existence Gilbert ever acknowledged. If a theatre critic had written what Sullivan had written *Bab* would have raged and threatened legal action. As it was the wounded sensitivity could find—as yet—no refuge in its usual defences. Sullivan could not be shouted at or sued or cut dead: he had to be faced. The second part of Gilbert's reply, assuming it is not mere cant, reveals that lack of self-knowledge which is necessary to success in art or indeed in any walk of life. If taken literally it would prove him insane, for no writer was ever more adept at treating tender and dramatic situations humorously. Examples are well-nigh superfluous, but one might cite the words of the chorus as Ralph Rackstraw is led off in irons in *H.M.S Pinafore*. In real life this would inded be a serious situation, but Gilbert turns it to burlesque:[15]

> He'll hear no tone
>   Of the maiden he loves so well!
> No telephone
>   Communicates with his cell!

Faced with his legal obligation to write a new work for the Savoy Sullivan now turned his attack to a different direction. He wished Gilbert to provide a libretto in a new style—essentially a comic opera in the normal sense, without Gilbert's characteristic twists and inversions. In particular he objected to the libretto Gilbert had already begun to sketch. This was the Lozenge Plot, familiar in its final form as *The Mountebanks*. We have seen how, at least in the final version, Gilbert had reduced his initial idea to pure mechanism. Sullivan seems to have perceived this quality from the outset, besides remarking on its similarity to *The Sorcerer*, then little more than six years old. Politely, but firmly, he refused to have anything to do with it.

Gilbert's response was a letter which deserves to be quoted as an expression of the rigid categories within which his mind worked. Finding both compromise and comprehension of Sullivan's position impossible, he proposed simply to withdraw:[16]

> What do you say to this - provided that Carte consents. Write your opera to another man's *libretto*. I will willingly retire for one turn. It may well be that you are cramped by setting so many *libretti* of the same author, and that a new man with a new style will start a new train of musical ideas. I suggest this because I am absolutely at a loss to know what it is you want from me. You will understand how faintly I grasp your meaning when I tell you that your objections to my *libretto* really seem arbitrary and capricious. That they are nothing of the kind I am well persuaded—but, for all that, I can't fathom them.

In a sense Gilbert's proposal is both generous and reasonable; one wishes Sullivan had acceded to it, if only to find out what sort of opera he would then have written. On the other hand consideration of Gilbert's stated reasons for retiring leads us straight to the centre of his extraordinary personality. Sullivan had expressed a wish to set a story of 'human interest and probability'. One would expect any man of letters to understand at once what was meant. Not so Gilbert. To him Sullivan's position was arbitrary and capricious and unfathomable. The words are as fantastic as anything Gilbert ever put on stage; and yet they come naturally from little *Bab*, the five-year-old who had reduced the whole human race to clockwork dummies.

Following the receipt of this letter Sullivan met first Carte (12 April) then Gilbert (15 April) in an attempt to find a solution to the problem. At the meeting of 15th Gilbert, fighting for the lozenge, proposed incongruously to *add* a 'very serious and tender' interest to the charm, while keeping both elements distinct.[17] Sullivan promised to look at this hybrid, but rejected it on 2 May. In the meantime Gilbert had begun to construct the libretto in the belief that he had won the day. Faced with Sullivan's latest rejection he began to produce arguments that would hold water only in his own Fairyland. Reduced to its essentials the argument was that because Sullivan was bound by contract to write an opera, and because he set the lyrics to music but not the plot, he therefore had no right to reject whatever plot Gilbert chose to present; the alternative would be to suppose Gilbert legally bound to carry on supplying plots until he found one to suit the composer.[18] It is a neat stroke of logic, once again symptomatic of the unreality of Gilbert's outlook. Sullivan was not deceived:[19]

> All that you say in reference to the respective positions of author and
> composer, and the positions which they individually and jointly hold, I
> cordially agree with, and I should be humiliated and grieved if anything in
> my words or manner had ever indicated that I claimed to see your librettos
> 'on approval'. This constitutes a striking difference between us and other
> writers. Another composer would concern himself with all those things....
> That you are responsible for the plot is indisputable, but you cannot blame
> me if my interest extends even to that for which I am not directly respons-
> ible.

The explosion from Gilbert which might have been expected to follow such
resistance did not appear. Instead he went away and on 8 May proposed the new
plot we know as *The Mikado*. Sullivan met him halfway:[20]

> If, as I understand you to propose, you will construct a plot without the
> supernatural and impromptu elements, and on the lines which you describe,
> I gladly undertake to set it without further discussing the matter, or asking
> what the subject is to be.

On the face of it, the about-turn by which Gilbert rescued the partnership is
most untypical. One would have expected him to hold his ground with greater
and greater tenacity until the moment came to sue Sullivan for breach of contract.
Yet the change is consistent with his psychology, and might have been invaluable
to Sullivan had he felt disposed to take advantage of it. The preposterous and
blustering front with which Gilbert faced the world protected his 'real' self, the
pallid masochist who had died of a broken heart. In standing up for himself
Sullivan pierced the Gilbertian armoury and won his way through to the soft
centre. In that moment Gilbert the masterful stood mastered; he was probably
capable of *enjoying* the situation; but Sullivan had no taste for dominance, even if
he had understood its use.

Artistically speaking Sullivan's victory had important consequences. Left to
himself Gilbert would undoubtedly have entered a wholly mechanical and bizarre
universe, peopled by marionettes and fuelled by lozenges. It did not lie in his
power to respond fully to the composer's desire for a human libretto, but Sullivan
nevertheless kept him from becoming too much like himself. It took a convulsion
to produce *The Mikado*, but who, given the choice, would exchange it for *The
Mountebanks*?

The Mikado itself was written without friction. Sullivan suggested musical
improvements which Gilbert accepted, and Gilbert suggested that the three
verses of 'I am so proud' might be set to different tunes—an idea accepted by
Sullivan *con fuoco*. *Ruddigore* too seems to have been written in amity, but it is a
relatively poor work on Gilbert's part. As a burlesque of melodrama it had the
potential to be a second *Pirates of Penzance* but Gilbert—deliberately perhaps—
failed to provide the requisite situations. Sullivan, preoccupied with the success
of *The Golden Legend*, may have lowered his guard. Though 'highly

accomplished', as Arthur Jacobs has it, and itself the sole reason for the survival of the work on stage, the score of *Ruddigore* is only a shadow of what it might have been. It represents a waste of Sullivan's powers just as they were at their height.

Before the writing of *Ruddigore* Gilbert had suggested an opera based on Dr Frankenstein and his monster, the idea being to extract fun out of the humiliations of Frankenstein at the hands of his brainchild.[21] After *Ruddigore* he again proposed the lozenge plot (charm and clockwork) and again Sullivan rejected it:[22]

> At night (4 September 1887) Gilbert read me a scenario for proposed new piece. Clear, but I think very weak dramatically; there seems no 'go' in it. The 1st Act promises to lead to something, but that something doesn't appear in the 2nd Act which is the old story over again of whimsical fancies and subtle argument, but it is a 'puppet-show', and not human. It is impossible to feel any sympathy with a single person. I don't see my way to setting it in its present form.

The potential for another impasse is clearly present in this entry from Sullivan's diary, but Gilbert spontaneously abandoned the lozenge in favour of the historical romantic subject now known as *The Yeomen of the Guard*. A surviving letter shows him in accommodating mood, offering to rewrite in all sorts of ways to help the composer. On his side Sullivan seems to have been unusually ready to come forward with objections—whereupon Gilbert's mood changed. Rehearsals had already begun when Sullivan found several places in the second act 'where the musical requirements had not been fully met.'[23] He wanted the act reconstructed, and wrote Gilbert a 'snorter' of a letter to say so. Gilbert snorted in reply, but changes agreeable to both parties were apparently made.[24] A disagreement over one song, 'Is life a boon?', raised issues of principle which require a certain amount of discussion here.[25]

> Is life a boon?
>   If so,it must befall
>   That Death, when'er he call,
> Must call too soon.
>   Though fourscore years he give,
>   Yet one would pray to live
> Another moon!
>   What kind of plaint have I,
>   Who perish in July?
>   I might have had to die,
> Perchance in June!

Sullivan made a total of three settings of this lyric, two of which were rejected by Gilbert. Of the first he said 'I know nothing about music, but it seems to me the wrong tune for an Elizabethan lyric'; on the second occasion he said nothing, but puckered his brow and puffed out his cheeks. Sullivan declined to make another setting, but eventually gave in after having been 'irritated beyond bearing' by Gilbert. The familiar setting was made three days before the opening of the opera.[26]

The nature of the first rejected setting is not known, but the second survives. It is expansive in treatment, making generous use of repetition and distorting the thread of the argument. Gilbert's reasons for disliking it require very little explanation—Sullivan had destroyed the author's carefully constructed word pattern in favour of purely musical expression. When he came to make the familiar setting he avoided any such practice, making the music a simple, and possibly contemptuous, run-through of the lyric.

In this incident we see encapsulated the tensions within the Gilbert and Sullivan partnership. Who is right, the author who wants the audience to hear every every syllable of his argument, or the composer, who wishes his music to 'intensify the emotional element' of that argument? Sullivan gave way because he believed that in the particular kind of opera he was writing with Gilbert the words probably should be heard. Equally the incident must have reinforced his desire to write an opera where such sacrifices would not be necessary.

For his part Gilbert deserves something close to artistic censure for having written a greedy and selfish lyric. The words have a certain (doubtful) merit as a contribution to the Elizabethan style, but such a closely developed verbal argument has no place in the operatic context. Sullivan no doubt recognised this when in his second setting he decided to ignore it; the third setting recognises the demand inherent in the lyric for closely matching musical articulation. The point is that Gilbert, by the very nature of his words, has denied to his collaborator the legitimate means of expression. In reviewing *Haddon Hall* in 1892 Bernard Shaw said much the same thing:[27]

> ... Mr Gilbert, whose great fault was that he began and ended with himself, and gave no really congenial opportunities to the management and the composer. He exploited their unrivalled *savoir faire* to his head's content; but he starved their genius, possibly because he did not give them credit for possessing any.

If the Gilbert and Sullivan operas have a consistent artistic weakness it lies precisely in those areas where—in any other opera or operetta—one would expect the musician to be expansive, and where one finds instead a lyric of argument or narrative whose words must be heard. Continental hearers of the operas are puzzled by this effect, especially as the purpose of Sullivan's respectful treatment is lost in translation. In the comic or patter songs the words are, of course, at the centre of attention; but to Gilbert *all* songs were patter songs to be respected. A revealing incident is narrated by the tenor Durward Lely, who played the part of Nanki-Poo in the original performances of *The Mikado*. Gilbert, whose face is said to have worn a savage expression whenever the music was played without his words, had been listening to Lely's performance:[28]

> 'Very good, Lely, very good indeed,' said Gilbert at a rehearsal; 'But I have just come down from the back seat in the gallery, and there were one or two words which failed to reach me quite distinctly. Sullivan's music is, of course, very beautiful, and I heard every note without difficulty, but I think my words are not altogether without merit, and ought also to be heard

without undue effort. Please pay particular attention to the consonants, the Ms, the Ns, and especially the Ss'.

To judge from the reference to Ms and Ns Lely appears to have been singing 'A wandering minstrel I' from the first act of *The Mikado*. Gilbert's request to him for close attention to the consonants has the effect of making singing more difficult. The M sound is made with closed lips, stopping the air stream altogether, while S is a fricative sound, essentially unmusical. In other words, this incident represents a minor skirmish in a major war.

During the prime years of the 1880s Sullivan was generally able to make bricks without straw when confronted by a musically ungrateful lyric; a fine example of success is 'Our great Mikado, virtuous man' (*The Mikado*), a conspicuous example of failure 'Come, mighty Must' (*Princess Ida*). 'Fair moon to thee I sing' (*H.M.S Pinafore*) is rendered musically impotent by Gilbert's introduction of narrative into what should be a serenade.

As it happens *The Yeomen of the Guard* contains the best known example of a lyric whose difficulty proved musically fruitful. This was 'I have a song to sing, O!', the expanding form of which baffled Sullivan until Gilbert himself hummed the traditional tune he had used in constructing it. There is a world of difference between this essentially musical lyric, and the self-gratifying literary artifice of 'Is life a boon?'.

Both Gilbert and Sullivan considered *The Yeomen of the Guard* their finest work. In theory, therefore, it should have been possible for them to continue in the same vein; in practice Sullivan's determination to avoid another 'Is life a boon?' had taken a firm hold. On 9 January 1889 he enlisted the aid of the telephone:[29]

> Called, Carte, then Gilbert. Explained to latter my views as to future, viz. that I wanted to do some dramatic work on a larger musical scale, and that of course I should like to do it with him if he would, but that the music must occupy a more important position than in our other pieces—that I wished to get rid of the *strongly marked rhythm* and *rhymed* couplets, and have words that would give a chance of developing musical *effects*. Also that I wanted a voice in the *Musical constructions* of the libretto. He seemed quite to assent to all this.

On 20 February Gilbert replied in what is perhaps the most purely reasonable letter of his life. He said he could understand Sullivan's wish to do something substantial. But whereas in 1884 he had expressed himself willing to be involved in such a project, he now said he must necessarily be 'swamped in the composer'. Any writer, he suggested, could provide a suitable libretto for such a purpose. In particular he put forward the name of Julian Sturgis (1848-1904), the librettist of Goring Thomas's Russian opera *Nadeshda* (1885) and the eventual librettist not only of *Ivanhoe* but of Stanford's *Much Ado About Nothing* (1901). Why could not Sullivan write his grand opera while continuing to work at the Savoy? He, Gilbert, would not be taken seriously even if he were to co-operate.

Gilbert certainly overestimated the ease with which any hack writer can produce a good operatic libretto, but the position taken here is by no means unjustified or ungenerous. If Sullivan had not been legally bound to write comic operas for five years from 1883 it might have been acted on earlier, and the history of Gilbert and Sullivan would have been very different. Those five years, however, had left indelible marks on the composer:[30]

> I have lost the liking for writing comic opera, and entertain very grave doubts as to my power of doing it. You yourself have reproached me directly and indirectly with the seriousness of my music, fitted more for the Cathedral than the Comic Opera stage, and I cannot but feel that in very many cases the reproach is just. I have lost the necessary nerve for it, and it is not too much to say that it is distasteful to me. The types used over and over again (unavoidable in such a company as ours), the Grossmith part, the middle-aged woman with fading charms, cannot again be clothed with music by me. Nor can I again write to any wildly impossible plot in which there is not some human interest. ... You say that in serious opera, *you* must more or less sacrifice yourself. I say this is just what I have been doing in all our joint pieces, and, what is more, must continue to do in Comic Opera to make it successful. Business and syllabic setting assume an importance which, however much they fetter me, cannot be overlooked. I am bound, in the interest of the piece, to give way. Hence the reason of my wishing to do a work where the music is to be the first consideration—where words are to suggest music, not govern it, and where music will intensify and emphasize the emotional effect of the words.

Gilbert now cast aside any sympathy he may have felt or assumed for Sullivan's position. The familiar reflexes of *Bab* were set in motion, and the composer learned in straight terms how matters stood (19 March):[31]

> If you really are under the astounding impression that you have been effacing yourself during the last twelve years—and if you are in earnest when you say you wish to write an opera with me in which 'the music shall be the first consideration' (by which I understand an opera in which the libretto, and consequently the librettist, must occupy a subordinate place) there is most certainly no 'modus vivendi' to be found that shall be satisfactory to both of us.

At this point Sullivan withdrew from the full rigour of his position—it was, after all, no light thing to lose the income from comic opera. Tacitly admitting the possibility of a future collaboration, he began to complain about the harmful effects on the music of Gilbert's repetitious rehearsals (his position was weak here, for he avoided all routine rehearsals). He then demanded a voice 'in the laying out of the *musical situation*', meaning the right to insist on changes at a late stage in preparation. A letter to this effect was sent to Carte on 26 March from Venice, drawing his reply from Gilbert on 31st, in London:[32]

> You say that our operas are Gilbert's pieces with music added by you, and that Carte can hardly wonder that 12 years of this has a little tired you. I say that when you deliberately assert that for 12 years you, incomparably the greatest English musician of the age - a man who can deal *en prince* with operatic managers, singers, music publishers and musical societies - when

you, who hold this unrivalled position, deliberately state that you have submitted silently and uncomplainingly for 12 years to be extinguished, ignored, set aside, rebuffed, and generally effaced by your librettist, you grievously reflect not upon him, but upon yourself and the noble art of which you are so eminent a professor.

The fine rhetorical flourish of this passage does nothing whatever to conceal the bogus nature of its content. Sullivan's nature laid him open to high-handed treatment, but Gilbert was, after all, the man who once asked Mrs D'Oyly Carte for a certificate of sanity:[33]

> I know how terribly busy you are, but if you will spare me an hour on Monday or Tuesday (when the trial will probably come on) to say that you have known me personally in business for 16 or 18 years—that . . . during that time you have had many opportunities of forming an opinion of my characteristics, and that you have seen nothing in me to suggest that I am a man in whom vanity and egotism have degenerated into a disease—that I do not desire (as far as you know) to dominate the universe—and that I am not in the habit of abusing and insulting the actors who play in the pieces, I shall be greatly indebted to you.

True justice in all the quarrels of Gilbert and Sullivan may lie more in the department of the Recording Angel than in that of the student of their relationship. The only unambiguous element in it was the desire of both men for money. Perhaps therefore it was lucre rather than light which now began to dissolve the animosities. Sullivan agreed to write a new work for the Savoy in addition to his ambitious opera, and Gilbert agreed to pay more attention to musical needs. On 8 May Sullivan proposed that Gilbert should develop a Venetian subject previously mentioned, thus calling into being *The Gondoliers*. Gilbert responded by spontaneously offering the long *durchkomponiert* introductory scene of the opera. His mechanisms are less in evidence than usual, so much so that the work sometimes seems like a glance in the direction of musical comedy (which did not then exist). In short, after years of struggle, *Bab* became a model collaborator insofar as it lay in him to do so.

Given the success of *The Gondoliers* and the slowly increasing effect of his pressure, Sullivan might eventually have got a thorough-composed libretto from Gilbert if *Ivanhoe* had not cast its shadow over their working relationship. As it was Gilbert's pyrrhic victory in the Carpet Quarrel and the embarrassing collapse of the Royal English Opera left Sullivan (and Carte) in a weakened position. In particular, Sullivan could neither claim an unsatisfied ambition nor threaten to achieve it. Unscathed by his colleagues' difficulties, Gilbert must have thought himself a very just man. His libretti of the 90s show increasing self indulgence, unaccompanied, now, by striking imaginative power.

Work on *Utopia Limited* proceeded on a friendly footing at first, with each man visiting the other at home, and generally trying to be helpful. As we have seen (page 97) Sullivan objected to Gilbert's proposed antic treatment of Lady Sophy, and Gilbert eventually made her sedate enough. We need not regret the loss of her frenzied love scene, though Sullivan hardly supported his own case when he provided for her music as feeble as he ever wrote. An interesting alteration to the text of the second act love duet, 'Words of love too loudly spoken', is recorded by John Wolfson. As it stands in the libretto today, this duet is 'straight', without irony or inversion. However Gilbert originally wished to deflate the sentiments by a descent into bathos; he was prevented from doing so by Sullivan who, we may imagine, pursued his customary line of argument in such matters. The original version of the four last lines runs as follows: [34]

'Tis a truth needs no refutal—
   Always whisper when you woo.
Sweet and low the ringdoves tootle;
   Sweetly let us tootle too.

At Sullivan's behest these lines became: [35]

Whisper sweetly, whisper slowly,
   Hour by hour and day by day;
Sweet and low as accents holy
   Are the notes of lover's lay.

If more evidence survived, it is probable that the earlier operas would furnish similar instances of Sullivan's 'straightening' effect on the lyrics. In general the treatment of love in the lyrics of the operas is Sullivanesque rather than Gilbertian. The archetypal Gilbertian lover is Princess Toto, who forgot the names of both her husbands and went off to live with the Red Indians (whose tomahawks, to her disgust, proved to be made in Birmingham). Outside his work with Sullivan Gilbert rarely treated love except in this amusing fashion. At the Savoy he wrote for the composer, but, because the lyrics do not express his true ironical bent, they are formal affairs, employing for the most part the conventions of the contemporary drawing room. 'None shall part us' (*Iolanthe*) is the most charming of them, but even here the antitheses come to life only through the music. It is *Iolanthe*, too, which contains the most obviously intrusive moment of sentiment in the shape of the heroine's plea to the Lord Chancellor, 'He loves'. The operas are undoubtedly the richer for these concessions to Sullivan's taste, but in strictly Gilbertian terms they represent an improper breaking of the seamless web of irony.

Unhappily 'seamless' is not a term one can apply to the libretto of *Utopia Limited*. Even more than *Ruddigore* it is a mess of loose ends and missed opportunities. The source play, *The Happy Land*, entertainingly shows the effects on Fairyland when it is run by a Popular Government of English ministers. The following description of England—not actually written by W.S. Gilbert—burlesques a speech from *The Wicked World*:

SELENE: With all their wickedness, with all their sin,
         They have a great and ever-glorious gift
         That compensates for every ill. It's called
         A Popular Government, whose ministers,
         Chosen exclusively upon the score
         Of intellectual pre-eminence,
         Are posted to such offices as they
         By dint of long and arduous 'prenticeship,
         Have shown themselves to be most fitted for.

ZAYDA: Oh for an hour of such a government,
To set us all to rights! Why, after all,
Great Britain is the type of Fairyland!

When they come, the British reforms simply turn Fairyland grey, dedicated to the good, the beautiful and the cheap. Before long the Upper Ten have struck, the Peers are singing the Marseillaise, the country is invaded, revolution is at the gates, bankruptcy threatens, and the government has a majority of 120 against it.

Self-evidently, a straighforward operatic reworking of this plot would have provided everything we think of as characteristic of a Gilbertian satire. In *Utopia Limited* Gilbert simply lost control of his material. Utopia is thoroughly Anglicised even before the British arrive, and government by party is saved as a *deus ex machina* for the dénouement, whereas dramatically speaking it should have been used to provide a basic tension and conflict of interests throughout the play. The theme of political reform is in any case lost in the love-plot which we have already discussed (page 91).

Nor is the composer well served. The finale to the first act is a conspicuous example of Gilbert selfishly failing to perform even his elementary duty as a librettist. This finale consists of nothing but a succession of comic songs as each of the British Flowers of Progress steps forward to explain himself. Except for a tiny moment of rebellion at the end, the musician is given nothing to do but convey supposedly funny words with clarity. Compare the pace and variety of the *Iolanthe* finale, and the power of Sullivan's response to it! Gilbert called the *Utopia* finale the best Sullivan had done. From his own point of view this was not an error of judgement; for the first time in their collaboration he had placed the composer exactly where he thought he ought to be—in the position of a purveyor of tunes to a series of comic words.

Every operatic composer may be forgiven if he writes one weak work. In the case of Sullivan the work in question is undoubtedly *Utopia Limited*. A couple of movements of great brilliance, the 'minstrel' scene and the trio 'With wily brain', do not redeem a score which in general terms fails to impress. The second act chorus, 'Eagle high in cloudland soaring', is a particularly unhappy importation from Sullivan's oratorios, where the same *a capella* style is handled much more convincingly.[36] This chorus was interpolated into the already obtrusive Drawing Room scene solely to give the composer a 'chance'. Nothing could better illustrate the decline of the great partnership than this condescending offer of a 'chance' from the librettist—and the 'chance'-starved willingness of the musician to accept it.

Gilbert and Sullivan might have been wiser to allow their collaboration to end after *Utopia Limited*. Gilbert was now rapidly going to seed. Both his prose and his verse became extremely prolix, while undergoing a process of attenuation of content. Questions of self-indulgence apart, he was aged 60 at the time of the production of *The Grand Duke* (1896); one would not expect from him the fresh whimsies of his prime. Sullivan set the *Grand Duke* libretto without recorded complaint. It contains much he must have disliked, but he seems to have been past caring. Nevertheless, *The Grand Duke* is a more satisfactory work than *Utopia Limited*, partly because the finale to the first act is decently constructed for music.

If the libretto of *Utopia Limited* has detectable faults, that is because one can at least grasp what it might have been. *The Grand Duke* libretto has no faults in this sense because the quality of the ideas is too poor to be analysed. The basics from which it is built up - the playing card duel, the sausage roll, the ducal meanness - are lifeless things from which no growth was ever possible. Most of all the language of the lyrics has lost distinction:[37]

> Come, bumpers—aye, ever-so-many—
> And then, if you will, many more!
> This wine doesn't cost us a penny,
> Though it's Pomméry, Seventy-four!
> Old wine is a true panacea
> For every conceivable ill,
> When you cherish the soothing idea
> That somebody else pays the bill!
> Old wine is a pleasure that's hollow
> When at your own table you sit,
> For you're thinking each mouthful you swallow
> Has cost you a threepenny bit!

This lyric is apparently intended as a drinking song, which is by nature a celebration of the joys of the grape. Gilbert however has developed it into a celebration of miserliness, thus negating its purpose. It is a characteristic piece of perversity, which leaves the sensitive composer hamstrung. What is the appropriate music for a niggardly drinking song? Sullivan still had a magnificent drinking song in him, as *The Rose of Persia* was to show, but here he falls wretchedly into the pit dug by Gilbert's self-absorption.[38] Perhaps a third of the *Grand Duke* lyrics are of the same refractory type, and in all cases Sullivan has simply set them for what they are worth. As in *The Light of the World* so here, textual abstractions drew from him empty music.

On the other hand *The Grand Duke* also contains verse whose undeniable merit is that it does at least call for the kind of response music can provide. As an example one might cite Lisa's song from the second act:[39]

> Take care of him—he's much too good to live,
>   With him you must be very gentle:
> Poor fellow, he's so highly sensitive,
>   And O, so sentimental!
> Be sure you never let him sit up late
>   In chilly open air conversing—
> Poor darling, he's extremely delicate,
>   And wants a deal of nursing!

Ignoring the irony Sullivan seizes on the tenderness—a human emotion—of this lyric to make a beautiful, touching song. Elsewhere the French words and racy subject matter of the Roulette Song enabled him to make brilliant use of the *café-chantant* style, and the Greek procession at the beginning of the second act opened the way to a fine chorus in the 'neoclassical' manner familiar from *Patience*. As we have remarked, the first act finale contains a variety of incident and stimulus for the composer, who has responded with a skill born of long experience. In short, where it is not altogether denied life by the libretto Sullivan's contribution to *The Grand Duke* is very good indeed.

For many years *The Grand Duke* lay despised and rejected by all who knew, or rather did not know, it. However the arrival of a recording by the D'Oyly Carte Opera Company has stimulated stage performance and led to a reappraisal of the work as a whole. There is a moral here for any student of the artistic tug-of-war between Gilbert and Sullivan. Study of the libretto alone had caused the work to be written off as worthless. Only after a proper presentation of the music did the merits of the words become apparent.

There can be no doubt that Gilbert's gifts were brought to their finest potential at the Savoy. He is often said to have stimulated Sullivan, and this is true; but at a deeper level Gilbert was much more dependent on Sullivan than was Sullivan on Gilbert. As we have seen, Gilbert had the psychological make-up of an infant; he was rigid, mechanical and domineering; his work as a collaborator was basically selfish - why else should the composer have found it necessary to fight him? If he had a *twin* mind among musicians that twin was probably Offenbach, whose Olympia, the mechanical doll in *The Tales of Hoffmann*, is no discordant match for the clockwork Hamlet and Ophelia of *The Mountebanks*.

But a collaboration between Gilbert and Offenbach is unthinkable, for two such dominant men would have parted for ever long before the first rehearsal. If Sullivan had been like Offenbach we would never have discovered what Gilbert had in him. In every sense Gilbert's supposed dominance was dependent on Sullivan's qualities of forbearance, patience and tact, and on the fecundity of a musical imagination which could clothe difficult texts not merely with music, but with immortal music. In Freudian terms one might say that the life instincts in Sullivan overcame the death instincts in Gilbert. It is impossible to love Gilbert as he was, but millions of people think they love him because the love Sullivan always attracted to himself overflows abundantly into the operas as a whole. If, therefore, the dominance of the composer is the Pathetic Fallacy of opera, then the dominance of Gilbert is the Pathetic Fallacy of Savoy opera, the artistic unity of which is actually the composer's achievement.

In return for so much Gilbert offered Sullivan an artistic (and financial) escape route from the stifling atmosphere of the Victorian church and the Victorian home. Sullivan dwelt there not by nature but by the accident of birth and the necessity of earning a living. As all his works show, he blossomed whenever the requirements of his text carried him away from religion and domesticity. He was, however, not properly qualified to rescue himself unaided. By releasing Gilbert he made it possible for Gilbert to release him. Though not able to make all the demands Sullivan was capable of meeting, Gilbert did, nevertheless, strike out sufficient fire to have satisfied generations of audiences. The status of his own works as literary classics helps to raise the Savoy operas *as entities* well beyond the range of those continental operettas which tend to go under the name of the composer alone. Sullivan, it may be said, not only equalled or surpassed Offenbach or Strauss, but he did so while coping with the musically abnormal demands of a literary genius.

The suggestion that Sullivan was a more capaciously gifted artist than Gilbert has been made several times in this study. This view is not the private fancy of the present writer; it was the universal judgement of Sullivan's contemporaries, who were able to hear live performances of the full range of his works. We have seen that his struggle with Gilbert always centred round his desire for the proper musical expression of human emotions, and in this matter we may well account him justified. Very few operas are about anything but the emotional reactions of the characters to the situations in which they find themselves placed. At the same time Sullivan was certainly not capable, in the literary sense, of producing the work for which he craved. His problem therefore resolved itself into the one which confronts every operatic composer—how to find the right libretto. During the last ten years of his life Sullivan wrote six operas with librettists other than Gilbert. If he did indeed possess qualities other than those Gilbert brought out, the evidence should be audible in these six operas. *Ivanhoe* (1891) is the most ambitious as well as the earliest of them. What, in truth, is it all about? In the opinion of Sullivan's great contemporary, Sherlock Holmes, the truth of any case is the residue left when all other possibilities have been exhausted. By this token it may be easier to define *Ivanhoe* by what it is not rather than by what it is. During an interview given to the *San Francisco Chronicle* in July 1885 Sullivan set forth his views on existing schools of opera, and on the type of work he himself wished to write:[40]

> The opera of the future is a compromise. I have thought and worked and toiled and dreamt of it. Not the French school, with gaudy and tinsel tunes, its lambent lights and shades, its theatrical effects and clap-trap; not the Wagnerian school, with its sombreness and heavy ear-splitting airs, with its mysticism and unreal sentiment; not the Italian school, with its fantastic airs and *fioriture* and far-fetched effects. It is a compromise between these three - a sort of eclectic school, a selection of the merits of each one. I myself will attempt to produce a grand opera of this new school.
>
> Yes, it will be an historical work, and it is the dream of my life. I do not believe in operas based on gods and myths. That is the fault of the German school. It is metaphysical music - it is philosophy. What we want are plots that give rise to human emotions and human passions. Music should speak to the heart, and not to the head.

Not French, not Wagnerian, not Italian, *Ivanhoe* is what Sullivan was always careful to call a 'romantic' opera; one might add in qualification that for Sullivan the word *romantic* did not have superhuman connotations. It is a fully sung work, divided into three acts, each of three scenes. The libretto does not extract a dramatic plot from Scott's novel, but epitomises it in a succession of scenes, each depicting a different aspect of the story. In Sullivan's own time this procedure was valid enough, because almost every member of the audience would have been

Ivanhoe 1891
Act 3 Scene 3 - Death of the Templar
(*Illustrated Sporting and Dramatic News*, 14 February 1891)

familiar with the book. Today, when Scott's works are not nearly so well known, the absence of a coherently developed plot stands out as an obvious weakness.

Within its carefully delineated artistic aims the music of *Ivanhoe* shows all Sullivan's familiar charactersistics. One notes the beautiful inflections of the vocal lines, the variety of resource, the splendid orchestral writing. One also becomes aware that the pace, determined by the libretto, is too slow and cumbersome; there is a lack of emotional tension or incident, and of the dramatic clash of personality, even within the tableau form. Rebecca the Jewess is however a human character of the kind Sullivan sought in vain from Gilbert. Her prayer in the second act, 'Lord of our chosen race', is both deeply moving and exotic in its use of Jewish musical formulae. The powerful confrontation with the Templar which follows demonstrates the opera Sullivan might easily have written to a properly dramatic libretto. In the main, however, *Ivanhoe* is dominated by pageantry, and by the individual songs, of which Friar Tuck's 'Ho Jolly Jenkin' is still remembered; there is a beautiful song for Rowena, drenched in orchestral moonlight, 'O moon thou art clad', and the passionate 'Woo thou thy snowflake' for the Templar.

A fair summary of *Ivanhoe* is hard to make. It is not nearly as bad as its critics have pretended, but neither is it as good as the composer's admirers would hope. An overdue revival was seen in 1973, but, being amateur, was too poorly sung and played to mean very much. Unless public taste comes again to enjoy the historical romantic style, it is hard to see how the work could ever enter the repertory of a professional opera company. Under modern conditions its best home would certainly be the gramophone record, where its many fine aural qualities could be appreciated in and for themselves.

The collapse of D'Oyly Carte's opera house drove Sullivan back to the Savoy Theatre as his operatic outlet. Here the great stumbling block before him was the enormous power of the stereotype created by the operas written in collaboration with Gilbert. Already by the 1890s the Gilbert-and-Sullivan 'fans' had established their familiar tunnel vision. Their refusal to accept anything from Sullivan which was unlike Gilbert-and-Sullivan did much to determine the nature of the works the composer was to write for their approval, and has affected the reputation of these works to the present day.

In 1892 Sullivan knew nothing of the defeats in store. The Royal English Opera had gone, but hope had not gone with it. Sullivan hoped to use the Savoy tradition as the basis for the operas of human feeling he wished to write. For *Haddon Hall*, written with Sydney Grundy, he evidently made his wishes very clear. Grundy was invited to the composer's flat, where Sullivan expounded to him earnestly and at length his desire for humanity in the libretto, which was to deal with an historical event—the elopement of Dorothy Vernon of Haddon Hall with John Manners, son of the Duke of Rutland.[41]

The effect of Sullivan's lectures can be seen in many places in the *Haddon Hall* libretto though not, perhaps, in quite the manner Sullivan had in mind. The work is prefaced by a motto from *Hamlet*, 'To thine own self be true.' All the characters are, in their various modes, true to themselves. Thus Dorothy Vernon is true to her love in eloping; McCrankie, the comic Scot, begins as a strict Puritan, but ends by dancing a highland fling; the chorus of Puritans throw off Puritanism in order to fall in love. From time to time the characters tell us they are human beings, and the Puritans amongst them exhibit at least one human failing - a weakness for the bottle.

Very little critical acumen is required to perceive the faults of the *Haddon Hall* libretto; the comedy of the Puritans is weak, the elopement plot is clumsily and ineffectively handled, and the verse is not of Gilbertian standard. However, as we have seen, verse of Gilbertian standard is not necessarily an asset to an opera. Sullivan expressed himself well pleased with Grundy's words, and never ceased to assure the librettist what a pleasure they had been to set. It is fair to Grundy to quote the following, sung by Sir George Vernon during the second act finale; the verse gives expression to the romantic view of the past so dear to Sullivan, but it also deals in the human qualities of laughter and warmth, so foreign to Gilbert:

> In days of old when men were bold,
> And the prize of the brave the fair,
> We danced and sang till the rafters rang
> And laughter was everywhere!
> Our lives were lives of stress and storm,
> But through our veins the blood ran warm -
> We only laughed the more!
> For mirth was mirth
> And worth was worth
> In the grand old days of yore!

All in all Grundy deserves credit for having understood what the composer wanted from him, and supplying it. In particular he provided an extended finale to the second act which enabled Sullivan to write a long stretch of thorough-composed music. Whereas in *Ivanhoe* the pace is slow, in this finale events press forward through a great variety of moods, ranging from the graceful lightness of the so-called 'Elopement Quartet' and the drama of a storm to the comedy of the Puritans' 'We were hae'in' a wee drappie' and the radiant 'Vain is all life'. From first to last, as in the *Iolanthe* finale, Sullivan's touch does not falter. At the beginning of the opera—clearly at the composer's behest—we find a succession of lyrics dealing in human emotions, and at the end the glorious contralto song 'Queen of the garden'. Arthur Jacobs, whose praise is not won lightly, calls *Haddon Hall* 'a considerable achievement'.[42] Bernard Shaw, who was even harder to please, went further still, 'I contend that Savoy opera is a *genre* in itself; and that *Haddon Hall* is the highest and most consistent expression it has yet attained.'[43]

Shaw's description of *Haddon Hall* as the 'highest' embodiment of Savoy opera is an endorsement of Sullivan's desire to get away from the Gilbertian régime. Those who think Sullivan had no business to get away from Gilbert will find little to please them in the opera. The open-minded *listener*—a person whose cause Sullivan often pleaded—will find much to delight. The score is not pretentiously operatic, but it is infused throughout with a certain ripeness and richness of orchestral colour. Memorable phrases abound, and if there is an occasional lapse

Haddon Hall 1892
Act 2 Finale - The Elopement
(*Illustrated London News*, 1 October 1892)

from plenary inspiration the same is true of any opera, whether or not by Sullivan. *Haddon Hall* has not been performed professionally in the present century, but selections from the music were still being recorded 35 years after the original production. A modern recording of good quality would show why.

After a *succès d'estime* with *Haddon Hall* and half-a-failure with *Utopia Limited*, Sullivan's next opera, *The Chieftain* (1894), was a casual bit of work produced to satisfy Carte. A reworking of the *Contrabandista* of 1867, it makes no attempt to continue the composer's journey into the world of humanity and emotion. The librettist, F.C. Burnand, a long-serving editor of *Punch*, was a genial fellow, helplessly enslaved by the pun. He was jealous of Gilbert's success, but in preparing the *Chieftain* libretto took no trouble to excel himself. As a result both plot and dialogue reflect the easy-going nonsense he used to pour into *Punch*; the kindest thing one can say of them is that they are better than no plot and dialogue at all. The lyrics, however, are a different matter. They make no pretence to literary or dramatic quality; nor do they exhibit Gilbert's sewing-machine regularity. On the contrary, they are irregular almost to the point of randomness. Irregularity, however, is not a defect in the eyes of a musician, who often welcomes uneven lines as a stimulus. Burnand also possessed a natural tendency to employ a vocabulary of the kind to which music is responsive. To put the point in an elementary way, a composer can deal well with the idea of 'rushing water', but the idea of 'Latitudinarianism' lies almost outside the scope of music altogether. Burnand's lyrics abound in musically suggestive ideas as thus defined:

> *Jumping* on a steed, I *gallop'd*,
>   *Gallop'd* faster than the wind!
> How I *kick'd*, and *spurr'd*, and *wallop'd*,
>   What I suffered—never mind!

The words in italics are all suggestive of action and physical energy; they are concrete, and easily translated into musical terms. Compare this verse from *Utopia Limited*:[44]

> In towns I make improvements great,
> Which go to swell the County Rate -
> I dwelling houses sanitate,
>   And purify the Halls!

Abstract and intellectual, Gilbert's verse offers only sanitation to the musician. Which helps to explain why the music of *The Chieftain* is very good, whereas that of *Utopia Limited* is mediocre. Part of the quality of the *Chieftain* score stems from its place in the early days of Sullivan's career, when his mind was fresh and everything he did a new discovery. Most of the additional music is found in the second act, where the composer has taken advantage of the Spanish setting to write a vigorous brassy bolero to Spanish words—'La Criada' (The Chambermaid). In an earlier duet the English lovers reminisce in school French about their first meetings; here Sullivan produces a charming essay after the manner of Messager, whose *Mirette* preceded *The Chieftain* at the Savoy. A sparkling sestet, 'We quite understand', makes its effect by means of a feather-weight rhythm. Two short musical scenes illustrate once again Sullivan's ability to weave pace and variety into a consistent whole. In short, if the libretto were remotely stageworthy *The Chieftain* would be as pleasing a comic opera as one could wish. As it is, it shares with the prototypical *Contrabandista* the melancholy distinction of being the only opera by Sullivan to have shown no powers of survival.

After the disaster of *The Grand Duke* (1896), Sullivan put his next major effort into the Jubilee ballet *Victoria and Merrie England* (1897). When he returned to the Savoy it was to make a further attempt to write his humane opera in *The Beauty Stone* (1898). The plot and dialogue of the opera are the work of Arthur Pinero, while the basic idea and the lyrics came from Comyns Carr. Unfortunately the considerable merits of the libretto are masked by its surface characteristics. It is written throughout in that species of fake Olde Englysshe which everyone despises but which no one can replace. Both prose and verse are lengthy, leading the casual reader of the libretto to reject them altogether. In fact *The Beauty Stone* represents— at last—Sullivan's cherished libretto of human motivation and credible characterisation.

Briefly the story concerns a cripple girl, Laine, living with her weaver parents in the Flemish town of Mirlemont at the beginning of the fifteenth century. Laine prays to the Virgin for Love, but her prayer is answered by the Devil dressed as a friar. The Devil gives Laine the Beauty Stone, a gem which makes the wearer of it surpassingly beautiful. At the same time Philip Lord of Mirlemont organises a beauty contest in the town to amuse himself because he is bored with his exotic Cephalonian mistress, Saida. The transformed Laine wins the contest, whereupon Philip seeks to instal her in his palace (she has long loved him from afar). However Laine rejects him, flees the palace, and surrenders the stone to her decrepit father, who now becomes a handsome youth. He in turn attempts to woo the lovely Saida, but she is interested only in winning back the love of Philip. At length she wheedles the stone from him, and uses it to recover her youth for the benefit of Philip. However he has been to the wars and returns home blind. He cannot see Saida, whose efforts are wasted. She flings away the stone, and the Devil picks it up again. On the other hand Philip cannot see the ugliness of Laine. She lives in his memory as a beautiful woman, and marries him as a beautiful soul—this being a favourite idea of Comyns Carr, who believed that a man does not know true beauty until he becomes blind.

Several commentators have thought that the magic Beauty Stone was merely Gilbert's magic lozenge writ large, but this is not the case. As Doctor Johnson put it in connection with Shakespeare, 'The event which he represents will not happen, but, if it were possible, its effects would probably be such as he has assigned.'[45]

Gilbert's plots are not only impossible—most opera plots are impossible—the reactions of the people in them are also impossible. The Stone of Beauty is impossible, but if such a Devil's gift were to exist real people would react to it much as Pinero represents them as doing. Essentially the stone has a malign influence, bringing out the selfishness of the characters (except Laine). The Devil acts throughout as a sly *agent provocateur*, tempting both Laine's father Simon and Saida to do that which may win for him their souls. Whereas Sydney Grundy's characters *say* they are human, those of Pinero *behave* in accordance with human impulses. They react upon each other, and the events of the play are the outcome of these reactions. Philip, the Lord of Mirlemont, even has a certain complexity of character; having been a man of action, he has become a dreamer, neglectful of everything but pleasure. Saida, too, is a person. She is beginning to lose her physical attraction for Philip, but being in love with him is desperate to win him back for herself. Only Laine lacks complexity, though her motivation—longstanding love for Philip—makes her sympathetic enough. In other words, the *Beauty Stone* libretto offers the composer the kind of psychological motivation one finds in opera at large. Though it contains individual songs it is constructed so far as the lyrical parts are concerned in substantial scenes, thereby allowing Sullivan to develop his ideas at length.

And what of Sullivan's response? As we have seen, he complained of the wordiness of the text, but in practice he triumphed over it, perhaps stimulated by the very difficulty of the task. A character named Guntran of Beaugrant is allotted stirring sentiments which do not quite stir; everyone else comes to life in music of great beauty, superbly written for orchestra. The great achievement of the opera is the characater of Saida, whose exotic nature is first established through a sensuous waltz. She is developed in a lengthy *scena* in the second act, 'Though she should dance till dawn of day.' Here she dances forlornly before Philip, hoping to recapture his attention, recalling at the same time her youth in the Greek island of Cephalonia where she first saw him. The music of this scene has a strong claim to be considered Sullivan's finest single operatic composition. The neat song-capsules of the Gilbert operas have given way with effortless ease to a rhapsodical form in which unfaltering inspiration goes hand in hand with mature orchestral mastery. The predominant emotion is nostalgia, but its expression is tinged throughout by awareness of Saida's eastern origin, and that of her servant-girls who have become exiled with her in the north. Just as it is Rebecca the Jewess who comes to life most fully in *Ivanhoe*, so it is Saida the Greek who breathes and has being in *The Beauty Stone*. Evidently the pagan and foreign origin of these women permitted Sullivan to endow them with a vigour he would have felt obliged to deny to Christian heroines.

Regret does not complete the character of Saida, however, for in the third act she is given a song of exultation when she finally obtains the Beauty Stone from Simon ('Ride on, my Lord'). Once again Sullivan has broken out of Victorian inhibitions to write music of greater power than one would have predicted. Finally she flings the stone back at the Devil with a yell of real fury. Pinero and Carr seem to have thought of her as a villainess, unsympathetic when compared with the virtuous Laine. Sullivan however has transformed her into the central character of the opera, finally giving substance to his long desire for humanity in music.

By comparison with Saida the other characters in *The Beauty Stone* are necessarily less prominent. Philip is effectively treated both as a dreamer of beautiful dreams and, later, as a martial hero. Laine is allotted some lovely music, notably a folk-song-like solo at the beginning of the third act. But she is denied fire by her Christianity. The Devil emerges as bluff and sardonic, with a magnificent rolling ballad in the first act in which he describes the history of the Beauty Stone. Joan and Simon, Laine's parents, open the opera with a weaving duet in which the monotonous clack of the shuttle is heard, and disconsolate horn calls express their unhappiness. There is also a comic character, a tomboy girl named Crazy Jacqueline, who is allotted a captivating duet with the Devil, and a piquant solo when she realises she has fallen in love with him.

The Beauty Stone achieved only fifty performances at the Savoy, though it was later produced by the Carl Rosa Opera Company. The reasons for its disappearance are not far to seek: audiences came to the theatre looking for patter songs and plenty of fun from the Grossmith character. Instead they found the language of Wardour Street and music which by no means yields up its secrets at a single hearing. Walter Passmore, the chief comedian of the Savoy, must have been horribly miscast as the Devil, and several other performers do not seem to have been equal to their parts. One recalls Wilde's epigram that the play succeeded but the audience failed. *The Beauty Stone* is not an umixed success—the language in particular presents an obstacle to appreciation—but it is an altogether more coherent work than *Ivanhoe* and, as such, a better indication of Sullivan's ability to compose opera. The orchestral parts are kept in the BBC Music Library, where they seem to have been deposited as part of the Carl Rosa archive. It would be pleasant to think that with the parts so readily available the BBC might be persuaded to put them to their intended use.

The public's rejection of *The Beauty Stone* must have made it clear to Sullivan that he would not find an audience at the Savoy for the kind of opera he wished to write. At the end of his life he asked Comyns Carr to prepare a libretto on the subject of King Arthur, but for the Savoy he evidently judged it necessary to revert to type. As a result *The Rose of Persia* (1899), libretto by Basil Hood, is as nearly as may be an addition to the Gilbert series. Hood was not Gilbert, but he possessed the powers of a librettist to a respectable degree. *The Rose of Persia* has a well managed plot with a charming dénouement. The spoken dialogue is prone to puns, but is superior in intelligence to that of most operettas. The atmosphere of comic-opera-Persia is maintained throughout, helped by the origin of the story in *The Arabian Nights*.

For his contribution Sullivan drew on memories of a holiday spent in Egypt in the winter of 1881/2. Several passages in the score, notably an hypnotic dance repetitions of the word 'Allah', reflect time spent listening to the music of the Dervishes, who are actually introduced on stage when the Sultan and his courtiers enter disguised as these dancing Holy Men. In Sullivan's more familiar idiom there is a splendid drinking song, 'I care not if the cup I hold', and the captivating 'There was once a small Street Arab'. On the whole the melody is not so immediately memorable as in the familiar operas, but this appears to be a matter of choice inasmuch as Sullivan was now beginning to discard the formula of tune plus accompaniment in order to create what one might call purely aural movements in which the voice is a strand of colour rather than the exponent of a text.

The orchestral writing throughout is of great beauty and finesse. A couple of excursions into the music hall manner, which have been censured, actually deserve praise as displaying the breadth and openness of the composer's mind. One of them, set to words which call for 'a popular Persian tune', is quite obviously a rattling good joke.

The Rose of Persia is the most immediately stageworthy of all Sullivan's operas of the 1890s. It has not been performed professionally since 1935, but it survives to this day in the amateur repertory. Though not indestructible, in a lively production it shows exactly why it was so successful. It is, moreover, the best suited of any of the Savoy operas to the production techniques of the contemporary musical theatre. The snappy production numbers and remorseless zest which do damage to Gilbert's shapely frigidities are actually in place here, for Hood's libretto is the work of a man who well understood how to profit from the example of musical comedy. The character of the Sultan Mahmoud is tailor made for the kind of performance given to the Pirate King in the Broadway *Pirates of Penzance*. It is certainly along such lines that any modern professional revival should proceed.

With *The Rose of Persia* Sullivan completed his last opera. He was working on an Irish subject, *The Emerald Isle*, again with Basil Hood, at the time of his death. He had completed the opening chorus and song (I'm descended from Brian Boru') in full score. Thereafter he had composed the vocal parts, including choral and concerted items, of a further fifteen numbers, plus the first act finale. The first act had been framed, which meant that the music paper had been prepared to receive the orchestration. There was, in short, enough indication of the composer's intent to enable the work to be completed by another hand. Edward German was engaged for this purpose and, as the saying is, did it very well. With the addition of ten numbers by German and his orchestration of Sullivan's unfinished work the opera took the stage at the Savoy on 27 April 1901. It became and remained popular, so much so that a concert edition of the vocal score was issued in 1930.

In spite of his ancestry Sullivan was an Englishman who knew Ireland only as a visitor. As a musician, however, he had more than enough resource to write attractively in the manner of the typical Irish jig. This he did. But he also found it in himself to capture something much rarer—the dreamy melancholy of the Celtic feeling, profoundly felt, but remote and steeped in the past. He did this twice, once in the refrain to a song, 'Da Luan, da mort', and again in the first act finale 'Come away sighs the fairy voice.' This latter is quite simply the most beautiful tune of his career; it is as lovely as the Londonderry Air itself. Like a genuine folksong it seems to spring forth unconsciously from Sullivan's race memory. And yet, with his great resource, it is *composed* for its place in the opera; there is no question of the libretto having been worked round a fortunate musical inspiration. Finally, as a curiosity, we may notice that the last song by Sullivan in *The Emerald Isle* is, like the first song in *Cox and Box*, a 'Rataplan' number. Between the two he had written nearly five hundred songs and self-contained movements for his operas, besides countless connecting, narrative, and introductory passages. Viewing them overall these would appear to constitute an achievement without parallel in English music for their scope and variety and sustained imaginative power.

Whether Sullivan finally fulfilled himself may be doubted. His search for humane opera during the 90s was complicated by the need to sustain not only the Savoy Theatre but his own squandered fortunes. [46] For one reason or another the libretti which would have effected the release of the imprisoned splendour never came his way, and he finally returned to the established Savoy formula, whereupon the audiences too came back to the fold. In spite of stern passages in *Ivanhoe*, *Macbeth*, and elsewhere, his gift did not run naturally in the direction of intellectual toughness or violence of expression. Only the most bloodthirsty academic will feel disposed to condemn him for this. What he required was a libretto which would have been to him what *Carmen* was to Bizet–something colourful and exotic, rapid and various. The clearest indications of what he might have done with such a libretto are to be found in the thorough-composed sections of his existing operas–in *Trial by Jury*, *The Gondoliers*, *Haddon Hall* and *The Beauty Stone*. Within the realms of the possible a competent libretto from one of Shakespeare's comedies should have brought from him a work at least to compare with Nicolai's *Merry Wives of Windsor*. His existing Shakespearean music, all highly sympathetic, confirms such a judgement. Looking further, we have the view of Ralph Vaughan Williams that he was capable of a *Cosi Fan Tutte* under the right circumstances. [47] Unhappily Victorian London seems to have contained no librettist more capacious than Gilbert to provide the necessary framework, and Sullivan was in any case committed to historical romance.

We return, inevitably, to Gilbert himself. When he chose, Gilbert was perfectly capable of providing the dramatic contrast, concentration, and drive necessary to a successful operatic libretto. After the row of 1889 had driven him to it he wrote the charming succession of musically-conceived scenes that opens *The Gondoliers*. To have written the entire libretto in the same technique would have cost him nothing more than an extension of a principle he had already conceded. Not his art but his ego stood in the way of such a step. Sullivan urged him to take it but he refused, and in doing so robbed himself of greater glory and the world of more perfect pleasure.

For this reason the artistic conflict between Gilbert and Sullivan is not simply a meaningless sideshow or a reprehensible interruption of the gaiety of nations. The Savoy operas are the best of their kind; but they are not the best comic operas Gilbert and Sullivan might have written. Study of the stresses within the partnership reveals a conscious desire by Gilbert to restrain the part played by music, and constant pressure from Sullivan to approach more nearly to comic opera as we understand it from the masterpieces of continental Europe. Being thus born of conflict the operas are not, as is sometimes said, the product of two minds which worked as one. The impression of unity derives from the resourceful sympathy with which Sullivan approached his task once the argument was over, not from a working process of mutual agreement as to the best way forward. Most admirers of Gilbert and Sullivan would probably say that the balance finally achieved was perfect, but it can hardly be coincidence that the two libretti which most offended Sullivan–*Princess Ida* and *Ruddigore*– are precisely those which have had most difficulty in sustaining a place in the standard Savoy repertory. Similarly

Utopia Limited and *The Grand Duke*, which have suffered a long period of eclipse, are the libretti in which Gilbert was at his most self-indulgent. All the operas contain lyrics whose verbal quality does not entitle them to be heard at all costs, jut as they contain music which would be more satisfactory if the composer had not felt obliged to restrain himself.

No other operatic collaboration has displayed the same tensions as that of Gilbert and Sullivan. We do not read how Hofmannsthal persecuted Strauss over an affidavit, nor do we read how Boito refused to write for Verdi lest his syllables be obscured by music. The partnership endured for as long as it did because Sullivan needed money, because he had great powers of tolerance, and because he was bound by legal contract to write for the Savoy. Gilbert, for reasons which should by now be apparent, never showed spontaneous dissatisfaction with his operatic career. In retrospect it is possible to see the agreement of 8 February 1883 as crucial. Sullivan's first attempt to break away from the Savoy was frustrated by this agreement, which bound him to D'Oyly Carte for five years, plus a month. By the time it expired public expectation had set in a pattern which has undergone little subsequent change. If Sullivan had been able to make his break before his own institutionalisation set in he might have met with a more sympathetic audience response. As it was he put his shirt on *Ivanhoe*—and lost. Subsequently he has come to be associated in the public mind with a single librettist, and the fruits of his wider endeavour have fallen from the repertory. Whether the fall was justified is another matter; we should at least remember that *The Martyr of Antioch* and its companions were sent on their way by a deliberate campaign of vilification launched by men like Fuller Maitland and Ernest Walker, which at this distance of time may be regarded as the musical equivalent of the campaign launched by the members of the Bloomsbury Set against the Victorians generally.

But it is time to turn from speculation and discord to the achievement that is. In Gilbert we have an original master of comic verse and plot whose works have come to stand as classics in their own right. Gilbert not only created original libretti; by his methods of production he made a revolution in the theatre—a revolution from which every well-produced play continues to benefit. By his unique talents he presented to Sullivan the only thoroughly workable escape the composer was ever to find from his unnatural place within Victorian domestic and ecclesiastical respectability.

For his part Sullivan contributed an outstanding native ability, and a Shakespearean quality of humility without which the partnership could not have continued. He was a master of the orchestra, who had access to a large and varied musical resource; he had humour and energy, and the power to write memorable tunes even when accommodating himself to a difficult text.

Men of genius are rare enough in any generation. That two men of such symbiotic genius should have been born in the same city at the same period must be accounted a gift of the gods. Only when the same gift is given again can we hope to see another Gilbert and Sullivan partnership. Until then the one we have seems likely to endure.

Notes

1: MAINLY BIOGRAPHICAL - NOTES

1. For the rise of the amateur operatic movement in Britain see Mackinlay, *Origin And Development Of Light Opera*; for U.S.A. see Bordman, *American Musical Theatre*.
2. Gilbert, *The Memoirs Of A Cynic*, 2: 46.
3. Pearson, *Gilbert—His Life And Strife*, p. 15.
4. Goodman, *Gilbert And Sullivan At Law*, p. 16.
5. It is not easy to say which is the first *Bab* ballad. See Ellis, *The Bab Ballads*, pp. 7,326.
6. See introduction by Terence Rees to W. Gilbert, *Uncle Baby*.
7. Reprinted in Rowell, *Plays By W.S. Gilbert*, p. 89.
8. So reads his army discharge certificate, dated at the Horse Guards 18 December 1821, after his return from Elba. Public Record Office ref. WO 97/796 ZC/A 8156.
9. For letters from Grove to Mrs Sullivan see Young, *George Grove*, p. 166.
10. See Emerson, *Arthur Darling*, and Wolfson, *Sullivan And The Scott Russells*.
11. Quoted in Stedman, *Gilbert Before Sullivan*, p. 21.
12. Gilbert, *Original Plays*, 1: 173.
13. The sequence of events can be followed in advertisements for the Gallery of Illustration in *The Daily Telegraph* for June/July 1870. *Ages Ago* and *Beggar My Neighbour* ended 18 June; *Our Island Home* and *The School Feast* commenced 20 June; *Ages Ago* revived 11 July. *Beggar My Neighbour* was an English version of Offenbach's *Les Deux Aveugles* (1875). An undated letter from German Reed to Sullivan (reprinted in Flower, *Sir Arthur Sullivan*, p.68) asks Sullivan to provide music for a one-act work by Gilbert. Gilbert wrote two one-act plays for Reed: *Our Island Home* (1870) and *Eyes And No Eyes* (1875). If Sullivan met Gilbert for the first time only *after* the production of *Our Island Home*, the inference would appear to be that Reed's letter refers to *Eyes And No Eyes*.
14. Hollingshead is strangeley unforthcoming about *Thespis* in his *Good Old Gaiety*, London: Gaiety Theatre Company, 1903.
15. See Rees, *Thespis*, p. 71 f.
16. Rees, *Thespis*, p. 116.
17. Several French dramatists produced their own plays. In England Gilbert was preceded by Tom Robertson (1829-71), from whom he learned the elements of stagecraft. Dion Boucicault (1822-90) was also an autocratic producer of his own work.

18.   The original version of *Trial By Jury* is reproduced in Ellis, *The Bab Ballads*, p. 157 f.

19.   Dark & Grey, *W.S. Gilbert—His Life And Letters*, p. 194.

20.   Pearson, *Gilbert—His Life And Strife*, p. 78.

21.   The Latin citation for Sullivan's degree is printed in *The Musical World*, 8 July 1876.

22.   Goodman, *Gilbert And Sullivan At Law*, p. 70 f.

23.   Goodman, *Gilbert And Sullivan At Law*, p. 102.

24.   Pearson, *Gilbert And Sullivan*, p. 124.

25.   See Ormond, *George Du Maurier*, chapter 7.

26.   Ormond, *George Du Maurier*, p. 254.

27.   Dark & Grey, *W.S. Gilbert*, p. 83.

28.   This draft is printed by Jane W. Stedman in Jones, *W.S. Gilbert, A Century Of Scholarship And Commentary*, p. 285 f.

29.   See Eyre M. Shaw, *Fires In Theatres*, E. & F.N.S. Spon, 1876.

30.   See Killham, *Tennyson And The Princess*, pp.147, 154, 162.

31.   Ibid. pp. 200, 209, 225.

32.   See *The Musical Times* May 1887.

33.   Flower, *Sir Arthur Sullivan*, p. 164.

34.   See Terence Rees, 'Ruddigore Rediscovered', in *Theatrephile* Vol 1 no 2 (March 1984), p. 27.

35.   This statement has often been doubted, but it appears as part of an interview with Gilbert published in the *Strand Magazine*, October 1891. The interviewer concerned, Harry How, became for ever afterwards an object of Gilbert's dislike.

36.   Jacobs, *Arthur Sullivan—A Victorian Musician*, p. 265.

37.   Pearson, *Gilbert—His Life And Strife*, p. 129.

38.   The text of the agreement is in Goodman, *Gilbert And Sullivan At Law*, p. 109.

39.   Pearson, *Gilbert—His Life And Strife*, p. 139.

40.   Ibid., p. 152.

41.   For the circumstances of the lawsuit see Morrell, *Lillian Russell - The Era Of Plush*.

42.   See *The Times* Law Report, 4 September 1890.

43.   Pearson, *Gilbert—His Life And Strife*, p. 143.

44.   Ibid., p. 145.

45.   Jacobs, *Arthur Sullivan*, p. 330.

46.   Flower, *Sir Arthur Sullivan*, p. 141.

47.   The damages were paid on 30 May 1878. (John Gardner - personal communication).

48.   Flower, *Sir Arthur Sullivan*, p. 217.

49.   Young, *George Grove*, p. 228.

50.   Bennett, *Forty Years Of Music*, p. 71.

51.   See Wolfson, *Final Curtain*, p. 68.

52.   Hearing a selection from *His Majesty* played by a park band, Mackenzie mistook the music for that of Sullivan. See Mackenzie, *A Musician's Narrative*, p. 202.

53.   See Baily, *Gilbert And Sullivan Book*, p. 392.

54.   See 'Sullivan And Miss Violet' by Wyn and Barbara Wade in *The Gilbert And Sullivan Journal*, Vol 10 no 13 (Autumn 1977), pp. 276-77.

55.   Allen, *Sir Arthur Sullivan*, p. 174.

56.   Ibid.

57.   See Tillett, *Victoria And Merrie England*.

58.   The tale of 'The Sleeper Wakened' is in Mathers, *The Book Of The Thousand Nights And One Night*, 3: 230 f. The tale of 'Alī Ibn Bakr and Shams al-Nahār' is in Mathers, *The Thousand Nights*, 1: 611f.

59.   Young, *Sir Arthur Sullivan*, p. 256.

60.   Pearson, *Gilbert And Sullivan*, p. 226.

61.   Pearson, *Gilbert—His Life And Strife*, p. 193 f.

62.   Quoted in Pearson, *Gilbert—His Life And Strife*, p.197.

63.   Quoted in Ibid., p.199. *The Circus Girl*: Gaiety Theatre 15 December 1896; 497 performances; music by Ivan Caryll and Lionel Monckton.

64. Quoted in Ibid.
65. For Mrs D'Oyly Carte see 'Who was Helen Lenoir?' by Paul Seeley, in *The Savoyard* Vol 21 no 2 (September 1982), pp. 16-18.
66. See Ellis, *The Bab Ballads*, p. 26.

2: GILBERT'S PERSONALITY - NOTES

1. Dark & Grey, *W.S. Gilbert*, p. 192
2. Pearson, *Gilbert And Sullivan*, p. 269.
3. Hicks, *Between Ourselves*, p. 49 ff.
4. Gilbert's text is partly reprinted in Goodman, *Gilbert And Sullivan At Law*, p. 51.
5. Pearson, *Gilbert And Sullivan*, p. 208.
6. Ibid., p. 42.
7. Ibid., p. 44.
8. Pearson, *Gilbert—His Life And Strife*, p. 178.
9. Ibid., p. 121.
10. Hicks, *Seymour Hicks By Himself*, p. 145.
11. Quoted in Gilbert, *The Savoy Operas*, 2: vii.
12. Altick, *Victorian Studies In Scarlet*, p. 215.
13. The book carried by Gilbert was probably Atlay, *Famous Trials*.
14. Pearson, *Gilbert And Sullivan*, p. 203.
15. Pearson, *Gilbert—His Life And Strife*, p. 265.
16. Ellis, *The Bab Ballads*, p. 201.
17. Ibid., p. 6 n. 7.
18. Gilbert, *Original Plays*, 3: 279.
19. Ibid., 3: 190
20. Ibid., 4: 173.
21. Ibid., 4: 107.
22. Pearson, *Gilbert And Sullivan*, p. 21.
23. Jones, *W.S. Gilbert - A Century Of Scholarship*, p. 168.
24. Ellis, *The Bab Ballads*, p. 14.
25. Ibid., p. 85.
26. Freud, *On Sexuality*, p. 110.
27. Ibid., p. 116.
28. Ibid., pp. 72, 116.
29. Ibid., p. 117.
30. Ibid., p. 209.
31. Gilbert, *Original Plays*, 4: 60.
32. Freud, *On Sexuality*, pp. 214, 299.
33. Gilbert, *Original Plays*, 4: 63.
34. Freud, *On Sexuality*, p. 71.
35. Haining, *Lost Stories of W.S. Gilbert*, p. 143 f.
36. Dark & Grey, *W.S. Gilbert*, p. 54.
37. Gilbert, *Original Plays*, 2: 3.
38. Ibid., 2: 5.
39. Ibid., 2: 37.
40. Ibid., 2: 182.
41. Ibid., 2: 201.
42. Ibid., 1: 3.
43. Ibid., 1: 43.
44. Ibid., 1: 4.

45. Pearson, *Gilbert And Sullivan*, p. 268.
46. Pearson, *Gilbert—His Life And Strife*, p. 204.
47. Pearson, *Gilbert And Sullivan*, p. 34.
48. Pearson, *Gilbert—His Life And Strife*, p. 64.
49. Gilbert, *Original Plays*, 3: 151.
50. Ibid., 3: 198.
51. Ibid., 4: 64.
52. See, for example, Berman, 'Gilbert's First Night Anxiety' and Brenner, 'The Fantasies of W.S. Gilbert,' in *The Psychoanalytic Quarterly*.

3: THE PRINCESS PLOT - NOTES

1. Gilbert, *Original Plays*, 1: 167.
2. Freud, *The Standard Edition Of The Complete Works Of Sigmund Freud*, 19: 162.
3. Gilbert, *Original Plays*, 1: 73.
4. Reprinted in Haining, *Lost Stories of W.S. Gilbert*, p. 106 f.
5. Gilbert, *Original Plays*, 1: 73.
6. A useful overview of aestheticism as it was, not as Gilbert and *Punch* would have us see it, will be found in Aldington, *The Religion Of Beauty*.
7. Gilbert, *Original Plays*, 1: 246.
8. Wolfson, *Final Curtain*, p. 18.
9. Johnson, *Selections From Samuel Johnson*, p. 204.
10. Gilbert, *Original Plays*, 3: 447.
11. Ibid., 3: 451.
12. Dark & Grey, *W.S. Gilbert*, p. 144.
13. Ellis, *The Bab Ballads*, p. 130.
14. Quoted in Moll, *The Sexual Life Of The Child*, p. 11.
15. Gilbert, *The Memoirs Of A Cynic*, p. 62 f.
16. Gilbert, *Original Plays*, 3: 105.
17. Ibid., 1: 137.
18. I have stolen the list of youthful lovers, and the reference to Flaubert, from Moll, *The Sexual Life Of The Child*, p. 11.
19. Gilbert, *Memoirs Of A Cynic*, Vol 1 pp. 69-70.
20. Ellis, *The Bab Ballads*, p. 81.
21. Gilbert, *Memoirs Of A Cynic*, 1: 42.
22. Ellis, *The Bab Ballads*, p. 99.
23. Pearson, *Gilbert—His Life And Strife*, p. 172.
24. Wolfson, *Final Curtain*, p. 30.
25. Sulloway, *Freud—Biologist Of The Mind*, p. 397.
26. Freud, *The Ego And The Id*, p. 43.
27. Ibid., p. 30.
28. Gilbert, *Original Plays*, 2: 5.
29. Dark & Grey, *W.S. Gilbert*, p. 169.
30. Morrell, *Lillian Russell—The Era Of Plush*, p. 68. In 1922 Lillian Russel reported that Gilbert said to her: 'You can't play it the way I want it played unless you come down to my room every night and rehearse the part with me.' See Jacobs, *Arthur Sullivan*, p. 186.
31. Pearson, *Gilbert And Sullivan*, p. 149.
32. Freud, *On Sexuality*, p. 248.
33. Pearson, *Gilbert—His Life And Strife*, p. 74.
34. Freud, *Complete Works*, 19: 162.
35. Gilbert, *Original Plays*, 2: 114.

36. Freud, *On Sexuality*, p. 296.
37. Gilbert, *Original Plays*, 2: 114.
38. Dark & Grey, *W.S. Gilbert*, p. 167.
39. Freud, *The Ego And The Id*, pp. 21-23.
40. Freud, *on Sexuality*, p. 319.
41. Freud, *Complete Works*, 19: 168.
42. Pearson, *Gilbert—His Life And Strife*, p. 78 f.
43. Gilbert, *Original Plays*, 3: 179.
44. Ellis, *The Bab Ballads*, p. 226.
45. Pearson, *Gilbert And Sullivan*, p. 302.
46. St John Stevas, *Obscenity And The Law*, p. 189.
47. Mr Patrick Kearney, in a private communication.
48. Legman, *The Horn Book*, p. 95; Ginzburg, *An Unhurried View Of Erotica*, p. 395.
49. Pearson, *Gilbert And Sullivan*, p. 302.
50. Dark & Grey, *W.S. Gilbert*, p. 210.
51. Ibid., p. 177.
52. Stedman, *Gilbert Before Sullivan*, p. 82.
53. There is no mention of Gilbert in either of Sala's essays in autobiography, nor in Straus, *Sala—The Portrait Of An Eminent Victorian*.
54. See Marcus, *The Other Victorians*, especially chapter 7.

4: THE DEATH OF JACK POINT - NOTES

1. Lytton, *The Secrets Of A Savoyard*, pp. 47-48.
2. Pearson, *Gilbert And Sullivan*, p. 181.
3. Gilbert, *Original Plays*, 2: 155.
4. Dark & Grey, *W.S. Gilbert*, p. 7.
5. Ellis, *The Bab Ballads*, p. 69.
6. Ibid., p. 87.
7. Quoted in ibid., p. 325.
8. Gilbert, *Original Plays*, 3: 299. A similar situation is posited by a line in Jack Point's second act song: 'Though your wife ran away with a soldier that day, And took with her your trifle of money.' The use of the word 'wife' seems to indicate just how sanguine were the hopes of Point/Gilbert; the word 'money' may be given a Freudian interpretation by anyone who feels inclined.
9. Gilbert, *Original Plays*, 4: 109.
10. Pearson, *Gilbert And Sullivan*, p. 226.
11. The 'Stroller's Song' printed by Ellis, *The Bab Ballads*, p. 310, was clearly intended to be sung by the Prince Regent on his entry as a strolling player in *His Excellency*. It should not therefore be included among the *Bab Ballads*. John Wolfson, *Final Curtain*, p. 85, allots this song to *The Grand Duke*, where it is wholly out of place. Its proper position would be Gilbert, *Original Plays*, 4: 109.

5: THE THEATRICAL BACKGROUND - NOTES

1. Interview with Gilbert in *The Strand Magazine* October 1892; *Illustrated Interviews* No 4, p. 333.
2. Booth, *Pantomimes, Extravaganzas And Burlesques*, p. 217.

3. Equally the burlesque—but for the censorship—might have matched the outspoken ridicule of Aristophanes.

4. Booth, *Pantomimes, Extravaganzas And Burlesques*, pp. 300-1.

5. Gilbert, *Original Plays*, 3: 86.

6. Traubner, *Operetta*, p. 74.

7. Ellis, *The Bab Ballads*, p. 41.

8. Ibid., p. 280.

9. Dark & Grey, *W.S. Gilbert*, pp. 238-39.

10. Gilbert, *Original Plays*, 3: 180. Pooh-Bah's ancestry seems to be derived from the writings of Ernst Haeckel (1834-1919), whose *Natural History Of Creation* (1868) traced the descent of man from protoplasm to the chimpanzee in 26 stages. The first stages were named globules or hollow spheres.

11. See Wolfson, *Final Curtain*, p. 69.

12. Quoted in Jones, *W.S. Gilbert—A Century Of Scholarship*, p. 194.

13. Frere, *The Plays Of Aristophanes*, p. ix.

14. Fitzgerald, *The Savoy Operas*, p. 14.

15. See for instance Walter Sichel, p. 69, and Edith Hamilton, p. 111, in Jones, *W.S. Gilbert—A Century Of Scholarship*.

16. Baring, *Punch And Judy*, p. 46.

17. Watling, *The Theban Plays*, p. 10.

18. Gilbert, *Original Plays*, 1: 228.

19. Bywater, *Aristotle On The Art Of Poetry*, p. 42.

20. Ibid., p. 65.

6: GILBERT'S SATIRE - NOTES

1. Gilbert, *Original Plays*, 1: 7.

2. Ibid., 3: 374.

3. Ibid., 2: 182.

4. Ibid., 2: 189.

5. Printed in Jones, *W.S. Gilbert—A Century Of Scholarship*, p. 32.

6. Ibid., p. 39.

7. Gilbert, *Original Plays*, 3: 387.

8. Ibid., 1: 226.

9. Ibid., 1: 233.

10. Ibid., 2: 318.

11. Ibid., 3: 102.

12. Ibid., 1: 259.

13. Ibid., 3: 138.

14. Ibid., 3: 192.

15. Ibid., 3: 316.

16. Wolfson, *Final Curtain*, p. 123.

17. Gilbert, *Original Plays*, 3: 410.

18. Ibid., 3: 432.

19. Thackeray, *Burlesques*, p. 7.

20. Gilbert, *Original Plays*, 2: 284.

21. Thackeray, *Book Of Snobs*, p. 6.

22. Ellis, *The Bab Ballads*, p. 274.

23. Gilbert, *Original Plays*, 1: 276.

24. Stedman, *Gilbert Before Sullivan*, p. 101.

25. Thackeray, *Burlesques*, p. 238.

26. Gilbert, *Original Plays*, 2: 333.

27. Thackeray, *Roundabout Papers*, pp. 243-44. Jack Sheppard (1702-24), a celebrated highway-man who made several daring escapes before being hung. Henry Fauntleroy, a banker executed for forgery in 1824. William Weare see p. 61. William Dodd (1729-77), chaplain to George III. He was executed for the forgery of a bond in the name of Lord Chesterfield.

28. Thackeray, *Book Of Snobs*, p. 93.

29. A further extract in Dark & Grey, *W.S. Gilbert*, p. 47.

30. Gilbert, *Original Plays*, 2: 296.

31. Ibid., 3: 226.

32. Ibid., 3: 433.

33. For Jeames de la Pluche see Thackeray, *Burlesques*, p. 100 f. For a hint of Pooh-Bah who would not say 'how de do' to any one under the rank of a stockbroker, see Thackeray, *Lovel The Widower*, p. 35, where 'Sargent never comes to his lodge-door with any man under a marquis.' For a hint of Ko-Ko's 'little list' song (*The Mikado*) see *Thackeray, Roundabout Papers*, p. 38: 'My Lord So-and-so, my Lord What-d'ye-call-'im, My Lord Etcetera.'

34. Printed by Stedman in Jones, *W.S. Gilbert—A Century Of Scholarship*, p. 307.

35. Thackeray, *Book Of Snobs*, p. 14.

36. Ibid., p. 24.

37. Ibid., p. 14.

38. Gilbert, *Original Plays*, 3: 252.

39. Thackeray, *Book Of Snobs*, p. 158.

40. Dark & Grey, *W.S. Gilbert*, p. 233.

41. Printed with music in Rees & Spencer, *Sing With Sullivan*, p. 18.

42. Ellis, *The Bab Ballads*, p. 240.

43. The king's song in the second act of *Utopia Limited* tells us that in Utopia 'poverty is obsolete and hunger is abolished', whereas by implication they persist in England. Gilbert, *Original Plays*, 3: 440.

44. Ibid., 1: 271.

45. Ibid., 2: 323.

46. See article by Jane Stedman in *The Savoyard* Vol 20 no 1 (March 1981), p. 4.

47. Gilbert, *Original Plays*, 4: 57.

48. See Baldick, *A History Of Duelling*, p. 113. Sullivan almost became involved in a duel in Egypt in 1882. See Jacobs, *Arthur Sullivan*, p. 169.

49. Pearson, *Gilbert—His Life And Strife*, p. 95.

50. Gilbert, *Original Plays*, 2: 281.

51. Thackeray, *Book Of Snobs*, p. 38.

52. See Dark & Grey, *W.S. Gilbert*, p. 149; Jones, *W.S. Gilbert—A Century Of Scholarship*, p. 8.

53. Gilbert, *Original Plays*, 3: 102.

7: THE COMPOSER - NOTES

1. Hicks, *Between Ourselves*, pp. 54-55.

2. Emmerson, *Arthur Darling*, p. 44.

3. See Carr, *Some Eminent Victorians*, p. 285.

4. Jacobs, *Arthur Sullivan*, p. 171.

5. See Girouard, *Life In The English Country House*, p. 268 f.

6. Quoted in Young, *Sir Arthur Sullivan*, p. 263.

7. Young, *George Grove*, p. 103.

8. Walker said, among other things, 'We can never recollect without shame that the composer who stood for contemporary English music in the eyes of the world could put his name to disgraceful rubbish like *The Lost Chord* or *The Sailor's Grave* or, in what purported to be serious artistic work,

sink to the abysmally cheap sentimentally of the opening tune of the *In Memoriam* overture.' Quoted in Jacobs, *Arthur Sullivan*, p. 402.

9. Findon, *Sullivan And His Operas*, p. 45.
10. Quoted in Moore, *Edward Elgar—A Creative Life*.
11. Lawrence, *Sir Arthur Sullivan*, p. 57 f.
12. Stoker, *Personal Reminiscences Of Henry Irving*, 1: 111.
13. Flower, *Sir Arthur Sullivan*, p. 182.
14. Sullivan's banjo accompaniment was compared by Bernard Shaw to Mozart's accompaniments to 'Soave il vento' (*Cosi Fan Tutti*) and the entry of the gardener in *Le Nozze di Figaro*; see Shaw, *G.B.S. On Music*, p. 144. Shaw also pointed out that Sullivan had made use of the plantation son *Johnny Get A Gun*, words by T. Clay, music by F. Belasco, an American import of about 1889. Sullivan has made some use not of the song itself but of the dance which follows it.
15. Hughes, *The Music Of Arthur Sullivan*, p. 84.
16. Allingham, *William Allingham's Diary*, p. 106.
17. Bennett, *Forty Years Of Music*, p. 78.
18. Wilson, *Brandy Of The Damned*, p. 135.
19. A perfect illustration of this point is the song 'When our gallant Norman Foes' (*The Yeomen of the Guard*). The words sing the praises of 'the heroes who have fought/For conscience and for home in all its beauty.' Gilbert, *Original Plays*, 3: 266.
20. Strong, *And When Did You Last See Your Father?*, p. 152 f.
21. Shaw, *G.B.S. On Music*, p. 135. (10 May 1893).
22. Raynor, *Music In England*, p. 172.
23. Wood, *Olympian Dreamers*, chapters 1 and 4.
24. Young, *George Grove*, p. 250. Grove wrote 'clear' for 'calm' in the last line.
25. Hotson, *Shakespeare By Hilliard*, p. 190.
26. Hazlitt quoted in Gittings, *John Keats*, p. 186.
27. Hotson, *Shakespeare By Hilliard*, p. 187.
28. Dark & Grey, *W.S. Gilbert*, p. 194.
29. Holbrook, *Gustav Mahler And The Courage To Be*.

8: THE CREATIVE CONFLICT - NOTES

1. Smith, *The Tenth Muse*, p. 3 f.
2. Ibid., p. 76.
3. *Grove's Dictionary Of Music And Musicians*, 5th ed, 3: 679.
4. Einstein, *Mozart*, p. 400.
5. Smith, *The Tenth Muse*, p. 174.
6. Ibid., p. xviii.
7. Statement by F.C. Burnand in his preface to the libretto of *The Chieftain* (1894).
8. Pearson, *Gilbert—His Life And Strife*, p. 108.
9. Pearson, *Gilbert And Sullivan*, p. 228.
10. Lord David Cecil in W.S. Gilbert, *The Savoy Operas*, 1: xvii.
11. Jacobs, *Arthur Sullivan*, p. 187.
12. Flower, *Sir Arthur Sullivan*, p. 140.
13. Ibid., p. 140.
14. Ibid., p. 140.
15. Gilbert, *Original Plays*, 2: 298.
16. Flower, *Sir Arthur Sullivan*, p. 141.
17. Ibid., p. 143.
18. Jacobs, *Arthur Sullivan*, p. 192.
19. Ibid., p. 193.

20. Flower, *Sir Arthur Sullivan*, p. 145.
21. Jacobs, *Arthur Sullivan*, p. 215.
22. Flower, *Sir Arthur Sullivan*, p. 172.
23. Jacobs, *Arthur Sullivan*, p. 270.
24. Flower, *Sir Arthur Sullivan*, p. 177.
25. Gilbert, *Original Plays*, 3: 270.
26. Baily, *The Gilbert And Sullivan Book*, p. 297.
27. Shaw, *The Complete Musical Criticism*, 3: 691. From *The World* 28 September 1892.
28. Pearson, *Gilbert And Sullivan*, p. 299.
29. Flower, *Sir Arthur Sullivan*, p. 184.
30. Ibid., p. 187.
31. Ibid., p. 188.
32. Ibid., p. 190.
33. Dark & Grey, *W.S. Gilbert*, p. 204.
34. Wolfson, *Final Curtain*, p. 35.
35. Gilbert, *Original Plays*, 3: 439.
36. In the ballroom scene of a Viennese operetta everyone would break not into an oratorio chorus but into a waltz. The best way to deal with the same moment in *Utopia Limited* would be to discard 'Eagle High' and dance one of Sullivan's waltzes. There is a good waltz for the purpose in the ballet *Victoria And Merrie England* (1897).
37. Wolfson, *Final Curtain*, p. 263. This song is cut in Gilbert's *Original Plays*, 4: 84.
38. The lyric of 'Come bumpers - aye, ever so many' is a reworking of a lyric, apparently not by Gilbert, which appeared in *Punch* 27 July 1861. See 'An Unidentified Gilbert Source' by David Mackie in *The Savoyard*, Vol 20 no 1 (March 1981), p. 10.
39. Gilbert, *Original Plays*, 4: 75.
40. Jacobs, *Arthur Sullivan*, p. 218.
41. The elopement of Dorothy Vernon took place in about 1563, during a ball held to celebrate the wedding of her sister Margaret. Dorothy, whose effigy may still be seen in Bakewell church, died in 1583. However, Grundy has advanced the story in time to the period of the Civil War (1642/9), apparently in order to introduce his comic Puritans. The story of Dorothy Vernon has been told in two novels: *Dorothy Vernon of Haddon Hall* by Charles Major, and *Sweet Doll Of Haddon Hall* by J.E.P. Muddock.
42. Jacobs, *Arthur Sullivan*, p. 341.
43. Shaw, *The Complete Musical Criticism*, 3: 691.
44. Gilbert, *Original Plays*, 3: 432.
45. Johnson, *Selections From Samuel Johnson*, p. 254.
46. Jacobs, *Arthur Sullivan*, p. 382.
47. Vaughan Williams, in *National Music*.

Bibliography

Aldington, Richard (ed) *The Religion Of Beauty*. London: Heinemann, 1950.

Allen, Reginald, *Sir Arthur Sullivan—Composer And Personage*. New York: The Pierpont Morgan Library, 1975.

Allingham, William, *William Allingham's Diary*. London: Centaur Press, 1967.

Altick, R.D., *Victorian Studies In Scarlet*. London: Dent, 1972.

Atlay, J.B., *Famous Trials*. London: 1899.

Baily, Leslie, *The Gilbert And Sullivan Book*. London: Cassell, 1952.

Baldick, Robert, *A History Of Duelling*. London: Chapman & Hall, 1965.

Baring, Maurice, *Punch And Judy*. London: Heinemann, 1924.

Bennett, Joseph, *Forty Years Of Music 1865-1905*. London: Methuen, 1908.

Berman, Leon E.A., 'Gilbert's First Night Anxiety' in *The Psychoanalytic Quarterly* 45: (1976) 110-27.

Bond, Jessie, *The Life And Reminiscences of Jessie Bond*. London: Bodley Head, 1930.

Booth, Michael R. (ed), *Pantomimes, Extravaganzas And Burlesques*, being vol 5 of the series *English Plays Of The Nineteenth Century*. Oxford University Press, 1976.

Bordman, Gerald, *American Musical Theatre*. New York: Oxford University Press, 1978.

Brenner, Arthur E., 'The Fantasies of W.S. Gilbert', in *The Psychoanalytic Quarterly* 21: (April 1952) 337-401.

Browne, Edith A., *W.S. Gilbert*. London: John Lane, 1907.

Bywater, Ingram (trans), *Aristotle On The Art Of Poetry*. Oxford University Press, 1959.

Carr, J. Comyns, *Some Eminent Victorians*. London: Duckworth, 1908.

Dark, Sydney, & Grey, Rowland, *W.S. Gilbert—His Life And Letters*. London:

Methuen, 1923.

Einstein, Alfred, *Mozart*. London: Panther Books, 1971.

Ellis, James (ed), *The Bab Ballads* by W.S. Gilbert. Cambridge (Mass): The Belknap Press of Harvard University, 1980.

Emmerson, George, *Arthur Darling*. Lòndon (Ontario): Galt House Publications, 1980.

Findon, B.W., *Sullivan And His Operas*. London: Sisley's, 1908.

Fitzgerald, Percy, *The Savoy Operas*. London: Chatto & Windus, 1899.

Flower, Newman & Sullivan, Herbert, *Sir Arthur Sullivan, His Life, Letters And Diaries*, 2nd ed. London: Cassell, 1950.

Frere, J.H., *The Plays Of Aristophanes*. London: Routledge, n.d. (c1900).

Freud, Sigmund, *The Ego And The Id*; being no 12 of *The International Psychoanalytical Library*. London: The Hogarth Press, 1962.

Freud, Sigmund, *The Standard Edition Of The Complete Works Of Sigmund Freud*, Vol 19. London: The Hogarth Press, 1961.

Freud, Sigmund, *On Sexuality*; being Vol 7 of *The Pelican Freud Library*. London: Penguin Books, 1983.

Gilbert, W., *Uncle Baby, A Comedietta*, edited with an introduction by Terence Rees. Privately Printed, 1968.

Gilbert, William, *The Memoirs Of A Cynic*. London: Tinsley Bros., 1880.

Gilbert, W.S., *Original Plays*, 4 Vols. London: Chatto & Windus, 1915.

Gilbert, W.S., *The Savoy Operas*, 2 Vols. Oxford University Press, 1962.

Ginzburg, Ralph, *An Unhurried View Of Erotica*. London: Secker & Warburg, 1959.

Girouard, Mark, *Life In The English Country House*. London: Penguin Books, 1980.

Gittings, Robert, *John Keats*. London: Heinemann, 1968.

Goodman, Andrew, *Gilbert And Sullivan At Law*. London: Associated University Presses, 1983.

Haining, Peter (ed), *The Lost Stories Of W.S. Gilbert*. London: Robson Books, 1982.

Hicks, Seymour, *Seymour Hicks By Himself*. London: Alston Rivers, 1910.

Hicks, Seymour, *Between Ourselves*. London: Cassell, 1930.

Holbrook, David, *Gustav Mahler And The Courage To Be*. London: Vision Books, 1975.

Hotson, Leslie, *Shakespeare By Hilliard*. London: Chatto & Windus, 1977.

Hughes, Gervase, *The Music Of Arthur Sullivan*. London: Macmillan, 1960.

Irving, Laurence, *Henry Irving: The Actor And His World*. London: Faber & Faber, 1951.

Jacobs, Arthur, *Arthur Sullivan—A Victorian Musician*. Oxford University Press, 1984.

Johnson, Samuel, *Selections From Samuel Johnson*, ed. R.W. Chapman. Oxford University Press, 1962.

Jones, John Bush (ed), *W.S. Gilbert - A Century Of Scholarship And Commentary*. New York University Press, 1970.

Killham, John, *Tennyson And The Princess - Reflections Of An Age*. London: Athlone

Press, 1958.

Klein, Herman, *The Golden Age Of Opera*. London: George Routledge & Sons, 1933.

Lawrence, Arthur, *Sir Arthur Sullivan*. New York: Duffield & Co., 1907.

Legman, Gershon, *The Horn Book*. New York: University Books Inc., 1964.

Lytton, Henry, *The Secrets Of A Savoyard*. London: Jarrolds, (n.d.) c1922.

Mackenzie, Alexander, *A Musician's Narrative*. London: Cassell, 1927.

Mackinlay, Sterling, *Origin And Development Of Light Opera*. London: Hutchinson & Co., 1927.

Marcus, Steven, *The Other Victorians*. London: Weidenfeld & Nicolson, 1966.

Mathers, Powys (trans), *The Book Of The Thousand Night And One Night*, 4 Vols. London: Routledge & Kegan Paul, 1972.

Milman, Henry, *The Martyr Of Antioch—A Dramatic Poem*. London: John Murray, 1822.

Moll, Albert, *The Sexual Life Of The Child*. London: George Allen, 1912.

Moore, Jerrold Northrop, *Edward Elgar—A Creative Life*. Oxford University Press, 1984.

Morrell, Parker, *Lillian Russell—The Era Of Plush*. New York: Random House, 1940.

Ormond, Leonée, *George Du Maurier*. London: Routledge & Kegan Paul, 1969.

Pearson, Hesketh, *Gilbert And Sullivan*. London: The Right Book Club, n.d. (1st Edition 1935).

Pearson, Hesketh, *Gilbert—His Life And Strife*. London: Methuen, 1957.

Raynor, Henry, *Music In England*. London: Robert Hale, 1980.

Rees, Terence, *Thespis—A Gilbert & Sullivan Enigma*. London: Dillons University Bookshop, 1964.

Rees, Terence, & Spencer, Roderick (eds), *Sing With Sullivan*. London: Cramer, 1978.

Rowell, George (ed), *Plays By W.S. Gilbert*. Cambridge University Press, 1982.

Sala, George Augustus, *Things I Have Seen And People I Have Known*. 2 Vols. London: Cassell, 1894.

Sala, George Augustus, *Life And Adventures Of George Augustus Sala, Written By Himself*, 2 Vols. London: Cassell, 1895.

Shaw, George Bernard, *The Complete Musical Criticism*, 3 Vols. London: The Bodley Head, n.d. (c1981).

Shaw, George Bernard, *G.B.S. On Music*. London: Penguin Books, 1962.

Simcoe, Augustine H., *Sullivan v Critic—A Study In Press Phenomena*. London: Privately Printed, 1906.

Smith, Patrick, *The Tenth Muse—A Historical Study Of The Opera Libretto*. London: Gollancz, 1971.

Stedman, Jane W., *Gilbert Before Sullivan—Six Comic Plays By W.S. Gilbert*. University Of Chicago Press, 1969.

Stevas, Norman St John, *Obscenity And The Law*. London: 1956.

Stoker, Bram, *Personal Reminiscences Of Henry Irving*. London: Heinemann, 1906.

Straus, Ralph, *Sala—The Portrait Of An Eminent Victorian*. London: Constable, 1942.

Strong, Roy, *And When Did You Last See Your Father? - The Victorian Painter And British History*. London: Thames & Hudson, 1978.

Sulloway, Frank, *Freud—Biologist Of The Mind*. London: Burnett Books, 1979.

Thackeray, W.M., *Burlesques*; being Vol 15 of *The Works Of William Makepeace Thackeray*. 26 Vols. London: Smith, Elder & Co., 1888.

Thackeray, W.M., *Lovel The Widower*: being Vol 24 of *The Works Of William Makepeace Thackeray*, 26 Vols. London: Smith, Elder & Co., 1888.

Thackeray, W.M., *The Roundabout Papers*; being Vol 22 of *The Works Of William Makepeace Thackeray*, 26 Vols. London: Smith, Elder & Co., 1888.

Thackeray, W.M., *The Book Of Snobs*; being Vol 14 of the Works Of William Makepeace Thackeray, 26 Vols. London: Smith, Elder & Co., 1886.

Tillett, Selwyn, *Victoria & Merrie England*. London: Sir Arthur Sullivan Society, 1980.

Traubner, Richard, *Operetta - A Theatrical History*. London: Gollancz, 1984.

Vaughan Williams, Ralph, *National Music*. London, 1934.

Watling, E.F. (trans), *Sophocles - The Theban Plays*. London: Penguin Books, 1947.

Wilson, Colin, *Brandy Of The Damned*. London: John Baker, 1964.

Wolfson, John, *Final Curtain*. London: Chappell/Andre Deutsch, 1976.

Wolfson, John, *Sullivan And The Scott Russells*. Chichester: Packard Publishing, 1984.

Wood, Christopher, *Olympian Dreamers—Victorian Classical Painters 1860-1914*. London: Constable, 1983.

Young, Percy M., *Sir Arthur Sullivan*. London: Dent, 1971.

Young, Percy M., *George Grove*. London: Macmillan, 1980.

Index